1990

Major Film Directors
of the American
and British Cinema

Major Film Directors
of the American
and British Cinema

Gene D. Phillips

Bethlehem: Lehigh University Press
London and Toronto: Associated University Presses

Associated University Presses
440 Forsgate Drive
Cranbury, JN 08512

Associated University Presses
25 Sicilian Avenue
London WC1A 2QH, England

Associated University Presses
P.O. Box 488, Port Credit
Mississauga, Ontario
Canada L5G 4M2

The paper used in this publication meets the requirements
of the American National Standard for Permanence of Paper
for Printed Library Materials Z39.48-1984.

Library of Congress Cataloging-in-Publication Data

Phillips, Gene D.
    Major film directors of the American and British cinema/Gene D. Phillips.
        p.   cm.
    Filmography: p.
    Bibliography: p.
    Includes index.
    ISBN 0-934223-08-4 (alk. paper)
    1. Motion picture producers and directors—United States. 2. Motion picture producers and directors—Great Britain. 3. Motion pictures—United States—History. 4. Motion pictures—Great Britain—History. I. Title.
PN1998.2.P55   1990
791.43′0233′092273—dc20
                                                        88-46163
                                                        CIP

For Adam Reilly

It is difficult to be freely creative in something that calls itself an industry.
—John Schlesinger

Contents

Acknowledgments

First of all, I am most grateful to the film makers who cooperated with me in preparing this book, thereby helping me to interpret their work more accurately. I conducted personal interviews with the following directors, most of whom discussed their work with me more than once during the long period in which I was engaged in the preparation of the present volume: George Cukor, Fred Zinnemann, Stanley Kubrick, Carol Reed, Joseph Losey, Bryan Forbes, John Schlesinger, and Ken Russell. In addition, I watched Alfred Hitchcock shooting his next-to-last film on location in London, and talked with Howard Hawks and with George Stevens at the Chicago International Film Festival, and with Francis Coppola at the Cannes International Film Festival. Moreover, Charles Chaplin and David Lean examined a draft of the chapters on their work. I also interviewed Karel Reisz and Lindsay Anderson about British Social Realism; cinematographer James Wong Howe about working with Howard Hawks; Alec Guinness about working with Carol Reed and David Lean; Olivia de Havilland about working with George Cukor; Evelyn Griffith Kunze, D. W. Griffith's second wife, in connection with the Prologue of this book; Bryan Foy, director of the first all-talking picture, about the advent of sound; and Fred MacMurray about working with George Stevens.

Of the many others who helped me, I also wish to mention the following: the Research Committee of Loyola University of Chicago for a grant with which to pursue this study; the staff of the Education Department and of the National Film Archive of the British Film Institute, the staff of the Motion Picture Section of the Library of Congress, and the staff of the Film Study Center of the Museum of Modern Art for the use of their research facilities. Research materials were also provided by William K. Everson of New York University, Stuart Kaminsky of Northwestern University, and Les Keyser of the City College of New York, and Robert Rosterman, an expert on film history.

Some material in this book appeared in a completely different form in the following publications: *Cinema*, copyright 1968 by Spectator International, Inc.; *Film Comment*, copyright 1969, 1970, 1971, and 1972 by Film Comment Publishing Corp.; *See*, copyright 1971 by the Screen Educators Society; *Alfred Hitchcock*, copyright 1984 by G. K. Hall Co.; and *Films in Review*, copyright 1989 by the National Board of Review.

This is the revised, expanded edition of this book. An earlier edition was published by Nelson-Hall Co., copyright 1973 by Gene D. Phillips.

Prologue:
Artists in an Industry

"Hollywood's like Egypt," the late producer David O. Selznick once remarked, "full of crumbled pyramids. It will just keep crumbling until finally the wind blows the last studio prop across the sands. . . . There might have been good movies if there had been no movie industry. Hollywood might have become the center of a new human expression if it hadn't been grabbed by a little group of bookkeepers and turned into a junk industry."[1]

These are bitter words indeed to come from the man responsible for producing films like *Gone with the Wind*. Nonetheless, Selznick has accurately expressed the perennial problem that has vexed motion picture makers since the movies developed from their humble beginnings into a full-scale industry: the problem of trying to make motion pictures that are personal, unified works of art which a director can truly call his own, despite the fact that he or she is working in a complicated commercial industry. Yet many a film maker has succeeded in this hazardous enterprise, as the following chapters aim to show.

Indeed, the premise of this book is precisely that the director alone can confer artistic unity on a motion picture. The director, after all, is the single controlling influence during the production of a motion picture; hence it is up to him to blend all of the varied contributions of cast and crew into a unified whole. Consequently, the director, more than anyone else involved in the making of a movie, is the one who leaves his personal stamp on the finished product.

Andrew Sarris, one of the most articulate champions of the film director's vital role in the movie making process, has written, "Only the director can provide a unity of style out of all the diverse ingredients at his disposal. The script writer will find his words chopped up into shots. The actor who performs continuously on the stage is recorded intermittently on the set, where his part is slowly eroded out of sequence into little bits and pieces."[2] Only the director, then, can create a unified work of art out of the corporate effort that characterizes the making of a motion picture. In describing the central role of the director in the production of a movie, another critic has said that the director's function is that of quarterback, orchestra leader, trail boss, company commander, and, at times, lion tamer.

When the role of the director is viewed in this fashion, moreover, as the guiding light of film production, it is clear that he is the true author of a film in much the same way that a writer is the author of a novel. A film director who merely puts together a motion picture as if he were a foreman on an assembly line would, of course, not be considered the author of a film that he has directed, and there are many such directors in the history of cinema.

But a film director who uses cinematic techniques to express his personal view of the human condition in film after film will build up a coherent body of work like that which the novelist produces. This is not say that a given film cannot be analyzed and enjoyed apart from the other films made by the same director; but one's appreciation of a given film can be greatly enhanced when it is examined in the context of the director's total body of work.

Making the film director the center of cinema study was initiated by a series of articles in the 1950s in the French journal *Cahiers du Cinema*. The *auteur* (author) theory developed in the pages of *Cahiers* was most easily applied to directors who work in relatively small industries like that of Great Britain, and hence can more easily control every aspect of the production of their films from beginning to end. At first it seemed that the *auteur* theory could not be applied so readily to the American director because directors working in a larger industry have found it so much more difficult to gain artistic control over their films.

On closer examination, however, it has become clear that some of the best American film makers have been able to impose their personal stamp on their films just as the British directors have done, and their work likewise warrants and repays further critical examination along the lines set by the *auteur* theory. As Peter Wollen remarks in *Signs and Meaning in the Cinema*, the *auteur* theory sprang from the conviction "that masterpieces were made not only by a small upper crust of directors, the cultured gilt on the commercial gingerbread, but by a whole range of authors, whose work has previously been dismissed or consigned to oblivion."[3]

Almost from its inception the *auteur* theory has from time to time been challenged by various film critics who have questioned its validity. One such critic is Pauline Kael, who once caricatured the *auteur* theory by describing the "ideal *auteur*" as "the man who signs a long-term contract, directs any script that's handed to him, and expresses himself by shoving bits of style up the crevasses of the plot."

Kael's difficulties with the theory really come down to two fundamental points. The first is that many a director does not personally compose his own screenplays, but, in her view, simply "directs any script that's handed to him." In this context she picks up on a remark that George Cukor once made, "Give me a good script and I'll be a hundred times better as a director," and endeavors to turn it to his disadvantage. "Cukor has a range of subject matter that he can handle," she writes; "and when he gets a good script within his range (like *The Philadelphia Story* or *Pat and Mike*) he does a good job." But he does not qualify for *auteur* status, she argues, because he is so dependent on the ideas of so many different screenwriters.

"The fact that most directors do not write their own scripts," Sarris counters, "is enough to discredit the role of the director in the eyes of the literary establishment," and, one might add, in the eyes of critics of Kael's persuasion. "Such discredit is often unjustified even on literary grounds simply because many directors decline to take credit for collaborating on the writing of their films." Furthermore, a director can still be considered the author of his succession of films, whether he has had a direct hand in script preparation or not, if he has consistently chosen material that is in keeping with his own personal vision and directorial style. A director of this kind, Sarris points out, has created in his films "a world of his own, a world no less unique for having been filtered through the varying verbalizations of scores of scriptwriters."[4]

As Cukor himself testified, it was his custom to hold script conferences with his writers prior to filming, in order to trade ideas about plot and dialogue. "I'm not a writer," he said; "but I know how to hector screenwriters and make suggestions that will help them improve what they have written." In fact, he would always go over the screenplay with the writer "scene by scene and line by line" before going on to the studio floor to shoot a movie.

Commenting wryly on the legend promoted by Kael and some other critics that film directors too often seek to usurp some of a screenwriter's credit by claiming that they supervise the scripts of the movies they make, British director Ken Russell told me, "One Hollywood writer I worked with, in fact, stole my screen credit. When the script came back from the printers with his name, and his alone, emblazoned all over the place, I naturally objected. 'But I did write it, Ken,' he protested. 'OK, so you dictated it; but I was the guy who typed it all out.'"

Pauline Kael's other basic objection to the *auteur* theory is that it is ultimately a defense of the Hollywood studio system, because it suggests, as I have already noted, that many directors have become genuine artists while working within the factory atmosphere of a large Hollywood studio. She dismisses this notion as portraying "the superior hack as hidden artist."[5]

Film making, it is true, involves a whole host of individuals, from actors to technicians, who collaborate with the director on a movie, a fact that more than one of the directors in this book reminds us of. Yet genuine *auteurs* are directors who have nevertheless been able to impress their films with their personal trademark, regardless of the number of collaborators involved with them on a given picture, by systematically influencing every phase of the production process, from script to scoring.

Alfred Hitchcock is a prime example of an *auteur* who left his mark on every facet of a production he directed, as his coworkers were the first to acknowledge. For example, Edith Head, costume designer for several Hitchcock films from 1954 to 1976, remarked that "every costume is indicated when he sends me the script. . . . There is always a story reason behind his thinking, an effort to characterize. He's absolutely definite in his visual approach, and gives you an exciting concept of the importance of color." Louis Levy, who scored five Hitchcock films in the mid-1930s, observed that, even though Hitchcock did not understand all the technicalities of the composer's craft, his directions were so precise that "I always left our music conferences with a tune written clearly in my mind, almost as though Hitchcock himself had written it."[6]

One suspects that working within the studio system presented an *auteur* like Hitchcock with a challenge to his artistic creativity, a challenge which sharpened his determination to turn out films that he could in some true sense call his own. The greatest individual directors, says film historian Gerald Mast, are those who are able to avoid the clichéd convention, or those who are able to inject their own personal insight into that convention. So much for Kael and company.

In order to understand the obstacles that the *auteurs* treated in this book have faced in their attempt to gain artistic control of their films, we must understand how film making developed into the complex industry that it has become. Because of the parallel development of the American and British film industries, the problems confronting the artist who wishes to make personal films within the motion picture industry are, for all practical purposes, the same in both America and Britain. As Gerald Mast points out in his *Short History of the Movies*, "The British film industry has maintained a symbiotic relationship with Hollywood since the end of World War I, . . . a relationship intensified by the sharing of a common language after the conversion to sound."[7] This relationship has been further intensified because American financing largely controls the British movie industry. Consequently, I shall deal in this Prologue with the growth of movie making into an industry in America alone. I shall focus on the British industry more specifically in treating the English directors who make up the second part of this book.

In the early days of Hollywood, when film making was still an infant industry as well as an infant art, a film maker was free to make a motion picture in the way he envisioned it. As Arthur Knight writes in *The Liveliest Art*, "Frequently the director was his own producer, not only making the picture but going out to find the financing and, ultimately, arranging for its sale and distribution."[8]

One thinks immediately of D. W. Griffith, the first *auteur*, conceiving, producing, and directing *The Birth of a Nation* in 1915, all the while being the only individual involved in the making of the film who had any idea of what the plot was, or how each of the scenes would eventually be integrated into the finished film, simply because it was his custom to work without a written script. Yet the film was carefully made. For example, in the course of the movie Griffith adroitly utilized extreme long shots to photograph battle scenes of epic scope, as well as close-ups to create love scenes of warm personal intimacy. What's more, he topped off his panoramic picture of the Civil War and its aftermath with the suspenseful last-minute rescue of a Southern family holed up in a cabin beseiged by Yankee troops, ingeniously crosscutting between the beleaguered family desperately hoping to be rescued and the rescuers galloping to save them.

It is true that Griffith did not necessarily invent each of the innovative cinematic techniques he employed in *Birth of a Nation*; but he did bring them all together for the first time in a single motion picture, thereby demonstrating that movies were no longer a toy, but a budding art form. Gerald Mast succinctly sums up Griffith's achievement by saying that *The Birth of a Nation* succeeds both as a "mammoth spectacle" and as a "touching human drama."[9]

With *Birth of a Nation* Griffith became the premier movie maker in filmdom. In order to preserve his artistic autonomy, Griffith in due course built his own studio at Mamaroneck, New York, near New York City, with a view to releasing the films he made there through United Artists, the distribution organization he had cofounded around this same time with Charles Chaplin, Douglas Fairbanks, Sr., and Mary Pickford to distribute the pictures each of them made. Griffith turned out some excellent films at Mamaroneck, like *Orphans of the Storm* (1923), a grand costume spectacle built around another civil war: the French Revolution.

But, as an independent producer, Griffith had to handle the overhead expenses of maintaining the Mamaroneck facility, which included meeting the weekly payroll. Unfortunately, Griffith was not a businessman, and simply lacked the know-how to manage a motion picture studio on a profit-making basis. For example, he lacked the business acumen to budget a production in a way that would make possible a reasonable return on the financial investment that had been made in the picture. *Orphans of the Storm* is a case in point; despite the fact that *Orphans* was lauded by the critics, it was a financial flop. This is because "the cost of the film had been immense," writes David Robinson; "the sets of revolutionary Paris covered thirteen acres. It was impossible for the film to recoup such a cost. After this, no Griffith film ever made a profit."[10] When his movies stopped making money, he inevitably lost his studio, and with it his creative freedom. For, after the Mamaroneck studio had closed its doors, Griffith simply became a staff director at Paramount Pictures in Hollywood.

By the time Griffith went to work for Paramount in the mid-1920s the Hollywood studio system had developed from a small-time operation into a large industry. The reason is that movie making had by now become a more complex, expensive operation, and the problems of administering a movie studio had likewise begun to grow. Hence the distance increased between the studio sets where a film was being shot and the "front office" where the decisions were made about budgeting a film's production in terms of its eventual distribution and exhibition. By the mid-1920s the studio had become a factory and the motion pictures turned out there were simply referred to as the product to be merchandised. The movies had become "big business," says Knight; "and since the very essence of big business is standardization and control, methods of production were introduced that would permit a close calculation of costs and a reasonably exact estimate of profits."[11]

The director became only one link in the complicated chain of command. The script had been written, the cast chosen, and the sets built before the director was called in to direct the picture. When shooting was completed, the footage was then passed on to the editing department, where it was shaped into a finished film. Under these circumstances it was difficult for any director to place his personal stamp on a film.

In Griffith's case, once he was employed by a major studio, it meant that, although he had been accustomed heretofore to carrying a scenario inside his head, he was now forced to use shooting scripts, sometimes written by others. "The result," to quote Louis Giannetti, "was startling impoverishment." That is to say that Griffith, who previously had often depended on the inspiration of the moment for his direction of a scene, found that "his inventiveness and spontaneity" had all but evaporated.[12] And so he fell by the wayside. In conversation with his second wife, Evelyn Griffith Kunze, it became clear to me that Griffith's decline was ultimately the result of his failure to reckon with the fact that the movie business is, after all, just that: a business.

In essence, the kind of director that the studio officials were now looking for was one whom they could count on to turn out a competently made film, while staying within the budget and shooting schedule set by the studio officials. When a director demonstrated his ability to turn out films to studio specifications and that made money, they were rewarded by being given an increasingly freer hand in choosing

their material and filming it in the way that they envisioned. In short, once a director proved to the studio officials that he knew how to use responsibly whatever
degree of independence they were willing to allow him, they would grant him more.

The studio, nevertheless, always kept an eye on even its most experienced directors during the production of a picture. The story is told of one veteran Hollywood
director, noted for bringing his films in on time and within the set budget, who
became irritated when he was reminded by a studio minion that he was two days
behind schedule. Confident that he would finish the picture on schedule, the director picked up a copy of the shooting script, tore out a couple of pages, and snapped
sarcastically, "Now I'm back on schedule."

The Hollywood studio system flourished throughout the years of World War II
because everyone needed and wanted to get away from the pressures of the war
effort whenever they could by spending a couple of hours in the cool darkness of a
movie theater. Up until the end of the war Hollywood could count on a huge,
largely undiscriminating audience of people who simply went to the movies every
week, regardless of what was playing.

By the late 1940s, however, the honeymoon was over, and Hollywood was faced
not only with the influx of superior adult films from abroad, but, more critically,
with the advent of television at home. Instead of trying to upgrade the quality of
their films, the studios first turned to technical innovations as a possible way of
saving their audience. Thus Hollywood seemed convinced that a wider screen with
the old traditional plots acted out on it would do the trick. But movie audiences
continued to defect to TV.

Since, by the early 1950s, television was providing more than enough routine
entertainment, the potential moviegoer was becoming more and more discriminating in choosing film fare. The big studios were at a loss to know what kind of films
to make, and so they began turning to independent producer-directors, whom
they allowed to lease studio space to make their own films. One of these, Stanley
Kubrick, has remarked that the source of the supremacy of the major studios was
their power to make money. When they stopped making money, they sent for the
independents.

These men were not interested in signing a long-term contract with any one
studio, if it meant that they were expected to machine-tool films according to studio
specifications, as some directors at the big studios were willing to do. Instead, they
preferred to make a deal with a given studio for one picture at a time. As a result,
the films turned out by these film makers became more personal in style and point
of view than had been customary for Hollywood films of the past. In sum, we have
come a long way from the days when motion picture companies sought to make
films that could roll off the studio conveyor belt as anonymous studio products.

The Italian film maker Bernardo Bertolucci has said that if all of the films of a
good director are laid end to end, what results is not a group of separate films, but a
series of installments in the same film. The following pages, then, pay tribute to a
group of film makers who have been able through their resourcefulness to place on
their films, not the stamp of the studio, but the stamp of their own directorial style

and personal vision of reality. And it is with tracing the thematic continuity in the work of each of these directors that this book is chiefly concerned.

While this book is not meant to be a formal history of the cinema in America and Britain, it can be considered a work of film history, since the films of the directors included in it cover a wide spectrum, ranging from the silent period up to the present, and represent various trends in film making that have evolved over the years, such as American Film Noir and British Social Realism. In sum, the present study is intended not only for the cinema specialist, but also for those filmgoers who have enjoyed the motion pictures made by these film makers, in order to provide them with a context in which they can appreciate the work of these men more fully.

Major Film Directors
of the American
and British Cinema

Part One
Film Directors in America

Charles Chaplin (center), with Harold Lloyd and Douglas Fairbanks, at the peak of their screen careers. (The Adam Reilly collection)

1
Charles Chaplin
The Little Fellow in a Big World

When the first Academy Awards were presented in 1928, a special award went to Charles Chaplin for "his genius and versatility in writing, acting, directing, and producing *The Circus*." At the 1972 award ceremonies Chaplin was on hand to be honored again, this time for "the incalculable effect he has had in making motion pictures the art form of this century." In addition, he was knighted in 1975, in recognition of his supreme importance in shaping the motion picture medium as an art form.

In more than half a century of film making Chaplin produced an impressive body of work that is uniquely his own personal achievement. He not only wrote, produced, directed, and acted in his films but composed musical scores for them and supervised the editing as well. Therefore Chaplin's films are surely the expression of his own personal vision, a vision developed throughout the years as he continued making films. Hence Chaplin is a classic *auteur*, in the sense explained in the Prologue.

The Tramp character, which he made beloved the world over, had its roots in his own poverty-ridden childhood. "Perhaps because of my early environment," Chaplin said, "the comedy in tragedy has always been second nature to me. Cruelty, for example, is an integral part of comedy. We laugh at it in order not to weep."

Chaplin was born in London on April 16, 1889.[1] Both of his parents were moderately successful music hall entertainers. When he was still a youngster, his father died of alcoholism, and his mother retired from the stage because of poor physical health and mental illness. Consequently, Chaplin was forced to earn his living in vaudeville before he reached his teens. Mack Sennett, the creator of the Keystone comedies, saw Chaplin perform while the comedian was touring the United States with Fred Karno's vaudeville company and invited Chaplin to go into pictures in 1913. Chaplin left the stage for a career in movies the following year.

One rainy afternoon Sennett heard that a children's auto race was to be held at Los Angeles's Venice Amusement Park, and he sent Chaplin and the rest of his troupe over to the park to make a short comedy. Chaplin had no idea what kind of costume to wear, so he borrowed various items from his fellow comics on the Sennett lot and put together an outfit. From "Fatty" Arbuckle he took a pair of baggy pants, from Mack Swain a false mustache, and from Ford Sterling a pair of oversized shoes. To this Chaplin added a coat that was too tight and a derby hat that was too small. "I had no idea of the character," Chaplin recalls in his autobiography. "But the moment I was dressed, the clothes and the make-up made me feel the person he was. I began to know him."[2]

In a 1923 interview Chaplin explained that Charlie the Tramp was his conception of the average man. "The derby, too small, is a striving for dignity. The mustache is vanity. The tightly buttoned coat and the stick and his whole manner are a gesture toward gallantry and dash and 'front.' He is trying to meet the world bravely, to put up a bluff, and he knows that, too. He knows it so well that he can laugh at himself and pity himself a little."[3] In short, the Tramp is an everyman, with whom we can all identify: the well-meaning but inept little man whose reach forever exceeds his grasp, but who is always ready to pick himself up, dust himself off, and continue down the road of life, twirling his cane with disarming bravado.

Chaplin eventually prevailed on Sennett to let him write and direct his own comedies, starting with the thirteenth short that he starred in for Sennett. But even with this increased artistic freedom Chaplin still felt constricted by the Keystone formula, in which gag followed gag at a frenetic pace with little thought given to character or plot development. Chaplin therefore was not able to evolve fully the personality of his Tramp character until he left Keystone in 1915, after a year of working for Sennett, and transferred to Essanay.

In his year at Essanay Chaplin had to make only fourteen short films, as compared to thirty-five at Keystone in the same length of time. Hence he was now able to make his films with more care and to explore further the possibilities of integrating a serious dimension into his comedy material from time to time. The Tramp character began to be more clearly defined as the pathetic outsider, longing for an acceptance from others that he will never achieve. In his sixth film for Essanay, *The Tramp*, Chaplin injected into a comedy film for the first time a clear note of pathos culminating in an unhappy ending, something unheard of at the time. In the film Charlie saves a beautiful young girl from being molested by other tramps. He mistakes her gratitude for love, but realizes the truth when she introduces him to her real sweetheart. He scribbles a note of farewell, doubly pathetic because of its misspellings, and saunters down the road with a shrug.

While at Essanay, Chaplin gained a firmer grasp on his art, and this would blossom still more in the films which he was now to make for Mutual in 1916–1917. Chaplin brought with him to Mutual a team of associates that he had built up at Essanay, including leading lady Edna Purviance, who was to appear in thirty-five of his films over a nine-year period, and cameraman Roland Totheroh, who would remain with Chaplin until 1947. With each new contract he negotiated at each new studio, Chaplin received still greater artistic independence. Thus, when his last Essanay film, *Burlesque on Carmen*, was re-edited and lengthened after he had left that studio, he then stipulated in his contract with Mutual that there would be "no mutilating, extending or interfering" with his finished work.[4]

Chaplin made his Mutual two-reelers with still greater care and creativity than he had expended on those he made for Essanay; indeed in his eighteen months at Mutual Chaplin produced twelve nearly perfect short comedies. The greatest of them is *The Immigrant* (1917), which dealt with a subject close to Chaplin's heart, since he had come to America himself as an immigrant in 1913. Moreover, because the immigrant is perhaps the quintessential example of the lonely outsider striving for acceptance in an alien milieu, the role fit the personality of Charlie the Tramp perfectly.

Charlie first meets the girl Edna aboard ship, where, ironically, they are roped together and tagged like cattle just as they pass the Statue of Liberty. As Chaplin describes the film in his autobiography: "When they arrive in New York they separate. Eventually he meets the girl again, but she is alone, and like himself is a failure. . . . And of course, in the end they marry on a doleful, rainy day."[5] Just as Charlie the Tramp symbolizes the eternal outcast, so the girl in a Chaplin comedy also has symbolic significance. She is sweet and innocent, representing all that is true and beautiful in an otherwise soiled and shabby world. As such, she is the one ray of sunshine in the Tramp's bleak existence. In each film the Tramp uses all of his resourcefulness to win the girl and sometimes he succeeds in doing so, as in *The Immigrant*. But usually she and all that she represents prove to be beyond his grasp.

When Chaplin left Mutual for First National in 1918, he took yet another step toward total artistic control of his films. Chaplin now became his own producer, as well as writer, director, and star. He was to make his films in his own small studio for distribution by First National, while he and First National would split the profits equally. Chaplin was now in a position to take his time in making each of his films and in fact made only eight films for First National distribution between 1918 and 1923.

On the other hand, most of the First National comedies were longer than the one- and two-reelers that he had made for other studios, since they averaged three reels apiece; as such, they were to become the prototypes of his later features. In fact, *The Kid* (1921), running to six reels, became Chaplin's first feature. Chaplin's new format obviously allowed him to develop the elements of plot and character in each of his films in more depth than had been possible in the past. The supporting characters, for instance, were now drawn more fully and seemed less like caricatures. In addition, the sets and decor were more realistic in detail.

The most popular film of this period was undoubtedly *Shoulder Arms* (1918), which anticipated *The Great Dictator* (1940) as a satire on war. Released a few weeks before the Armistice, *Shoulder Arms* gave the ordinary enlisted man's feelings about being a soldier—the regimentation, homesickness, privations, and dangers of life in the trenches. Nevertheless, the film is unfailingly funny. When Charlie is asked how he managed to capture thirteen soldiers single-handedly, he explains without hesitation, "I surrounded them."

Prior to his First National films, Chaplin had portrayed the Tramp as a rambunctious ragamuffin who felt that he had to cheat to survive in a cold and brutal world. In the First National films, particularly *The Kid*, Charlie emerges as a gentler kind of person, one who receives the kicks that life administers to him with more resignation and less of a will for retaliation than he had exhibited in his earlier comedies. In *The Kid* the Tramp finds an abandoned child (Jackie Coogan) and cares for him until his mother is discovered. The story takes place in an authentically grimy slum setting, reminiscent of the circumstances in which Chaplin himself grew up. In fact, more than any film which Chaplin has ever made, *The Kid* is deeply rooted in Chaplin's own wretched childhood.

That Chaplin by this time could make a film which sprang so intimately from his own personal experience was an indication that now more than ever his films were the expression of a single artistic mind. Working with complete indpendence in his own studio, he would first conceive an idea for a plot and then set about developing it into a scenario. While the film was in production, Chaplin encouraged improvisation on the set, for the inspiration of the moment often provided just the right finishing touch for a scene. Because Chaplin was not burdened with the huge overhead of a large studio complex, he could afford to shoot bits of action over and over again until they were done to his satisfaction. Then, in editing the film, he would pare down the miles of footage that he had shot until he got the film as close to perfection as possible.

"Chaplin's films are indeed one-man jobs," Theodore Huff has written. "Nearly every significant milestone of the screen has been the work of one man. . . . Hollywood, however, prefers the factory method of many 'experts' assembling their products, instead of one man's work, as leading to more certain box office returns."[6] By working almost totally outside the Hollywood factory system in his own studio, which was geared to make one film at a time, Chaplin was able to create a continuous series of films, linked together because they all had their origin in his own creative imagination.

Chaplin was able to maintain this same kind of control over his motion pictures when he began making full-length features. In 1919 he had formed the United Artists Corporation, in partnership with D. W. Griffith, Douglas Fairbanks, Sr., and Mary Pickford, to distribute the films that they each turned out. Because of prior commitments to First National, however, Chaplin was not able to make a film for United Artists release until 1923.

Chaplin's first film for United Artists was a serious drama in which he did not star. It was called *A Woman of Paris*. His primary reason for making the film was to reward his long-time leading lady Edna Purviance with stardom, and to launch her on a career of her own. In addition, since a serious element had for some time been creeping into his comedies, Chaplin perhaps also wanted to try his hand at writing and directing a straight drama in order to gain experience in handling serious material. *The Kid* had been criticized because the dramatic scenes, which centered around Miss Purviance as the mother of the lost child, were not as deftly done as the rest of the film. *A Woman of Paris* was Chaplin's chance to prove that he could direct a drama with as sure a hand as he could direct a comedy.

The preface of *A Woman of Paris* sets the tone of the film to follow, and indeed could be taken as part of the philosophy that underlies every Chaplin film: "Humanity is composed not of heroes and villains, but of men and women; and all their passions, good and bad, have been given them by God. They sin only in blindness, and the ignorant condemn their mistakes, but the wise pity them."

The story concerns Marie St. Clair (Edna Purviance), a young girl from a French village who goes to Paris in search of a career and becomes swallowed up in the half-world of Parisian night life. When her fiancé comes to Paris and discovers that

Marie is being supported by Pierre, a wealthy playboy (Adolphe Menjou), he despairs of winning her back and commits suicide. Grief-stricken, Marie renounces Paris and returns to her village. One day she is riding down the road on a haywagon when Pierre passes her by in his smart sports car. Neither recognizes the other as they go their separate ways, and on this ironic note the movie ends.

Chaplin, who had never made a serious social satire before, had brought this genre to a new level of sophistication in *A Woman of Paris*. He had discovered, for example, that the suggestion of sexual implications in a scene could be more interesting than graphic portrayals of such a situation. The nature of the relationship between Marie and Pierre is subtly implied when Pierre casually goes to Marie's bureau drawer and takes out one of his own handkerchiefs.

In another sequence, Chaplin suggests that a strip-tease is in progress at a Paris party by holding his camera on the man who is winding a girl's costume around himself as she twirls out of it. The sophistication of Chaplin's film immediately made it stand out as superior to the brash commercial romances and melodramas that were coming out of Hollywood at the time. Although the film might seem commonplace when seen today, this would be only because it has been so often imitated since it was made.

Chaplin brought with him to the making of his next film the experience gained in directing a drama like *A Woman of Paris*. *The Gold Rush* (1925) has scenes that are almost straight drama, in which Chaplin becomes more of an actor and less of a clown. Most important, the plot of *The Gold Rush* is more than a mere thin strand on which to hang comedy routines, as many feature-length comedies of the time were. Instead, the humor in *The Gold Rush* rises directly from the serious situations in the story. This weaving together of comic and serious elements into an integral whole, foreshadowed in earlier films such as *The Immigrant* and *The Kid*, was for the first time fully accomplished in *The Gold Rush*, which Chaplin subtitled "A Dramatic Comedy." Theodore Huff notes that the film "plumbs the depths of pathos. Its laughs, drawn out of tragedy, have a magnified force and meaning. Its principal character symbolizes the good, kind, and pitiful core of humanity. Moments of the film reach the sublime."[7]

Chaplin said that he got the idea for the story from reading a book about the Donner expedition, which got lost in the Sierra Nevada Mountains: "Some resorted to cannibalism, eating their dead; others roasted their moccasins to relieve their hunger. Out of this harrowing tragedy I conceived one of the funniest scenes. In dire hunger I boil my shoe and eat it, picking the nails as though they were bones of a delicious capon, and eating the sholelaces as though they were spaghetti."[8] Elsewhere he added that at first he hesitated to use this routine, fearing that he might be going too far: "But I said, no, no, this is based on a fact and it will be funny. We must laugh in the face of our helplessness against the forces of nature— or go insane."[9]

In *The Gold Rush* Charlie the Tramp is called the Lone Prospector, again emphasizing his status as an outsider. He hopes to gain society's acceptance by becoming wealthy through the discovery of gold in the Klondike. In the sopken commentary that Chaplin wrote and recorded for the rerelease of the film in 1942, he refers to Charlie the Tramp as the Little Fellow; and that name, too, fits the Tramp's character.

That Charlie is a social outcast is emphasized repeatedly in the movie. When the Little Fellow goes to a dance hall, we see him with his back to the camera standing outside and looking through the window at the people inside. Then, when he finally goes inside, he stands momentarily on the edge of the crowd before summoning the courage to seek companionship at the bar. When he does so, one of the hostesses and her boyfriend make fun of him. Charlie nevertheless gets the mistaken notion that Georgia, the hostess (Georgia Hale), likes him and he invites her and some of the other girls to a New Year's Eve party in his cabin. The girls accept his invitation and then promptly forget all about it.

On New Year's Eve the Little Fellow sits alone in his cabin, waiting for the guests who will never come. Chaplin cuts to the dance hall festivities, which present a dramatic contrast to the Tramp's loneliness. When the scene shifts back to the Little Fellow, Chaplin gives us one of the truly great moments in motion picture history. Charlie falls asleep and imagines that his party is in full swing, with the girls all in attendance. In response to their calling for a speech from their host, Charlie offers to dance the "Oceana Roll." He spears two bread rolls with forks, then guides them through a little soft-shoe routine on the table top. The scene is so lit that only his head and the little "shoes" are emphasized. Hence Charlie looks like a living caricature—a clown who has a life-sized head but little feet. His eyes follow the tiny shoes as they kick this way and that and finally dance sideways "off stage" at the conclusion of the number, in a kind of "Shuffle Off to Buffalo."

Chaplin's genius for combining humor and pathos is brilliantly illustrated in this dream sequence, for the comic dance is set in the pathetic context of Charlie's rejection by the thoughtless girls who have forgotten him. Of course Charlie is forced to face this harsh reality once more when he awakens from his dream. Indeed, throughout *The Gold Rush* Chaplin takes us from reality to fantasy, from comedy to near tragedy and back again with incomparable ease.

The theme that emerges from the film epitomizes the vision that is implicit in all of Chaplin's films: man's struggle for survival in a tough world, as evidenced in the Lone Prospector's resourcefulness in coping with whatever obstacles life puts in his way. That struggle has never been more concretely visualized for us than in the first appearance of Charlie in the film: overloaded with gear and shambling along a snowy mountainside, blithely unaware that he is being followed by a huge bear. "Thus we meet the Little Fellow," comments Bosley Crowther, "overburdened but plainly ill equipped for such a vicious country and venture. . . . He is an innocent in a cruel environment, cut loose among avaricious men, blithely pursuing his reckless fancy—and about to be eaten by a bear!"[10]

Charlie dauntlessly escapes the bear and all of his other adversaries in the film, and goes on to strike it rich and even win the girl. But he and Georgia are united only after they have left the brutally acquisitive atmosphere of the Klondike, which had stifled the capacity for love and friendship in everyone there—except Charlie, whose spark of true humanity never flickers out.

That spark of humanity is very much in evidence in *The Circus* (1928), in which

Charlie befriends a bareback rider (Merna Kennedy) who is mistreated by her father, the owner of the circus in which the Tramp is employed as prop man. Without realizing it, Charlie becomes the most popular clown in the show, as he hilariously ruins the act of every performer he is supposed to assist. In the end he unselfishly disowns his genuine love for the girl and encourages her to marry the handsome tightrope walker, whom she really loves. After the circus rolls out of town, the Tramp sits alone on the deserted fairgrounds for a while, dejectedly tracing a circle in the dust. Then he rises and, with a twirl of his cane and a shrug of his shoulder, wanders off once more into the distance.

At the time that Chaplin was making *The Circus* he was involved in a scandalous divorce suit brought by his second wife, Lita "Lolita" Grey Chaplin. At the close of the film, Theodore Huff observes, Chaplin "had the daring to turn his personal troubles to advantage before the camera. The last scene was deliberately photographed in the harsh, early morning light to bring out the careworn lines of his face. This adds a great poignancy to his representation of the tragic emotions of the eternal frustrated misfit."[11]

While Chaplin was preparing his next film, *City Lights* (1931), talking pictures took Hollywood by storm. Chaplin personally was not impressed by the faulty sound quality of the early talkies, however. Recalling one early sound epic, he says in his autobiography, "When the handle of the boudoir door turned I thought someone had cranked up a farm tractor, and when the door closed it sounded like a collision of two lumber trucks. At the beginning they knew nothing about controlling sound."[12] Therefore Chaplin decided to make *City Lights* as a silent film. The only concession that the picture made to the advent of sound was the addition of a musical score Chaplin composed himself, something he likewise did later on for the rerelease of his major films that were made before the sound era, such as *The Gold Rush* and *The Circus*. That Chaplin composed musical scores for his films further marks them as the product of a single creative intelligence.

Another such mark is the continuity in the personality of the Tramp over the years. One of the constants in Charlie's character is that he is always kind to women, especially if they are stray waifs like himself. In *City Lights* the Tramp befriends a blind flower-girl (Virginia Cherrill) who mistakenly thinks that he is a rich man. The Tramp in turn is befriended by a millionaire (Harry Meyers) who, when drunk, generously gives the Little Fellow money, but when sober does not recognize Charlie at all. Fortunately for the Tramp, the millionaire is drunk often enough to provide him with sufficient money to keep up his pretense, with the blind girl, of being rich.

Chaplin chose Cherrill for the role of the blind girl because she had the ability to look as if she were blind, without grotesquely rolling her eyes back in her head, as so many of the actresses who had tried out for the part had done. "I instructed her to look at me but to look inwardly and not see me, and she could do it," says Chaplin.[13] The scenes with the blind girl could have been very maudlin, had Chaplin not undercut their potential sentimentality with humor. An excellent example of Chaplin's ability to mingle humor and pathos in this way occurs early in the film, when the Tramp watches the blind girl affectionately without her knowing that he is

Charlie the Tramp in the final scene of *The Circus* (1928). (Author's collection)

Charlie brings groceries to the blind girl (Virginia Cherrill) in *City Lights* (1931). (Author's collection)

nearby. He is abruptly shaken from his dreamy mood when she empties a vaseful of water in his face.

Although *City Lights* was conceived as a silent film, Chaplin nonetheless included some comic routines that depended, to some extent at least, on sound effects, indicating that he was beginning to think in terms of sound, as well as in visual terms, while making the film. In one scene the Little Fellow attends a party given by his rich friend and desperately seeks to be accepted by the millionaire's social set. As luck would have it, he swallows a whistle, which causes him to hiccup little peeps that are audible on the sound track and, to his chagrin, bring every dog in the neighborhood galloping into the house and into his lap, thereby completely disrupting the party.

In another scene Charlie enters a prizefight in order to raise money for the blind girl's eye operation. The fight itself is almost balletic, as Charlie dances around, endeavoring to keep the referee between himself and his opponent. When he is knocked against the ropes, the Tramp gets the cord of the bell that calls the rounds tangled round his neck, so that, when he jerks his head, he starts and stops each round at the most inopportune moments.

Although certain gags like these depend on sound effects, *City Lights* nevertheless remains substantially a silent film. That dialogue is all but superfluous to Chaplin's art is most clearly demonstrated in the final sequence. Charlie has just been released from prison, where he served a term for stealing money from his wealthy friend. Actually the millionaire had given Charlie the money to secure an eye operation for the blind girl and then did not remember his generous gesture when he was sober. Now that the girl has had her sight restored, she has opened a successful flower shop. Through the window of the shop she sees Charlie staring at her; and she goes outside to offer a flower and a coin to the pathetic Tramp, who she does not know is her real benefactor. As she gives him her alms, she touches his hand and in this way realizes who he really is. The final close-up of Charlie that ends the picture is one of the finest in the history of cinema. The Tramp's face reflects several conflicting emotions all at once: he is glad that she recognizes him, but ashamed that he is not the handsome, wealthy man that she imagined him to be; he hopes that she will accept him as he is but is afraid that she will not. On this note of uncertainly *City Lights* ends.

"I did several takes of that close-up," Chaplin recalls; "but they were all overdone. This time I was looking at *her*. It was a beautiful sensation of standing outside of myself. The key was exactly right: slightly embarrassed, delighted about meeting her again, apologetic. He was watching and wondering what *she* was thinking. It was one of the purest close-ups I've ever done."[14]

The considerable risk that Chaplin took in releasing an essentially silent film more than three years after the arrival of talking pictures paid off handsomely when *City Lights* became one of the most popular films of 1931. Chaplin therefore confidently decided to make his next film, *Modern Times* (1936), in the same format. The inspiration for this film came to Chaplin while he was touring an auto factory and noted its time-saving but man-killing devices. The film, initially entitled *The Masses*, developed into a satire on man's dehumanization by the machine. The prologue announces that *Modern Times* is "a story of industry, of individual enterprise—of humanity crusading in pursuit of happiness." The shot that follows this statement shows a flock of sheep going down a runway and dissolves to workers pouring into a factory. The social comment implicit in the juxtaposition of these two images sets the tone of the motion picture that follows.

Chaplin himself said at the time he made *Modern Times* that he wanted "to say something about the way life is being standardized and channelized, and men turned into machines."[15] Yet the film uses machinery as a source of comedy as well as for symbolic social comment, and sometimes for both at once. For instance, Chaplin's vision of man being dominated by the machines over which he should be master is reflected in a comic routine in which a workman is literally swallowed whole by the machine he is supposed to be repairing. This situation touches off a series of comic complications in which Charlie tries to extricate his fellow worker from his plight, with hilarious inefficiency.

As Peter Cotes and Thelma Niklaus have noted, Chaplin never indicates precisely what product is being manufactured in the plant where the Little Fellow works. This point underscores Chaplin's satire on the factory system with its shining, sterile, inhuman machinery, "endlessly working at producing nothing."[16]

Toward the end of the movie Charlie gets a job in a cabaret as a singing waiter. Just before he is to do his number, he discovers that he has lost his copy of the

Chaplin as Adenoid Hynkle, the dictator of Tomania, in *The Great Dictator* (1940). (Author's collection)

lyrics, which he had scribbled down beforehand. He therefore does a little panto-mime dance and sings in gibberish. When the film was first released, some critics saw this scene as a satire on talking pictures, implying that the dialogue in talkies was not always clear. But it is more likely that Chaplin wanted to avoid limiting the Tramp's universality by having him express himself in a language that could be identified with any specific country or culture. That song is as close as Charlie the Tramp ever came to speaking; and, significantly enough, *Modern Times* was the last film in which the Tramp character appeared.

"Some people suggested that the Tramp might talk," Chaplin says in his auto-biography. "This was unthinkable, for the first word he uttered would transform him into another person. Besides, the matrix out of which he was born was as mute as the rags he wore."[17] In Chaplin's first talking picture, *The Great Dictator* (1940), he plays two roles: a little Jewish barber, who at times is reminiscent of the Tramp in his well-intentioned bungling of his affairs, and Adenoid Hynkle, the dictator of Tomania, who has a strong resemblance to Adolf Hitler. In playing a dual role in *The Great Dictator* Chaplin demonstrated his ability to handle other roles besides the one he had enacted exclusively since 1914.

In this, his first film with spoken dialogue, Chaplin expertly integrates verbal with visual humor. Examples of the former are found in the satiric puns that punctuate the script, beginning with the name of the dictator and of the country he rules and going on to the designation of his political party as the Sons and Daughters of the Double Cross.

The visual humor of the film is best epitomized in the scene in which the barber and his companions plot the assassination of the dictator. The conspirator who finds a coin in his pudding is to perform the deed. Unknown to them, the barber's girl friend (Paulette Goddard) has placed a coin in each of the puddings, in order to discourage the risky assassination attempt. As the conspirators "courteously" pass the puddings back and forth, hoping to avoid choosing the one that contains the fatal coin, the barber winds up finding the coin in each pudding that comes to him; and he surreptitiously swallows them one by one. In a variation on the swallowed whistle in *City Lights*, the barber begins to hiccup; and each time he does so there is a clinking noise on the sound track. Finally he spits the coins out and—in a final Chaplinesque touch—pockets them all.

As in *Modern Times*, the serious social implications of the film are interwoven with the comedy material into one fabric. Earlier in the picture the barber is about to buy a lapel button honoring the dictator from a street vendor, when a loud-speaker booms out with a speech by Hynkle denouncing the Jews. Hearing this, the barber hurriedly returns the button to the vendor and jumps head first into an ash can.

Referring to the serious racial theme of the film, Chaplin, who was of Jewish descent, said at the time *The Great Dictator* was released, "I did this picture for the Jews of the world. I wanted to see the return of decency and kindness. I'm no Communist, . . . just a human being who wants to see this country a real democracy, and free from the infernal regimentation which is crawling over the rest of the world."[18] Chaplin underlined this idea at the close of the film when the barber, who at that point is impersonating the dictator, delivers an impassioned plea for brotherhood directly to the audience. At a time when the world was on the brink of war, Chaplin said in the speech:

> we think too much and feel too little. More than machinery we need humanity. More than cleverness we need kindness and gentleness. Without these qualities life will be violent and all will be lost. . . . To those who can hear me I say, "Do not despair. . . . The hate of men will pass, and dictators die, and the power they took from the people will return to the people."

Despite criticism in some quarters that the speech had no place in a comedy film, Chaplin was applauded by many moviegoers for having the courage to make a plea for humanity to a world in the mood for war. His next film, *Monsieur Verdoux* (1947), was a more implicit but still unmistakable indictment of war, dealing as it does with a man who murders rich widows for their money, but who feels that he is a piker in comparison with war profiteers.

In Chaplin's earlier films Charlie the Tramp felt that he had to cheat to survive in a hostile world. The world which Chaplin pictures in *Verdoux* is still worse, for it has brutalized the central character to the point where he believes that he must kill to survive. Verdoux is a middle-aged man who lost his job as a minor bank clerk in the Depression and has taken to marrying and murdering rich widows in order to support his invalid wife and his small son.

When *Verdoux* first appeared, moviegoers were not prepared to see Chaplin in the role of the dapper murderer Verdoux, who had finally gained some measure of the affluence that Charlie the Tramp had always craved—but at a grim price. The Little Fellow had always wanted to be a lady killer, and that is literally what Verdoux has become. In essence, audiences were not equipped to appreciate black comedy, that genre of storytelling which finds humor in situations usually reserved for serious treatment. Chaplin, one of the oldest veterans in Hollywood, had proved with *Verdoux* that he was really ahead of his time, for only in the wake of later cinematic essays in black comedy like Stanley Kubrick's *Dr. Strangelove* in 1964 could audiences truly appreciate in retrospect the artistry of *Monsieur Verdoux* in this genre.

About making the picture, Chaplin commented, "I saw a great chance to take a tragedy and satirize it, as I did with Nazi Germany. Crime becomes an absurdity when it is shown incongruously, out of proportion. It is a phenomenon of life, thank God, that a thing when it is overstated becomes ridiculous. This is the salvation of man's sanity."

If *Verdoux* was ahead of its time in terms of its content, it has been criticized as old-fashioned in its cinematic techniques. "I don't twist the camera upside down and twirl it around and hurt your eyes," Chaplin countered. "Complexity isn't truth. We get things so cluttered up, get so damn clever that it hides the simple truth in a situation."[19] Chaplin always avoided employing unusual camera angles and clever cutting, in favor of concentrating as much meaning and movement as possible into a single shot. This visual economy is evident in *Monsieur Verdoux* in the scene in which Verdoux shows a real estate agent and his client around the home of his most recent wife and victim. As Verdoux enters a bedroom and explains that this was his late wife's room, he pushes a huge dressmaker's dummy out of sight, indicating with a single gesture his feeling of relief that this overwhelmingly large lady is now out of his life.

Verdoux is studded with comic vignettes of this kind. In an inspired bit of casting, Chaplin chose comedienne Martha Raye to play the brash Annabella Bonheur, who unwittingly foils every attempt that Verdoux makes to kill her. The funniest of their encounters takes place in a rowboat. In a parody of the famous scene in Dreiser's *An American Tragedy* (later filmed by George Stevens as *A Place in the Sun*), Verdoux's efforts to drown Annabella end with his falling into the lake and being hauled out by the indestructible lady.

As the picture reaches its conclusion, Verdoux meets a young woman whom he had befriended earlier when she was a helpless and hopeless outcast. Now she is the mistress of a rich munitions manufacturer who is becoming even wealthier, as European nations step up their armament programs with the approach of World War II. In contrast, Verdoux's fortunes have waned. He tells her forlornly that his wife and child have died and that accordingly he no longer has any real purpose in life. Shortly afterward, he deliberately allows himself to be captured by the police.

In defending himself at his trial Verdoux says sardonically, "Mass killing—does not the world encourage it? I'm an amateur in comparison. . . . Wars, conflict—it's all business. One murderer makes a villain; millions, a hero. Numbers sanctify." To the priest who visits him in his death cell, Verdoux explains, "I am at peace with God; my conflict is with man." When the priest prays that God will have mercy on Verdoux's soul, the latter responds with his customary bravado, "Why not? After all, it belongs to him."

With these somber remarks as a prelude, Chaplin concludes the film with a scene that represents a stark variation on the way the Tramp used to saunter away from the camera, as he continued down the road of life. Instead, Verdoux marches off into the distance, on his way to his death by the guillotine. For the first time in his entire career, Chaplin allowed the central character in one of his films to die.

Limelight (1952) not only ends with the death of its hero, but it is permeated throughout with an elegiac quality, as it tells the story of Calvero, a dying English music hall comedian, played by Chaplin.

Although a has-been, Calvero is still a trooper. He saves a young ballet daner (Claire Bloom) from suicide, restores her determination to continue with her career, and then dies himself after appearing in a benefit show given in his honor. There is much more of Charlie the Tramp in Calvero than there was in Verdoux; in fact, it almost seems that, in Calvero, Chaplin is portraying the Little Fellow as grown old and tired in his struggle for survival before Chaplin wistfully lays him to rest. At one point, when his fortunes have reached their nadir and he has become a street singer, Calvero quips, "There's something about working in the street that I like. It's the tramp in me, I suppose."

Charlie the Tramp is certainly very much present in the vaudeville turns that Calvero does in the film. "In the various performances," Cotes and Niklaus have written, "the whole Charlie is there, from the earliest slapstick days, through the pathos and defiance of the Little Tramp, to the anger and bitterness of Verdoux, haunting the song and dance and mimicry of Calvero on stage and looking sometimes with sick eyes on the cruelty of man towards his fellow man."[20]

Again Chaplin has skillfully mixed comedy and pathos as he did in his greatest films. For example, the sublime humor of Calvero's last comedy number—done with Buster Keaton, Chaplin's only real rival in silent screen comedy—ends with Calvero tumbling into the base drum in the orchestra pit and dying of a heart attack. *Limelight*, like *Verdoux*, failed at the box office; but both films were rediscovered by critics and audiences alike when Chaplin reissued his major films throughout the world in the 1970s.

When Chaplin set sail for Europe in September, 1952, for the European premieres of *Limelight*, he was informed in mid-ocean by a cable from the United States Attorney General that he would not be permitted to re-enter the country without facing an investigation into his personal character and political beliefs. Chaplin continued on to Europe and settled down in Switzerland. This incident was the climax of a controversy about Chaplin that stretched back to the early 1940s, when he had championed a second front during the Second World War to help Russia ward off the Nazi invasion. In the Cold War years that followed the hot war, when Senator Joseph McCarthy was conducting his anti-Communist witch-hunt, such gestures toward our former allies were not remembered benignly. Chaplin was labeled a Communist sympathizer and further criticised because he had never become an American citizen, although, as he had often explained, his patriotism "rests with the whole world, the pity of the whole world and the common people."[21] But the humanitarian sentiments which Chaplin had expressed in his *Great Dictator* speech in 1940 were not patriotic enough in postwar America.

Graham Greene addressed to Chaplin an open letter at this time, in which he demolished the charges against Chaplin's loyalty to the United States, adding, "Intolerance in any country wounds freedom throughout the world." Greene goes on in the letter to remind Chaplin that, when he had visited with Chaplin a few days earlier, he had suggested that Chaplin make a film about his recent brush with McCarthyism. In Greene's proposed film the Tramp would be summoned from obscurity to answer for his past before the House Un-American Activities Committee. Greene records that Chaplin had laughed the suggestion away; but in point of fact the sentiment in Chaplin's next film, *A King in New York* (1957), is in some ways very similar to Greene's original suggestion.

Chaplin plays a deposed monarch exiled in America, who reduces an investigating committee hearing to a shambles with the help of a fire hose. Chaplin always maintained that the film is not anti-American. He rather implies in the picture that the witch-hunting hysteria of the 1950s is a phase of the American mood which would pass, as indeed it did.

Chaplin's last film was *A Countess from Hong Kong* (1967), which he wrote and directed and scored, but in which he did not appear, except in a cameo role as a seasick steward. "The *Countess* has been quite an adventure for me because I've never directed stars before," said Chaplin when he finished the film. He was referring to Marlon Brando and Sophia Loren, who play the film's principal roles. "I've always been my own star, and I could always do what I liked with me."[22] The picture is about a refugee from a Hong Kong dance hall (Sophia Loren) who claims that she is an aristocratic refugee from Russia. She stows away in the stateroom of an American diplomat (Marlon Brando), and mishap follows mishap from that point onward. Andrew Sarris has given the wisest and most succinct assessment of the film: "Few reviewers have bothered to observe that Chaplin's role is being played by Sophia Loren, the Tramp with oversized men's pajamas and a heart of gold. Chaplin had problems with both Loren and Brando simply because neither is Chaplin, but the movie still generates a surprising amount of charm and wit."[23]

Chaplin began his film-making career in the days when it was possible for a director to make a film that was solely the product of his own creative ingenuity. He was able to maintain this kind of personal artistic control over his films throughout his career, even after the motion picture industry had become a factory system. When Chaplin saw this happening, he warned that Hollywood was doomed unless it decided, once and for all, to give up standardizing its films; unless it recognized that "masterpieces cannot be mass-produced in the cinema, like tractors in a factory."[24]

Although no film director ever again would have the total artistic independence that Chaplin enjoyed during his career, some film makers have succeeded in creating personal films, depsite the studio system in which they have worked. For them Chaplin has proved an abiding inspiration. In the course of *Limelight* Calvero the clown muses that entertainers are "amateurs—that's all any of us are—amateurs. We don't live long enough to be anything else."

Chaplin lived long enough.

2
Howard Hawks
Lonely Are the Brave

Cinema critics for a long time did not view Howard Hawks as an important director, simply because they did not consider action films, with which his name had
over the years become virtually synonymous, as worthy of serious consideration.
Hence it was relatively late in his career that Hawks was acknowledged as a significant *auteur* director with an impressive corpus of work. The first American critic
to give Hawks and his films serious consideration was Manny Farber, who wrote in
the mid-1950s about a trend in American cinema that he christened "underground
films," and named Hawks as one of its key figures. Farber was describing a style of
movie making that began in the 1930s, peaked in the 1940s, and has since passed
from the film-making scene, at least as a definable movement; nonetheless, it has
left its impact on contemporary cinema.

The term *underground film* has also been applied to the cheaply made, sometimes
pornographic, films made by Andy Warhol and other experimental film makers.
But the term as Farber coined it referred to movies made by certain Hollywood
directors who would "tunnel" beneath the surface of the routine scripts they were
given to direct and seek to illuminate in a shrewd and unsentimental fashion deeper
truths, usually about the unglamorous side of the human condition. "With striking
photography, a good ear for natural dialogue, an eye for realistic detail," a director
like Hawks created films that seemed to take "private runways to the truth," said
Farber, while other directors "took a slow, embalming surface route."

Underground films did not get bogged down in "significant" dialogue but told
their stories in a straightforward fashion that nonetheless implied subtle thematic
implications beneath the surface of their basically action-oriented plots. Essentially
the people who made these films moved about easily in the world of their often
shabby subjects, adds Penelope Houston. The settings of these films included run-
down hotel rooms, private detective's offices, and barrooms. "The heroine was
usually discovered propped against a piano, singing an insolent dirge. The hero was
a cynic who had been pushed around once too often," a character best exemplified
by Humphrey Bogart in his two Hawks films, *To Have and Have Not* and *The Big
Sleep*.

Although Hawks's name was frequently associated with action films like the two
just mentioned, he was successful in making comedies and musicals as well. Despite
this variety of subject matter, Hawks's films nevertheless reflect a consistent

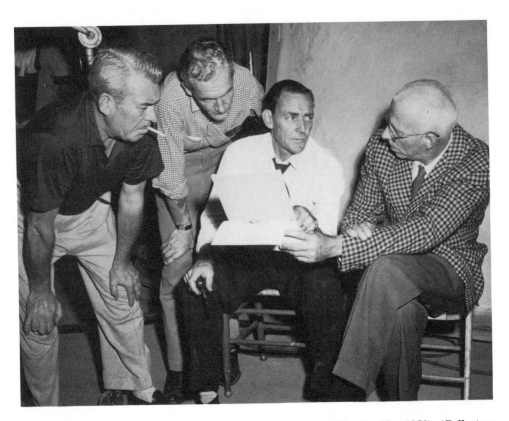

Howard Hawks (right) conferring with his crew on the set of *The Big Sky* (1952). (Collectors Book Store)

personal style and view of the world. This is because, as Andrew Sarris has said, Hawks "retained a surprising degree of control over his assignments, choosing the ones he wanted to do, and working on the scripts of all his films," usually without screen credit. "The Hawksian hero acts with remarkable consistency in a predominantly male universe," Sarris continued. Like his heroes, Howard Hawks "lived a tightrope existence, keeping his footing in a treacherous industry for more than forty years without surrendering his personal identity. . . . That one can discern the same directorial signature over a wide variety of genres is proof of artistry."[1]

When serious film scholars finally began analyzing Hawks's films, they discovered that the secret of Hawks's success, both artistic and popular, lay in the fact that he was able to work comfortably within the established Hollywood genres of film making such as the Western and the detective story and at the same time unobtrusively use these genres to express his own personal vision and directorial style. "My recipe for making movies," he said when I spoke with him, "has always been to give an audience two or three really top-notch scenes in every film and to try not to annoy them the rest of the time. If you can do that you will have made an entertaining picture."

Robin Wood points out in his book on Hawks that the director was always free of the kind of pretensions or ambitions that usually bring a director into conflict with the commercial considerations which underlie the functioning of the studio system. Hawks always looked for stories that appealed to him personally, and that therefore showed promise of appealing to the mass audience as well. "I know the kind of story I can tell," he said; "and if it's fun for me to do, I'll do it well. There are only a few times that I've done a favor for somebody and made a picture, and usually it hasn't been good."

Hawks, who was born in Goshen, Indiana, in 1896, began his apprenticeship in the picture business in the silent days. He worked in the story departments at Paramount and at MGM in the mid-1920s; then he moved to the Fox studios, where he directed his first film. It was a silent picture, to which he was assigned, called *The Road to Glory* (1926), about a girl who goes blind after an auto accident, and it was not a success. "Then I suggested to the studio that I make a movie about Adam and Eve waking up in the Garden of Eden and call it *Fig Leaves* (1926)," he recalled. "It made back its cost in one theater. Fron then on the studio asked me what I wanted to do."

In the first sequence of *Fig Leaves* Adam (George O'Brien) and Eve (Olive Borden) are pictured at the dawn of the human race; but then the film moves up to the twentieth century with a transitional title that comments, "Thousands of years later women hadn't changed a bit." Just as Eve was fussy about making an outfit of fig leaves look attractive in the Eden scenes, so the modern Eve Smith becomes so clothes-conscious that her extravagance almost causes her to lose the modern Adam. Not a very profound story by any standard, but the success of *Fig Leaves* did earn Hawks the right to choose his own projects from then on. In fact, from 1929 onward Hawks was not under contract to any studio and was therefore able to work with an independence not common in the days when most film makers served as staff directors under long-term contracts to the studios that employed them.

The first of Hawks's silent films to treat subject matter that points ahead to his later work is *A Girl in Every Port* (1928), with its preoccupation with male comradeship, a subject that turns up in most of Hawks's major films. Here he handles this theme somewhat simplistically, however, in a film that seems to be a trial run for movies to come, such as *Only Angels Have Wings*, *Air Force*, *Red River*, and *Rio Bravo*.

In *A Girl in Every Port* Spike (Victor McLaglen) and Bill (Robert Armstrong) are sailors who are frequent rivals for the same girl, as they go from port to port. Bill has the custom of tattooing each of his conquests with the heart-and-anchor symbol on his signet ring. When he and Spike slug it out over the possession of one young lady in a bar, Bill clouts Spike on the chin and, significantly, leaves the imprint of his signet ring on Spike's chin. This signals the beginning of their friendship and the end of Bill's compulsive pursuit of girls. Spike, however, still has an eye for the ladies. He takes Bill to meet a girl with whom he has fallen in love (Louise Brooks), who turns out to be one of Bill's old flames. Bill insists that she is a tramp—and she is. Spike nonetheless suspects that Bill is trying to poison his mind against her for selfish motives. A crisis develops in their friendship; but the two men are reunited in a barroom brawl, after which they decide that no "dame" will ever come between them again.

Some critics have inferred a hint of homosexuality in the theme of this film, but such a reading of a Hawks picture misconstrues the value that Hawks places on male companionship in his films. In the present instance, Spike and Bill have never experienced a deep relationship in their lives, since their love life consists of picking up girls in the ports that they visit. Hence, like the two men in John Schlesinger's *Midnight Cowboy*, they are experiencing in their friendship a relationship that is fulfilling for them on an emotional level that has nothing to do with sex. Bill and Spike are really like two adolescent boys who must first know what true male friendship can be before they can go on to experience a meaningful relationship with a member of the opposite sex.

In later films like *Only Angels Have Wings* Hawks will show how the female becomes integrated into the masculine world of his heroes, but *A Girl in Every Port* ends before that process begins for Bill and Spike. In this sense *A Girl in Every Port* is a prologue to the male-friendship theme of Hawks's later films.

Most of Hawks's silent films have nothing particularly distinctive about them that would mark them as the work of the same director. *Fazil* (1928) is a silent film that film historian William K. Everson in some unpublished program notes for the picture has called "a tongue-in-sheik" parody of the popular Rudolph Valentino films of the period.[2] "The entire picture has the look of a Victorian pornographic novel from which all of the pornography has been removed," he continues, "although the harem scenes retain a definite eroticism." Nevertheless, *Fazil* begins to take itself much more seriously as it moves toward its climax and ends up a rather turgid parable about how westerners will never understand the inscrutable East. The film was made on the threshold of the sound era, and a synchronized musical score was added before it was released.

With the coming of sound, Hawks's personal style began to assert itself. His first talking picture was *The Dawn Patrol* (1930). Hawks thinks that the primary reason he was chosen to direct the movie was that he had a considerable amount of flying experience and was therefore able to shoot several of the flying scenes himself while piloting the plane at the same time.

"I had not worked since the coming of sound," Hawks remembered, "because the producers didn't know if I could work with dialogue. I had never had any theatrical experience," in contrast to a director like George Cukor, who came to Hollywood from Broadway in the early 1930s. Hawks wrote the scenario for the film himself, eschewing the stagy kind of dialogue commonplace in the early talkies in favor of a more natural kind of conversational speech. "During shooting everyone kept telling me that the dialogue wasn't dramatic enough," he said. "What they meant was that it wasn't theatrical enough."

When the picture turned out to be one of the best films of the year, studio officials frequently screened it for other directors, telling them that *Dawn Patrol* was an example of what good screen dialogue should be. "I've gone ahead working on the dialogue of my pictures ever since," Hawks concluded. In fact, he developed the custom over the years of sitting down with a yellow pad each morning before shooting began and changing any dialogue that no longer fit the flow of the shooting as it had been progressing. He was not really improvising, he explained; he was simply modifying the dialogue "to fit the action of the scene."

An abiding theme of Hawks's action films is the stoical courage with which men face both life and death; and this theme is obvious in *Dawn Patrol*, which tells the story of a fighter squadron in World War I that has a high death rate. One squadron leader replaces another, but the mortality rate continues to remain as high as ever. "It's part of the game," Hawks said. "Men take planes up and test them, for instance; and having been schooled to the army, they accept commands, no matter what the command. And that's what makes an army function." In Hawks's male universe the virtues most prized are courage and loyalty to one's duty and to one's comrades, and this code is much in evidence in *Dawn Patrol*, as well as in Hawks's other great aviation films, *Only Angels Have Wings* and *Air Force*.

In *Only Angels Have Wings* (1939) Jeff Carter (Cary Grant) runs an air mail service in the remote South American town of Barranca. Death is a fact of daily existence, and Jeff's pilots have learned to live with it just as he has. They have also learned to live with each other in a spirit of friendship in their isolated outpost. For most of the film the airfield is enveloped in fog, a circumstance that underlines still more the way the men are cut off from the rest of the world.

Into this male milieu comes Bonnie (Jean Arthur), who is attracted to a pilot named Joe (Noah Beery, Jr.). When Joe is killed in a plane crash, Bonnie is shocked by the apparently casual manner in which Jeff and the others take his death, until she realizes this is only their way of coping with their loss of a comrade and with their awareness that their common profession requires that they live daily in the shadow of death. As the evening goes on, Bonnie begins to understand and accept the code by which the flyers live and die. She even joins Jeff in singing "The Peanut Vendor." The song, says Robin Wood, "becomes a shout of defiance in the face of the darkness surrounding human life and the chaos of the universe." The comradeship that develops in the course of carrying out a joint task seems to be the only comfort that Hawks's heroes have in the face of that outer darkness, a darkness which becomes almost palpable in *Only Angels Have Wings* in the form of the fog that encompasses the airfield.

One is always aware in a Hawks film of what Wood calls "the extreme precariousness of everything. In the background, never far away, is the eternal darkness surrounding human existence, against which the Hawksian stoicism shines."[3] That stoicism is embodied in the insistence of Hawks's heroes on the virtues of courage and endurance, through which man achieves self-respect. Jeff sums up that stoicism when he says after Joe's death, "What's the use of getting upset about something that couldn't be helped?"

In *Air Force* (1943) the comradeship of the group is organized around the *Mary Ann*, a bomber with a devoted crew. The film is, therefore, not a mere "warbond seller," as many wartime American films were, but a study of a group of men under stress, in the very same way as *Only Angels Have Wings*. The plane in *Air Force* becomes the concrete embodiment of the mutual loyalty that unifies its crew. Hence, as Wood notes, the *Mary Ann* becomes the symbol of order preserved in a chaotic world by a teamwork to which each member of the group contributes. Yet this group spirit does not cause the members of the crew to lose their individual identity; for, in contributing to the group effort, each man earns the respect of his comrades, which in turn confirms his own self-respect.[4] It is this mutual dependence that binds the crew of the *Mary Ann* together and enables them to live their dangerous existence.

This group solidarity is best reflected in the moving scene in which the captain of the plane dies. The delirious skipper believes that the *Mary Ann* is taking off on a mission. As he goes over his take-off checklist, each member of the crew standing around his bed contributes to the illusion by enacting his usual role aboard the plane. As the navigator says that the course is "due east," the captain murmurs, "That's right into the sunrise," and expires. This particular scene was contributed to the script by William Faulkner, who collaborated with Hawks on other films, as shall be seen shortly.

Air Force was photographed with documentary-type realism by cinematographer James Wong Howe. Shooting on location, outside the controlled conditions of a studio sound stage, sometimes increases the technical problems of shooting a scene. In *Air Force*, for instance, there was a scene in which some bombers had to land in a clearing in the jungle because they had just heard that Pearl Harbor had been bombed and could not return to their base. "On the night we were to shoot the landing," Howe recalled, "the generator that supplied the power for the lights broke down. When I told Howard Hawks about it, he said, 'That's your problem; you're photographing the picture.' I collected all of the flares that I could find and arranged them along the runway and made them all go off at once. We got a flash of light followed by smoke from each of the flares, and it gave the effect of planes landing on an airfield that had been bombed. When Hawks saw the rushes, he said that he was tempted to send the generator back to the studio and finish the picture with flares."

There is a flavor of authenticity in Hawks's two other important war films, both of which deal with the First World War: *The Road to Glory* and *Sergeant York*. *The Road to Glory* (1936)—which is not to be confused with Hawks's silent picture of the same name—is really a companion piece to *Dawn Patrol*, in that it treats the inescapable cycle of death by which war separates comrades and loved ones. Like the squadron leaders in *Dawn Patrol*, Captain Laroche (Warner Baxter) is obsessed by his sense of responsibility for sending men to their deaths in battle. His position is made even more intolerable when his own father (Lionel Barrymore) becomes a soldier in his company.

Death eventually claims Captain Laroche himself, and the film ends with his replacement (Fredric March) repeating virtually the same speech to the new recruits that Laroche had given earlier in the picture. The cycle of death goes on, but each soldier's unflinching dedication to duty and to his comrades keeps him stoically going onward. In Hawks's world the road to glory is a very private one, which each man must travel alone even when he is in the company of others who are dying with him. He must confront death face to face, and no one can do that for him.

"The best drama for me is the one which shows a man in danger," says Hawks. "There is no action when there is no danger. To live or to die? What drama is greater?"[5] In *Sergeant York* (1941), Hawks's other war film with a World War I setting, the director illustrates this conviction by portraying a real-life war hero, Sergeant Alvin York. The film was released in September, 1941, on the eve of the Second World War, and went on to become one of Hawks's biggest commercial successes and also to win Gary Cooper an Academy Award for his performance as York.

York becomes a Hawksian hero in the movie long before his exploits on the battlefield. In the early scenes of the film, set on the Tennessee farm where York grew up, we see him striving to wrest a living from the rocky soil, so that he can prove himself worthy of marrying his sweetheart. York's insistence on proving himself to his girl—and to himself—reflects the kind of determination that will serve him well as a soldier, the film suggests.

Hawks achieved a striking realism in the film, not only in the battle scenes, but also in the earlier sequences of York's life in the small farming community. A strong sense of realism has always been a hallmark of Hawks's films, as in *Tiger Shark* (1932). That film is about a group of fisherman and begins with shots of the men at work that are worthy of any documentary about the sea.

Edward G. Robinson plays Mike Mascerena, a fisherman who is the rival of another, younger man for the love of Mike's ward. After shooting began, Hawks decided to lighten the whole tone of the film by rewriting the central character's part. "When we started the film," Hawks recalled, "Robinson's part was written as a very dour, sour man. At the end of the first day of shooting I said to Eddie, 'This is going to be the dullest picture that has ever been made.' I told him about a man that I knew that covered up his shyness by talking a great deal and very fast. 'If you're willing to try it with me,' I said to Robinson, 'let's make your character happy-go-lucky and talkative throughout the picture.' So every day I gave him a sheet of yellow paper with his new lines on it. He did a great job."

A note of Hawksian stoicism reverberates throughout *Tiger Shark*. After Mike, in a fit of desperation, pushes his rival overboard in the hope that he will be eaten by a shark, he ominously explains to the girl, "The sharks took my hand and gave me a hook to replace it; they took your father and gave you to me; and now they'll take him; the sharks, they settle everything." But the young man is saved; and later it is Mike who is gored by a shark. He dies in the arms of the girl and the man whom she is now going to marry, repeating, "The sharks, they settle everything." The sharks, of course, stand in Hawks's thematic context for an inscrutable Destiny or Fate, which man must stoically accept but cannot understand.

Hawks's stoic view of life is tinged with a cynicism that comes to the surface in his crime melodramas, *Scarface*, *To Have and Have Not*, and *The Big Sleep*. *Scarface* (1932) was the last and the best of the cycle of gangster films in the early 1930s. It was based on the career of Al Capone and incorporated episodes from the racketeer's life, including the Saint Valentine's Day Massacre.

Ben Hecht agreed to write *Scarface* for Hawks only after the latter told him that he wanted to pattern Tony Carmonte, the Capone character played by Paul Muni, after Cesare Borgia and Tony's kid sister after Lucretia Borgia. "This analogy permeates the script," said Hawks, and it "affects all the scenes." This twist interested Hecht, who finished the script in eleven days, basing it on news stories of the time. For example, he had a professional killer (George Raft) perpetually flip a coin because there had been several corpses found in Chicago with a nickle in one hand, which the murderer had put there as a mark of disrespect, Hawks explained.

"We also exploited another little-known fact," he continues. "The papers that published the photos of a murder indicated 'X marks the spot where the body was found.' So we designed fifteen or twenty scenes around the X, finding all sorts of ways to use the X when a murder occurred."[6] In the scene in the bowling alley where a rival gang leader (Boris Karloff) is killed, there is a shot of Karloff marking an X on the scoreboard, which, in terms of the film's symbolism, signals that he is to die. Then he throws his ball, and we watch it hit the bowling pins just as we hear gunfire off-screen. The camera holds on the last bowling pin still standing until it wobbles and falls over, and we know that Karloff is dead.

In the Saint Valentine's Day Massacre sequence, the camera focuses on the shadows cast on the wall by the seven victims who are about to be shot; then it pans upward to a pattern of Xs on the rafters above, as the sound of machine gun blasts are heard from below, and then downward to the bloody bodies of the seven dead. To round out the X symbolism in the movie, the scar on Tony's face is X-shaped, marking him too for eventual extermination.

Tony Carmonte dies as violently as he lived, but more significance can be attached to the finale of *Scarface* than the obligatory implication that "crime does not pay," which is found in other gangster films of the period. As Tony and his sister (Ann Dvorak) are holed up in his apartment, engaged in a last desperate gun battle with the police, Tony gradually realizes that the "protective" love he has had for her all along is basically incestuous. Tony becomes increasingly overwrought as this recognition forces itself on him, and he becomes even more hysterical when his sister is killed by a police bullet. He rushes through the clouds of tear gas that surround him and that serve as an apt metaphor for his own foggy state of mind, and flings himself defiantly into the hail of bullets that meets him as soon as he steps into the street. In a final cinematic touch, the camera pans from Tony's corpse on the pavement up to a neon sign advertising Cook's Tours that reads, "The world is yours."

Hawks continued to make superior crime films throughout his career. Two of his best, *To Have and Have Not* and *The Big Sleep*, starred Humphrey Bogart and Lauren Bacall and listed William Faulkner among the scriptwriters. *To Have and Have Not* (1944) was based on a novel by Ernest Hemingway and represents the only time in film history that two Nobel Prize–winning authors were involved in a film story. "I tried to get Ernest Hemingway to write for pictures as Bill Faulkner had done for me on several occasions," Hawks told me; "but Hemingway said that he was going to stick to the kind of writing that he knew best. Once, on a hunting trip, I told him that if he would give me the worst story that he had ever written, we would make a good movie out of it. He asked me what I thought was his worst novel; and I said *To Have and Have Not*, which I thought was a bunch of junk. He said that he had written it when he needed money, and that he didn't want me to make a movie out of it. But finally he gave in, and so Faulkner and Jules Furthman did the script."

With Hemingway's agreement, new scenes were devised to show what had happened to the main characters before the actual beginning of the novel. Hawks says that ultimately there was enough material in the novel left over to serve as the basis of two more films: Michael Curtiz's *The Breaking Point* (1950) and Don Siegel's *The Gun Runners* (1958). "Later, when I told Hemingway how much money we made from *To Have and Have Not*," Hawks concluded, "he didn't speak to me for six months."

To Have and Have Not is the film in which Lauren Bacall made movie history by saying to Bogart, "If you want anything, all you have to do is whistle." "I wrote that line as part of her screen test and it went over so well that we wanted to find a place to put it into the picture," Hawks remembered. "Faulkner decided to put it in while Bogart and Bacall were in a hotel room with no one else around, so that the audience wouldn't miss the implication." They didn't then and don't now.

"I told Bogey that I was going to make Bacall more insolent than he was, and he was the most insolent character in pictures. He could be insolent off camera too. The first day that I worked with him he got tough with me, so I grabbed him by the lapels, pushed him against the wall and said, 'I tell you how to get tough in the picture; you don't get tough with me.' He said okay. He had drunk his lunch that day, and he never did that again—while he was working for me."

In *To Have and Have Not* Bogart plays Harry Morgan, a self-styled adventurer in Martinique during the early years of the Second World War. Morgan gets involved in smuggling to safety Frenchmen who are fugitives from the pro-Nazi Vichy government, but the film also centres around the relationship of Harry and his girl Marie (Lauren Bacall), whom he casually calls Slim. Both Harry and Slim are tough and are therefore evenly matched from the start. "They seem to do even their kissing out of the corners of their mouths," quipped James Agee.[7]

**Lauren Bacall, Marcel Dalio, and Humphrey Bogart in *To Have and Have Not* (1944).
(Museum of Modern Art/Film Stills Archive)**

Faulkner was good at writing dialogue, but he was the first to admit that Jules Furthman, who worked on this and other Hawks films, had a way of telegraphing a great deal to the audience with little or no dialogue at all. According to Faulkner, Furthman suggested the kind of girl that Slim was, and how Harry would react to her accordingly, by having her look to Harry to light her cigarette the first time that they meet. Harry sizes her up for a moment, "then tosses her the matches to light her own cigarette." Later she proposes to Harry with the exact words that Bonnie uses to Jeff in Furthman's screenplay for *Only Angels Have Wings*: "I'm very hard to get; all you have to do is ask me."

Although the Bogart-Bacall team struck cinematic sparks, *To Have and Have Not* really belongs to Bogart, who is able to show in his performance how Harry develops by the film's end into the typical Hawksian hero: a man wo achieves self-respect by stoically maintaining his integrity. Despite the fact that in the past Harry has consistently refused to commit himself to any cause, he eventually decides to help the Free French at the cost of grave personal peril because his own stubborn sense of independence is revolted by the fascist methods employed by the agents of the Vichy government in tracking down the Free French fugitives. When one of the latter asks why Harry has finally agreed to aid them, Harry answers laconically, "Because I like you, and I don't like them." Beneath Harry's tough exterior, Bogart neatly implies in his performance, is a humanity that can be reached. Indeed, journalist Pico Iyer, in describing the Bogart persona as it appears in Hawks films like *To Have and Have Not*, has said that Bogart embodies the "figure of the tough-but-tender hero cracking wise to cover up his soft spots."[8]

Bogart continued his portrayal of the Hawksian hero in *The Big Sleep* (1946), this time as Raymond Chandler's detective, Philip Marlowe. Hawks again got Faulkner to work on the script, along with a young lady named Leigh Brackett, who would collaborate on Hawks's films for many years to come. Hawks told them to revise Chandler's story wherever necessary in order to provide plenty of action. "It doesn't have to be great art," he said to them; "just keep it moving." And so they did.

"It was basically an entertaining film and was a success, even though I never could figure out who killed who," Hawks noted. "When I was asked who killed the man whose car is fished out of the river, I said, 'I don't know. I'll ask Faulkner.' Faulkner didn't know either. So I asked Chandler, and he said that the butler had done it; and I said, 'Like hell he did; he was down at the beach house at the time.' The picture was a success, so I never worried about logic again. But I've always been concerned about the overall structure of a film, since the audience has to be able to follow that, whether or not some of the details get lost along the way." As Chandler himself once said about writing crime fiction, when in doubt about what to do next, you simply open a door on a man with a gun in his hand. Faulkner and Brackett employed that solution to the plot complications in *The Big Sleep* more than once.

In discussing his association with Faulkner over the years, Hawks told me, "Bill worked with me on several pictures. I could call on him any time and ask him for a scene, and he always gave it to me." Faulkner's admiration for Hawks was mutual. Once, when Hawks asked Faulkner to help him with a script, Faulkner's publisher objected because the novelist was in the midst of finishing a novel. Faulkner is said to have replied, "Mr. Hawks has carried me in pictures, seen that I got screen credits that I really did not deserve." Whenever he needed money, Faulkner concluded, Hawks was always very good to him; and if Hawks needed him, he was going.[9]

To Have and Have Not and *The Big Sleep*, as mentioned, epitomize perfectly the underground films of the 1940s; for the brutal violence in both pictures is balanced by a tough, cynical humor in the dialogue. An interchange between Marlowe and Vivian (Lauren Bacall) in *The Big Sleep* provides a sample of the brand of humor to be found in these films. In the course of a conversation ostensibly about horse racing, Marlowe quips that Vivian looks to him like a slow starter; and she responds in kind that it depends on who is in the saddle. By this point in their interchange, it is clear that they are discussing neither horses nor racing.

Robin Wood suggests that Hawks sought to balance the theme of responsibility and commitment found in his serious films with a sort of whimsical predilection for irresponsible behavior in his comedies, and this theory certainly holds up under close inspection. "Comedy is virtually the same as a serious adventure story," said

Hawks. "The difference is in the situation—dangerous in an adventure, embarrassing in comedy. But in both we observe our fellow human beings in unusual situations. . . . Whenever I hear a story, my first thought is how to make it into a comedy, and I think of how to make it into a drama only as a last resort."

Referring to Hawks's films, Peter Wollen adds, "Whereas the dramas show the mastery of man over nature, . . . over the animal and the childish, the comedies show his humiliation, his regression. The heroes become victims; society . . . breaks in with eruptions of monstrous farce."[10] In Hawks's first major comedy, *Twentieth Century* (1934), Oscar Jaffe (John Barrymore), a stage director, is victimized by Lily Garland (Carole Lombard), the star of the play he is directing who also happens to be his estranged wife. During their frequent battles, both in and out of rehearsals, Oscar and Lily hurl objects at each other as dexterously as insults. "It was the first time that the romantic leads, instead of the secondary comics, played for laughs," Hawks pointed out; and in Barrymore and Lombard, Hawks had a perfectly matched comedian and comedienne.

Many screen actors have given some of their best comedy performances for Hawks. Among them is Cary Grant, who appeared in *Bringing up Baby*, *His Girl Friday*, and *I Was a Male War Bride*. In *Bringing up Baby* (1938) Grant plays paleontologist David Huxley, who has just discovered the last bone needed to complete the skeleton of a dinosaur he is reconstructing, only to have it stolen by George, a dog belonging to Susan, a scatterbrained heiress (Katharine Hepburn). Susan also owns a leopard named Baby, and before the madcap farce ends, Huxley chases George, Baby chases Huxley, and the dinosaur skeleton collapses.

The latter catastrophe occurs when Susan climbs up the scaffolding adjoining the gigantic skeleton in order to talk to Huxley, who is sitting atop his reconstruction. In so doing she causes vibrations that start an avalanche, bringing the whole structure tumbling down. But Huxley winds up with Susan as a more-than-compensating consolation prize for the collapse of his project. The delightfully irresponsible Susan has succeeded in winning Huxley away, not only from his singleminded concentration on his work, but also from his soberly serious fiancée. In Hawks's comic world, man is no longer his own master, as he is in the director's serious films.

Although Hepburn and Grant never appeared again as a team in a Hawks film, they were to costar in some other sophisticated comedies of the period for George Cukor. After *Bringing up Baby*, Grant's next comedy for Hawks was *His Girl Friday* (1940), based on the Ben Hecht–Charles MacArthur play *The Front Page*, which had already been filmed in 1931 by Lewis Milestone under its original title.

Grant was set to play the domineering newspaper editor, Walter Burns; and Hawks was searching for someone to play the star reporter, Hildy Johnson. "One day I was saying that Ben Hecht and Charlie MacArthur were the best dialogue writers in the business," Hawks remembered. "To prove my point I had a secretary read through one of the scenes of *The Front Page* with me. I realized that Hildy Johnson's lines were better when they were read by a woman. I called Hecht and he agreed, so the part of the reporter was rewritten for Rosalind Russell." Miss Russell gave one of the best performances of her career in the movie. In fact, Pauline Kael has written that the difference between the Rosalind Russell of *His*

Girl Friday and of a later vehicle like *Auntie Mame* "is the difference between a comedienne and an institution."[11]

This time Grant played the character with a penchant for irresponsible behavior. Walter Burns is both Hildy's boss and her ex-husband, and he is bent on keeping her from marrying a respectable business man (Ralph Bellamy) and giving up the newspaper game for good. As was the case in *Bringing up Baby*, the lure of irresponsibility proves irresistible, and Hildy is reconciled with Burns, both professionally and personally.

A major innovation in *His Girl Friday* was Hawks's introduction of overlapping dialogue to keep the farce moving at a fast tempo. "Actors don't usually jump on one another's lines," Hawks explained; "so I told them that I'd fire them if they didn't. But I made sure that the lines that I wanted the audience to hear came out over the scramble. As a result, the film turned out to be better than the earlier version."

Although Hawks's comedies are often racy, he can never be accused of bad taste. *I Was a Male War Bride* (1949) had Grant as Henri Rochard, a French captain who can enter the United States with his wife, an American army officer (Ann Sheridan), only by posing as a war bride. "*I Was a Male War Bride* was a sensitive subject, but no one complained about the way we handled it," said Hawks. He

Rosalind Russell and Cary Grant in *His Girl Friday* (1940). (Museum of Modern Art/Film Stills Archive)

recast the dialogue of some of the scenes during shooting, in order to ensure that the lines would be funny and not merely embarrassing. "That's the good thing about Cary Grant," Hawks added. "You say, 'Cary, let's try this scene another way. It will change your dialogue, but don't let it worry you. Say anything you think of, and if you can't think of the right thing, I'll write something down for you on my yellow pad.' But usually he would think of the right thing and we would go ahead and shoot it."

This is an indication of the rapport that Hawks was noted for establishing with his actors. "I worked with Marilyn Monroe in the musical comedy *Gentlemen Prefer Blondes* (1953) and found that she was really a frightened girl. You had to convince her that she was good. Once you got her out of her dressing room, you could work with her. When I couldn't get something across to her, Jane Russell would talk to her for me; and they would work it out."

Hawks really saw comedy and drama as two sides of the same coin, and that helps to explain why he was comfortable in making both kinds of films. "Humor often comes close to tragedy," he pointed out. "The only difference between comedy and tragedy is the point of view. In *Red River* (1948) I wanted to have a scene where the hero's men get him drunk, so that they can amputate his finger after an accident. But John Wayne refused to do it, because he thought it was crazy to play a scene like that for comedy. So I had Kirk Douglas do it in *The Big Sky* (1952). When Wayne saw that picture, he called me and said that, if I told him that I wanted a funeral scene to be funny, he would do whatever I wanted."

Hawks's Westerns often have comic moments of this kind, even though they are essentially serious. In his Westerns, the Hawksian hero again appears as a man who wishes to prove himself to himself, with the support of the group to which he belongs, by living up to the responsibilities that life imposes on him. Perhaps more than any other genre in which he worked, Hawks's Westerns remain his most characteristic films. As William Faulkner said of *The Land of the Pharaohs* (1955), a film about ancient Egypt on which the writer worked for Hawks, "This is the same movie Howard has been making for thirty-five years. It's *Red River* all over again. The Pharaoh is the cattle baron, his jewels are the cattle, and the Nile is the Red River. But the thing about Howard is that he knows it's the same movie, and he knows how to make it."[12]

In discussing his Westerns, Hawks is quick to acknowledge his debt to John Ford, who began his career in films a few years before Hawks and who made such fine Westerns as *Stagecoach* and *My Darling Clementine*. "I never directed like Ford, but I learned a lot from him," Hawks said. "Every time I would run into a scene that he did well, I would think what he would have done. He knew how to use everything that happens—bad weather or whatever else comes along unexpectedly. During the burial scene in *Red River* we saw a cloud crossing the mountain while John Wayne was reading the prayer over the grave. I told him to stay where he was and keep talking until the cloud passed overhead, because it added to the gloom of the whole scene. I called Ford when the picture was finished and told him to catch that scene, because it was the kind of thing that he would have done. Afterwards he said that it was."

Red River centers around cattle baron Tom Dunson (John Wayne), who symbolizes the passing of the old order that refuses to change with the times. The key event in the film is a cattle drive from Texas to Missouri, where Dunson hopes to sell his cattle. By the time the cattle drive reaches its destination, it was become increasingly clear, even to Dunson, that the tough, stubborn qualities of the pioneer—qualities that enabled him to bring his men and his cattle through the ordeal of the drive—make him more and more of an anachronism in the more civilized territory away from the frontier. The railroad, symbol of civilization moving west, will soon be able to transport cattle without the need of men like Dunson.

This growing realization has caused Dunson to become a bitter and intractable boss, and his men have transferred their loyalty to his stepson Matthew (Montgomery Clift). The hostile rivalry of Dunson and Matthew threatens to erupt into a shootout; but when it comes to a showdown, Dunson cannot bring himself to fire on his stepson, the only person to whom he feels a real closeness.

"Hawks has returned repeatedly to the subject of close relationships between men, and he himself is explicit in calling it 'love,'" writes Robin Wood. But, as noted above, one should be wary of the word *homosexual*. For, as Wood explains, "The close male friendships of Hawks's films are invariably presented as thoroughly healthy and natural. Their essence is a deep and strong mutual respect." Implicit in this respect is the awareness on the part of Hawks's males that they need each other to fulfill the common task to which they are committed, whatever it might be.

This strong strain of friendship is visible in the trilogy of Westerns that Hawks later made starring John Wayne, and on which Leigh Brackett worked as writer: *Rio Bravo*, *El Dorado*, and *Rio Lobo*. "The style of writing and the use of the same part of the country are the same in all three films," Hawks pointed out; "but there are variations. *Rio Bravo* had a boy who was a good gunman, so in *El Dorado* we had a boy who couldn't shoot at all. I got the idea for *El Dorado* from *Rio Bravo*, but I got the idea of *Rio Bravo* from seeing *High Noon*, which was made by another director. I said to myself that a good sheriff wouldn't run around begging for help to face a gun battle; besides, in *High Noon* the hero winds up doing the job himself anyway. I made *Rio Bravo* to show the opposite kind of western hero, who is willing to stand up for himself."

Yet in *Rio Bravo* John Chance (John Wayne) is very much supported by his friends in facing the villain and his gang in the climactic gun battle. Perhaps in Hawks's view the difference between Chance and the marshall in Fred Zinnemann's *High Noon* is that Chance always confidently radiates the impression that, if no one offers to help him, he can carry on alone, while the marshall in *High Noon* is not so sure of himself.[13]

The opening scene of *Rio Bravo* (1959) effectively sets the tone of the film. Chance finds his friend Dude (Dean Martin) dead drunk in a saloon and is saddened to see the wreck that Dude has become. The economy with which Hawks tells us so much about the relationship of the two men, in a scene that is almost wordless, demonstrates how direct and straightforward the director can be. Hawks said that he always tried "to tell a story as simply as possible with the camera at eye level," because that gives the viewer the sense of being an actual witness to the action taking place before him.

As a matter of fact, when Hawks first started directing pictures, his simplicity of style got him into difficulties with producers, who complained that he did not shoot enough footage for the editor to work with in putting the film together. "I don't want you to make the movie in the cutting room," he would reply. "I want to make the film myself on the set." Hawks would consequently not shoot a surplus of material from which the editor could choose the shots that he wanted to include in the finished film. Instead, he would shoot only enough footage for the editor to be able to put the scene together one way—Hawks's way. For example, if Hawks did not want a close-up in a given scene, the editor would find, when he came to put the scene together, that Hawks had not shot any close-ups when filming the scene.

In any event, from the opening scene onward, *Rio Bravo* presents the rejuvenation of Dude's integrity and self-respect, supported all the way by Chance, whom he joins in the final gun fight. Together they ward off a gang of desperadoes who are determined to free one of their companions from the local jail before the marshall can arrive to claim him. Chance and Dude and two other comrades move into the jailhouse to hold off the gang until the marshall arrives. By so doing, they form a small, isolated male community similar to that of the flyers in *Only Angels Have Wings* and other Hawks films, a camaraderie that is deepened by the ultimate accomplishment of their common task.

While he and his scriptwriters were developing the scenario for *Rio Bravo*, Hawks said, they discovered that they had enough material for another film. In *El Dorado* (1967) they built on this material to tell the story of Cole Thornton (John Wayne), a middle-aged gunfighter who helps his old friend Sheriff Harrah (Robert Mitchum) get over his bout with the bottle, just as Chance had helped Dude in *Rio Bravo*. Then Thornton and Harrah join forces in a common cause, this time to stop selfish rancher Bart Jason from victimizing a fellow rancher into signing over to him the rights to a precious water supply for cattle that Jason covets. Once again the hero and his friends hole up in the jailhouse to confront the enemy, and once again their joint effort wins the day.

The same mellow humor that characterized the group of men in *Rio Bravo* can be found in their counterparts in *El Dorado*. For example, Thornton's efforts to sober up Harrah for the big gunfight with a concoction brewed by one of his sidekicks are genuinely funny. But the humor in *El Dorado* is tinged with an air of melancholy, rooted in the mutual recognition of Cole and the sheriff that age is catching up with them. This realization is crystallized by the periodic spasms of pain that Cole suffers because of a past wound, which in turn is symbolic of a long and arduous life. As Robin Wood comments, one senses in *El Dorado* that the darkness which often seems to surround the characters in a Hawks film is beginning to close in on them as they grow older.

The frontier humor that punctuates the film throughout reasserts itself, however, in the lasts scene, an ending that *Time* magazine saw as a sly comment on the state of the contemporary Western: "At the final fadeout, Wayne has been pinked in the knee, and Robert Mitchum in the thigh. With crutches as swagger sticks, they limp triumphantly by the camera—two old pros demonstrating that they are better on one good leg apiece than most of the younger stars on two."[14]

It is not surprising that, as Hawks himself grew older, the theme of age should

Christopher Mitchum, John Wayne, Jack Elam, and Victor French in *Rio Lobo* **(1971). (Author's collection)**

find its way into his work, as it found its way into the later films of Chaplin like *Limelight*. In the third film in the trilogy, *Rio Lobo* (1971), Wayne is Colonel Cord McNally, an aging veteran of the Civil War, who again saves a threatened frontier town from bandits by organizing a defense when no one younger is around to take the initiative. *Rio Lobo*, like the other films of the trilogy, and indeed most of the films Hawks made, once more expresses his admiration for the masculine virtue of loyalty to one's duty and to one's comrades.

Undoubtedly, it is a tribute to Hawks's talent that he was able to survive in the Hollywood studio system for more than forty years, creating a canon of films that are peculiarly his own. To put it another way, Hawks proved in more than four decades of film making that a director of exciting action films could also be a genuine artist.

James Stewart, Grace Kelly, and Alfred Hitchcock on the set of *Rear Window* **(1954). (Author's collection)**

3

Alfred Hitchcock

Through a Glass Darkly

One of the reasons that the career of Alfred Hitchcock is so fascinating is that he was one of the very few directors in the history of motion pictures whose name has always been as important on a movie marquee as that of any actor appearing in one of his films. His perennial popularity with the mass audience means that, in effect, Hitchcock, like Hawks, was discovered by his public as a maker of entertaining movies long before movie critics got around to realizing that he was also, as indicated in the Prologue to this book, an *auteur* of the first rank.

There are a number of reasons for his abiding appeal for audiences; and these elements, taken together, are essentially what comprise "the Hitchcock touch"—a phrase that is often used but rarely defined. For one thing, moviegoers easily identify with his heroes, because they are usually not people whose profession is by nature dangerous, such as spies or detectives. Instead, his protagonists are ordinary people who get drawn by circumstances into extraordinary situations. "My hero," he said, "is the average man to whom bizarre things happen, rather than vice versa."

Often his hero cannot confide in the police, because they wrongfully suspect him of having committed a crime. (Hitchcock's own mistrust of the guardians of the law goes back to a childhood incident in which his father had a constable lock the lad in a jail cell briefly, to teach him where naughty little boys wind up.) As a result, the hero is thrown back on his own resources; and we sympathize with his plight in a way that we cannot with a superhuman hero of the James Bond variety.

Not only his central characters, but also the settings of his movies are quite ordinary on the surface, thereby suggesting that evil can lurk in places which superficially seem normal and unthreatening. Hitchcock's villains commit their mayhem in brightly lit amusement parks and respectable restaurants, places where filmgoers might often find themselves, and not in locations we tend to avoid in order to escape potential harm, such as dark alleys and dives. Nor are Hitchcock's villains obviously menacing, criminal types. "The really frightening thing about villains," he pointed out, "is their surface likeableness."[1] How else, he asked, could they win the confidence of their victims?

All of these elements combine to make the spectator feel that what is happening to the hero up there on the screen could conceivably happen to him; for Hitchcock aims to make us aware that catastrophe surrounds us all and can strike when we least expect it. And it is precisely this unsettling reflection that holds one's interest in watching a Hitchcock picture, even after repeated viewings.

Alfred Hitchcock was born in London in 1899 and was brought up with a rather strict Catholic background, notably at Saint Ignatius, a Jesuit preparatory school in London. After graduating from secondary school, Hitchcock became fascinated with the cinema; and in 1920 he went to work at an American-owned British studio, Famous Players–Lasky (later Paramount Pictures). The aspiring movie maker gained experience at the studio in all the various phases of film production.[2]

The Americans who staffed the studio were professional craftsmen whose work and equipment were far superior to any found in other studios in Britain at the time. Hitchcock was the first to admit how much he learned about every facet of the picture business by serving his apprenticeship under the tutelage of the studio's American personnel. In point of fact, he always considered himself an American film director, not only because he worked for more than thirty years in Hollywood, but because of the American technicians who did so much to teach him his craft at the outset of his career.

Working in silent pictures, Hitchcock learned to place a great deal of emphasis on telling a story visually. Hence, at this early point in his career he began to think primarily in visual terms when mapping out a film, a practice he continued for the rest of his days.

In 1925 the front office promoted Hitchcock to the rank of full-fledged director, and he made his first movie in Munich at the Emelka Studios, with which his home studio in London had made a coproduction deal. *The Pleasure Garden* (1925) was a tale of madness and murder that presaged the films of his later career. But it was *The Lodger* (1926), which he made after he came back to Britain, that really established Hitchcock as an important film director. The film was based on the legend of Jack the Ripper, a subject to which he would return four decades later in *Frenzy*. *The Lodger* not only demonstrated incontestably Hitchcock's talent for telling a taut suspense tale efficiently, but also marked his first appearance in one of his own films as an extra, a phenomenon that would become a trademark of his work. His reason for placing himself in the newspaper office scene in *The Lodger*, however, was purely economic; he needed another person in the foreground of a shot to help give the impression of a crowded office, and his budget would not allow him to hire another extra.

The Lodger found favor with both press and public; and he compounded his good fortune after the film opened by marrying Alma Reville, who had been working with him in different capacities, from script supervisor to assistant director, from his earliest days as a director. She would continue to work on the screenplays for his films for years to come.

In 1929 Hitchcock made *Blackmail*, which has the distinction of being the first major British talking picture, since the only other British talkie which had preceded *Blackmail*, *The Clue of the New Pin* (1929), had been crudely made. *Blackmail* had been shot silent; but when it became clear that talking pictures were here to stay, Hitchcock went back and reshot several scenes with spoken dialogue. But he was able to incorporate into the finished film a number of action scenes, such as the climactic chase through the British Museum, just as he had originally filmed them, with only the addition of background music and sound effects.

From the very dawn of the sound era Hitchcock showed that he realized sound should complement image in a movie in an imaginative way. His smooth integration of the techniques of silent and sound pictures, a hallmark of his films from then on, is demonstrated by the fact that some scenes in *Blackmail*, like the British Museum sequence, are essentially visual, while others depend on the creative use of sound.

One scene in the film that reflects a shrewd manipulation of the sound track takes place after the heroine, Alice White (Anny Ondra), stabs to death an artist named Crewe with a bread knife when he attempts to rape her. The following morning Alice tries to behave naturally while eating breakfast with her parents. A gossipy neighbor joins them to discuss the murder that is in all of the morning papers. As Alice prepares to slice a piece of bread for her father, the chatterbox's voice fades into an incomprehensible babble on the sound track, with only the work *knife* clearly audible. The word is repeated a little louder on the sound track each time it recurs, until it reaches a crescendo that causes Alice to scream hysterically and throw down the knife she is holding, as if it were the one she had wielded against Crewe the night before. No one present, however, guesses the true import of her behavior.

Nonetheless Alice's fiancé, Frank (John Longden), who is a police detective, knows of Alice's implication in the artist's death, as does Tracy (Donald Caltrhop), a seedy criminal who threatens to expose her to the police. But Frank turns the tables on Tracy by making him think that he is himself the police's prime suspect. Tracy flees in panic, and Frank organizes a manhunt to track him down. Cornered atop the British Museum, the blackmailer falls to his death through the glass dome of the Reading Room. Later, Hitchcock would stage similar scenes of disorder and violence on the top of other symbols of order and culture, such as Mount Rushmore in *North by Northwest*.

The premiere of *Blackmail* was an unqualified success and formally inaugurated the era of sound pictures in England. During the 1930s Hitchcock continued to make low-budget, high-quality thrillers, epitomized by *The Thirty-nine Steps* (1935), which still remain exciting cinema. One of the reasons that his films continue to involve moviegoers, even on repeated viewings, is that Hitchcock customarily take the audience into his confidence early in the course of the picture by sharing with them information that other directors might withhold for the sake of a surprise ending."I believe in giving the audience all the facts as early as possible," he explained, because that way a director can "build up an almost unbearable tension."[3] When the viewer knows about a danger of which the characters themselves are unaware, he almost wants to blurt out a warning to them. Surprise lasts only a moment, Hitchcock concluded, but tipping off the audience to what is really going to happen allows the director to nurture excitement that lasts throughout the whole movie.

The Thirty-nine Steps, as much as any of Hitchcock's films, exemplifies this approach to the thriller genre, as shall shortly be seen. What's more, the film also incorporates all the fundamental elements that constitute the Hitchcock touch.

Richard Hannay (Robert Donat) is the typical Hitchcock hero, an ordinary man drawn against his will into an extraordinary situation. He befriends Annabella Smith (Lucie Mannheim), a young woman whom he meets at a vaudeville show; and she turns out to be a secret agent committed to keeping some vital Air Ministry secrets out of the hands of an organization of spies known by the secret code name of the Thirty-nine Steps. When Annabella is murdered in Hannay's apartment by emissaries of the Thirty-nine Steps, he decides to go after the ringleader of the spy group, who is based in Scotland, and foil his attempt to steal the state secrets.

One of the most celebrated examples of Hitchcock's creative use of the sound track occurs when the scream of the housekeeper who discovers Annabella's corpse in Hannay's flat turns out to be the screeching whistle of a train barreling out of a tunnel, anticipated from the next scene. The train is, in fact, the Flying Scotsman rushing northward, carrying Hannay away from the scene of the crime of which he is wrongly accused.

In a Hitchcock movie the villain, we know, is usually an individual endowed with misleading charm and respectability. In the present film the chief of the enemy espionage agents is revealed to be Professor Jordan (Godfrey Tearle), an apparently amiable country squire living in a baronial manor in the highlands. For reasons already given, Hitchcock lets the audience know the identity of the leader of the spy ring early in the film. Moreover, Hannay in due course discovers, with the aid of Pamela (Madeleine Carroll), a feisty female with whom he gets involved along the way, that the classified information that Jordan and his co-conspirators covet is the design of an improved airplane engine. The specifications of the engine have been memorized by a memory expert who calls himself Mr. Memory (Wylie Watson), whom Hannay had watched perform in the music hall at the beginning of the picture. Hannay's mission comes to an end, then, in what is once more a most unlikely place in which to play out a danger-fraught adventure: a London vaudeville theater, where Mr. Memory is now appearing.

Hannay puts a crucial question to Memory by asking him to identify the Thirty-nine Steps. A look of dismay crosses the performer's face as he hesitates, on the one hand, between refusing to reveal that the term is the code name of the organization of foreign operatives with which he is covertly associated or, on the other hand, maintaining inviolate his peerless public image as an unlimited reservoir of information and thus giving the game away. Mr. Memory is photographed at the moment of his decision from a titlted camera angle, to dramatize how Hannay's seemingly innocuous inquiry has caught him off balance. The professional artist in him finally opts to vindicate his cherished reputation, and he begins to explain the meaning of the phrase when he is struck down by a bullet fired by Jordan from his box overlooking the stage.

The Thirty-nine Steps, besides being an excellent example of the Hitchcock touch, also illustrates the director's use of a narrative technique which he called the MacGuffin, a term he defined as a device that sets the plot in motion and keeps it

Robert Donat and Madeleine Carroll in *The Thirty-Nine Steps* **(1935). (Bennett's Book Store)**

going. The MacGuffin is simply the thing that preoccupies the hero and the heroine, and because of which they are thrown into danger, such as a vital secret formula. "The characters on the screen worry about what they're after," he explained; the audience, however, does not care about the MacGuffin directly at all, because "they only care about the safety of the hero and the heroine."[4] In the present film the MacGuffin is, of course, the secret plans for an aircraft engine, which Hannay wants to keep Jordan and his cohorts from turning over to a foreign power.

In summary, *Thirty-nine Steps* remains one of Hitchcock's finest achievements. And it is worth noting that the two remakes of the film, done by other directors in 1960 and 1978, both lack the panache and flair that Hitchcock invested in the original.

By the late 1930's major films like *The Thirty-nine Steps* had placed Hitchcock in the front rank of British directors. These films include such other action movies as *Blackmail*, *The Man Who Knew Too Much* (which will be taken up later, in tandem with Hitchcock's own remake of the same movie), and *The Lady Vanishes*. The last film, made in 1938, is a nifty thriller about an attempt on the part of enemy spies to kidnap a British agent aboard a transcontinental express as it speeds across Europe. Like *The Thirty-nine Steps*, it enjoyed considerable popularity in the United States. It is therefore not surprising that Hitchcock was invited to Hollywood to continue his career.

Naturally it would take some time for a director accustomed to working in the relatively intimate surroundings of a small British studio to adjust to the factory atmosphere of the larger and more complex Hollywood accommodations. He recalled that, while visiting another director's set during his first days in Hollywood, he was astonished to find the film maker bellowing at every one through a public address system. By contrast, Hitchcock preferred his own formal businesslike method of shooting a scene to such officious behavior. His custom was to confer privately with members of the cast and crew about a given scene in advance, all in accordance with the careful plans he had drawn up long before the cameras turned. In this regard he had no intention of changing his ways to coincide with those of other Hollywood directors.

What's more, when I watched Hitchcock shooting a scene for *Frenzy* in the heart of London in the summer of 1971, he conducted himself in the same formal, unobtrusive way that customarily characterized his manner when filming in the more controlled atmosphere of a studio sound stage.

Looking back on Hitchcock's best British thrillers, one can characterize them for the most part as straightforward, fast-moving chase melodramas, with a minimum of plot and character development and a maximum of excitement. By contrast, his American movies, starting with *Rebecca* (1940) tended to be longer films, that alloted more screen time for a deeper probing into the psychology of the principal characters.

Thus *Rebecca* presents an in-depth portrait of its key characters, Maxim de Winter (Laurence Olivier), a wealthy, aloof widower, and his youthful bride (Joan Fontaine). Once she takes up residence with Max in the forbidding family castle of

Manderley, the disconsolate heroine finds that she is constantly living in the shadow of Rebecca, Max's deceased first wife, with whom, she assumes, he was exceptionally happy. Max, however, eventually reveals to his second wife that the faithless Rebecca had sadistically sought to make his life a veritable hell, summed up by her attempt to goad him into murdering her by cruelly informing him that she was pregnant with the child of another man. Later the real reason for Rebecca's suicidal death wish is brought to light: she wanted to be spared a prolonged and unglamorous death from cancer by having Max in effect put her out of her misery.

When Mrs. Danvers (Judith Anderson), the dour, demonic housekeeper who had adored Rebecca, learns the terrible truth about her deceased mistress, the crazed woman puts a torch to the house and is herself burned up in the blaze. Hitchcock adroitly creates the final destruction of Manderley in all its compelling visual detail. When the flames ravaging Rebecca's sumptuous bedroom reach her ornate bed, they devour her monogrammed pillowcase. The embroidered *R* disappears behind a curtain of fire, a visual metaphor which implies that Rebecca's spirit is at last dispelled from the lives of Max and his new wife.

The brilliant visual imagery that characterizes the film's final sequence is a vivid reminder of the emphasis which Hitchcock, who joined the motion picture industry long before the movies learned to talk, placed on visual storytelling. He believed that the images should be allowed, as often as possible, to speak for themselves, as they do here in the closing scene of *Rebecca*, a superbly crafted film which won the Academy Award for best picture of the year.

Shadow of a Doubt (1943) was always one of the director's personal favorites, largely because he had as his principal collaborator on the screenplay the distinguished playwright Thornton Wilder (*Our Town*), who bestowed on the film a richness of characterization seldom equaled in Hitchcock's other movies. The villain of the piece is Charles Oakley (Joseph Cotten), a psychotic gigolo who has romanced and murdered a succession of wealthy widows and whom the press has hence sardonically dubbed the Merry Widow murderer.

Charles Oakley is first seen reposing on the rumpled bed in his seedy room in a Philadelphia boarding house where he is hiding out from the law. The dark, brooding atmosphere of the film, coupled with the equally somber vision of life reflected in this tale of obsession and murder, marks *Shadow of a Doubt* as belonging to the class of films French critics christened Film Noir (dark cinema). This trend in American cinema, which also includes later Hitchcock films such as *Spellbound* and *Strangers on a Train*, was already flourishing when he made *Shadow of a Doubt*. The pessimistic view of life exhibited in such movies, itself an outgrowth of the disillusionment spawned by World War II, a disillusionment which would continue into the period of uncertainty known as the Cold War that was the War's aftermath, is evident in the movie.

Also in keeping with the conventions of Film Noir is the movie's air of spare, unvarnished realism, typified by the stark, newsreellike quality of the cinematography, especially the grim scenes that take place at night. The milieu of Film Noir is essentially one of shadows and is exemplified in the present, appropriately named film in the scene where Charles is holed up in his cell-like room, lying on his bed like a prisoner on a cot. As his intrusive landlady solicitously pulls down his window shade to encourage him to take a nap, the shadow that gradually envelops his face suggests the morbid, murky world in which his madness has imprisoned him.

With the police hot on his heels, Charles decides to take sanctuary with his doting sister, Emma Newton (Patricia Collinge), and her family in the sleepy little town of Santa Rosa, California. Charles remains safe in Santa Rosa until Charlie (Charlotte) Newton, his namesake (Teresa Wright), comes to notice her Uncle Charles's increasingly suspicious behavior and begins to nurture the shadow of a doubt that he is in actual fact the Merry Widow murderer for whom the police are combing the country. After her ghastly suspicions are verified, Charles devilishly manipulates her into keeping his true identity a secret, to spare their family the grief and scandal of his exposure. In exchange for her silence, he agrees to leave town for good.

When, for the sake of appearances, young Charlie goes to the railroad depot to see her Uncle Charles off, he attempts to kill her and thus shut her up for sure. As they struggle, he loses his balance and falls backward into the path of an oncoming train and is crushed beneath its wheels. Charles's hideous fate is an example of genuine poetic justice, since it is the kind of horrible death he had had in store for young Charlie. It is supremely ironic, consequently, that, after Charles Oakley's demise, his relatives, who know nothing of his true nature, will continue to call his niece by his name in loving tribute to his memory.

Spellbound (1945) turned out to be another superlative psychological thriller in the grand tradition of *Shadow of a Doubt*. Its hero, John Ballantine (Gregory Peck), is obsessed with the notion that he murdered his psychiatrist, Dr. Edwardes, while they were skiing together. A victim of amnesia, Ballantine unconsciously assumes the identity of Edwardes at Green Manors, the private sanatorium of which Edwardes was to have been the new superintendent, had his untimely death not intervened. When John Ballatine's real identity is inevitably discovered, Dr. Constance Petersen, one of the staff psychiatrists (Ingrid Bergman), pledges herself to help him find out what really happened during Edwardes's fateful skiing expedition. To uncover the true facts about the incident, Constance must interpret John's recurring dream about Edwardes's death.

Hitchcock brought in the Spanish surrealist painter Salvador Dali to design the bizarre dream sequence, which starts with John and Edwardes playing cards in an eerie setting that suggests the Green Manors asylum. A further covert reference to the institution is made when a faceless individual insists to Edwardes that he is himself the sole owner and proprietor of the establishment. This is a veiled allusion to Dr. Murchison (Leo G. Carroll), the outgoing director of the sanatorium, who was known to be deeply disturbed by the prospect of being supplanted by Edwardes.

The next time the anonymous proprietor materializes in this fantasy sequence, he is holding a wheel in his hand, which suggests a revolver, and is hiding behind a chimney on a slanted roof, as he watches Edwardes slide off the roof to his death. Constance rightly reasons that this last episode of John's nightmare is a disguised representation of how the crazed Murchison, in a last desperate attempt to retain his position of authority at Green Manors, stepped from behind a tree and shot Edwardes while the latter was skiing down the hillside with John Ballantine, and then left John to take the blame.

When Constance confronts Murchison with this explanation, the demented psychiatrist pulls out a pistol and threatens to shoot her on the spot. The camera is behind Murchison while it photographs the gun in his hand, as the revolver slowly turns away from Constance and toward himself, and then fires straight at the lens. The explosion of the pistol in the filmgoer's face is a startling surprise, as is the discovery that the dapper, staid Dr. Murchison has been revealed to be the proverbial lunatic who has taken over the asylum.

Because of the success of Hitchcock films like *Spellbound*, movie moguls were willing to concede a greater degree of artistic freedom to him than they had accorded him during his first years in Hollywood. As a matter of fact, by the late 1940s Hitchcock had earned the right to act as his own producer; and he did so for the rest of his career, regardless of what studio held his contract.

Strangers on a Train (1951) was the first major success Hitchcock had after he began to produce his own motion pictures. It begins with a railway journey, in the course of which Bruno Anthony, a wealthy homosexual (Robert Walker, in an immaculate performance), ingratiates himself with Guy Haines, a handsome tennis champion (Farley Granger). The slightly effeminate Bruno has all the earmarks of a textbook case in abnormal psychology, since he combines a deep-seated implacable hatred of his domineering father with a curious attachment to his eccentric mother. As the two lunch together on the train, it is evident that Guy, who is unhappily married to a conniving, promiscuous spouse, is fascinated by this coy creature.

Before they part company at journey's end, Bruno tries to manipulate Guy into agreeing to exchange a murder with him, with Guy killing Bruno's father and Bruno doing away with Guy's wife Miriam. Since neither of them has an ostensible motive for committing the other's crime, they would both, according to Bruno's logic, successfully elude detection. This Proposal appeals to Guy more than he is prepared to admit even to himself, since he would like to be rid of his hateful wife. Consequently, he does not decisively reject Bruno's plan. Taking Guy's hedging for tacit approval, the deranged Bruno soon dispatches Miriam and demands forthwith that Guy keep his part of the bargain, which Guy in a moment of panic agrees to do, just to put Bruno off.

One of the tensest scenes in the picture is that in which Bruno strangles Guy's estranged wife in a secluded corner of the amusement park to which he has followed her. The murder is ironically accompanied by the distant music of the merry-go-round's calliope, as it grinds out its cheery rendition of "The Band Played On." Horrified, we watch the murder as it is reflected in Miriam's glasses, which have fallen to the grass during her struggle with Bruno. Photographed in this grotesquely distorted fashion, the strangling looks as if it were being viewed in a fun-house mirror, another reminder of the grimly incongruous carnival setting of the crime.

Given the fact that Guy subconsciously wanted Miriam dead, he has, in effect, indirectly accomplished her death through the mediation of Bruno as his proxy.

That Guy has become, however unwittingly, allied with the perverse force for evil that Bruno represents is concretized in the scene in which the two men stand on opposite sides of an iron fence, as Bruno informs Guy that he has taken Miriam's life. When a squad car appears across the street, Guy instinctively joins Bruno on the same side of the barrier, and thus implicitly acknowledges his share of the guilt for Miriam's demise. Moreover, the image of Guy's troubled face barred by the sinister shadows of the gate grill signals his imprisonment by Bruno in an unholy alliance from which he finds himself, for the time being, powerless to escape.

Guy is suspected of slaying his wife; but he is given the chance to redeem himself by pursuing Bruno back to the scene of Miriam's murder and forcing him to confess the truth about her death. As they wrestle each other aboard the carousel, the mechanism suddenly goes berserk, changing what is normally a harmless source of innocent fun into a whirling instrument of terror. The carousel is thus still another reflection of Hitchcock's dark vision of our chaotic, topsy-turvy planet. As the runaway merry- go-round continues to spin at top speed, its rendition of "The Band Played On" is also accelerated to a dizzying tempo and mingles with macabre persistence with the screams of the hysterial riders trapped on board. A mechanic at last manages to bring the carousel to a halt, but it stops so suddenly that the riders go sailing off in all directions as the machinery collapses into a heap of smouldering wreckage. As the movie draws to a close, Bruno dies in the debris, unrepentant to the last.

Another film which shows Hitchcock in top form is *Rear Window* (1954). Jeff Jeffries (James Stewart), temporarily incapacitated by a broken leg, indulges his press photographer's inclination to spy on other people's private lives by peeking into the windows of the apartment dwellings across the courtyard from his own Greenwich Village flat. Since Hitchcock's camera remains in Jeff's room throughout the picture, we see the inhabitants of the other apartments largely from his point of view. In fact, the wall of windows that faces Jeff's own rear window becomes for him a bank of television monitors, by means of which he is able to keep his neighbors under his voyeuristic surveillance without their being aware of it. In this manner Hitchcock extends the border of the movie's confined setting in a most ingenious way.

Among the assortment of people Jeff observes is Lars Thorwald, an adulterous husband (Raymond Burr), whom Jeff comes to suspect of having killed his invalid wife. Thorwald's ugly deed is eventually brought to light by the efforts of Jeff and his fiancée Lisa (Grace Kelly), who finds Jeff's morbid curiosity catching. Ultimately, they are not entirely proud of their meddling in other people's lives, however. In fact, Lisa shamefacedly confesses that both she and Jeff were deeply disappointed when it appeared for a time that Thorwald was not actually guilty of homicide after all.

Furthermore, Jeff's increasingly unwholesome interest in the affairs of the other tenants is mirrored in his switching, as his curiosity increases, from a simple pair of binoculars to a high-powered telescope as his means of prying more and more deeply into their personal lives, at as close a range as possible. Jeff's nurse (Thelma Ritter) wryly comments on his "window shopping" with his "spy glass." "We have become a race of Peeping Toms," she says. "People ought to get outside and look at themselves for a change."

By film's end, Jeff has learned his lesson. In the last scene we see Jeff, who has finally given up keeping tabs on his neighbors, sitting with his back to the window.

In *Vertigo* (1958) Stewart plays Scottie Ferguson, a veteran detective, who suffers from vertigo. Gavin Elster, an old school chum, asks Scottie to shadow his wife Madeleine (Kim Novak), who he says may be contemplating suicide. Scottie agrees; but he ultimately feels he has failed his client when he is unable to keep Madeleine from apparently hurling herself out of the bell tower of an old California mission church, because his acrophobia prohibited him from climbing to the top of the tower to save her.

As was mentioned earlier, Hitchcock usually opts for suspense over surprise by giving moviegoers as much advance information as possible. Thus the audience learns long before Scottie does that Elster actually counted on Scottie's vertigo to keep him from interfering with Elster's own plans to do away his wife—under circumstances that falsely imply she committed suicide.

As things develop, Scottie meets Judy Barton (Kim Novak again), who he eventually discovers is both Elster's former mistress and his accomplice in an elaborate hoax to murder his wife. Judy for a time impersonated Mrs. Elster to establish in Scottie's mind the mistaken impression that the real Madeleine harbored suicidal tendencies, so that he would testify at the inquest that Madeleine took her own life. When Scottie forces Judy to re-enact for him her part in Madeleine Elster's death at the scene of the crime, she becomes hysterical and herself falls from the belfry just as the real Madeleine had done. On this note of ironic poetic justice, the film concludes.

Stewart's other Hitchcock film, *The Man Who Knew Too Much* (1956) was a remake of the film of the same title that the director had originally done back in 1934. The action of the first film version begins with Bob and Jill Lawrence (Leslie Banks and Edna Best) as an English couple vacationing with their daughter Betty at a winter resort in Saint Moritz. While Jill is dancing in the ballroom with Louis Bernard, a Frenchman who is also staying at the lodge, Bob playfully attaches a ball of knitting wool to a button on Bernard's coat. As he and Jill dance, they become hopelessly entangled in the unraveling string of yarn. Bernard smiles good humoredly when he notices what has happened, but his face is abruptly drained of expression when he is mortally wounded by a gunshot. Hitchcock employed the gimmick of the ball of yarn as a visual symbol of the manner in which Bob and Jill have inadvertently become enmeshed in international intrigue by associating with a fellow vacationer who is in reality a French secret agent.

In the wake of Bernard's death, young Betty Lawrence is abducted by Abbot (Peter Lorre) and his gang of anarchists in order to silence Bob, who had learned earlier from Bernard about the impending assassination of a foreign diplomat visiting London. The search for Betty takes Bob and Jill from the fashionable vacation resort in Switzerland where they were staying to the slums of London, where danger seems to pounce at every turn. In a scruffy nonconformist chapel, which turns out to be a front for Abbot's mob, a modest-looking, middle-aged woman suddenly produces a revolver from her shopping bag and forces Bob to drop his weapon into the collection plate. With that, the doors of the chapel slam shut with a menacing echo, and Bob is temporarily shut in with the kidnappers.

Meanwhile Jill has gone to the Royal Albert Hall, where the assassination of which Bob had been warned is scheduled to take place in the course of a concert. The featured piece on the program is "The Storm Cloud Cantata," and the assassin is to fire at his target at the precise moment when a cymbal crash will drown out the sound of the gunfire. Jill screams out just when the killer is about to shoot and thus saves the statesman's life. The police then help her to trace Bob and Betty to the anarchists' citadel, where an exciting gun battle brings the film to a close.

More than twenty years after the release of the original movie, Hitchcock decided that the time was right to film this tried and true story a second time. In the version of the story, Ben McKenna (James Stewart) and his wife Jo (Doris Day) have a son Hank, rather than a daughter, and they go on a vacation to Morocco rather than to Switzerland. But once Hank is kidnapped in the Casbah and his parents pursue the kidnappers back to London, the basic plot line of the first version holds true. The American remake is about forty-five minutes longer than the British version, because Hitchcock concentrates more on character development this time around and on scrupulously tying up the loose plot strands he had left dangling in the 1934 movie.

To cite one example, in the earlier movie the exact nature of Abbot's curious, emotionally dependent attachment to the woman of indeterminate age called Nurse Agnes, who is his constant companion, is never clarified. In the remake, however, they are established as husband and wife, both of whom have clearly defined personalities. Yet the 1956 film is not automatically a better film because of this and other refinements in its heavily revised, more substantial screenplay.

If the earlier picture left some things unexplained, the filmgoer was kept sufficiently breathless by this fast-moving, seventy-five-minute movie not to notice. As a matter of fact, the *London Observer* judged the 1934 film at the time of its release to be Hitchcock's most promising movie since *Blackmail* five years before, simply because of the director's frank refusal to indulge in subtleties that would have got in the way of the forward movement of the exciting plot. In any event, the high point of both films is the almost intolerably suspenseful concert sequence—in which the heroine must decide whether or not to stop the assassination that she knows is about to take place, when it might well mean further imperiling the life of her child, still detained as a hostage by the terrorists.

In Hitchcock's opinion, the remake possessed a professional polish lacking in his earlier attempt. Thus, in the first version the plot goes into overdrive before the moviegoer really gets a chance to become acquainted with the principals and consequently to sympathize with them to the degree one can in the second movie. On the other hand, because the remake is less tightly constructed than its predecessor, it contains a few slow-paced, talky stretches that may cause the viewer's interest temporarily to flag, something that never happens in the original.

The ongoing debate about the relative merits of the British and American periods of Hitchcock's career can be summed up by the comparison of the two

Cary Grant and the crop-duster in *North by Northwest* (1959). (Bennett's Book Store)

versions of *The Man Who Knew Too Much*. Whether one believes that Hitchcock's British thrillers are superior to his American suspense dramas largely depends on whether one prefers fast-paced action movies, with a modicum of plot and character development, to longer, somewhat slower, but denser films that reflect a more thorough analysis of the psychology of character. In the last analysis, an individual filmgoer's choice in this matter basically says more about his or her personal cinematic taste than it does about the relative merits of the films themselves.

In *North by Northwest* (1959), one of Hitchcock's biggest hits, the director eschews the shadowy ambience of London's dingy back streets, which are a key setting in both versions of *The Man Who Knew Too Much*, in favor of staging several scenes of violence in the cold light of day. He does so in order to suggest that, in the nasty world of the film, evil is no less likely to strike in broad daylight than under cover of darkness.

In the movie's most renowned sequence, Roger Thornhill (Cary Grant) is lured out into the country by foreign spies, whose leader (James Mason) mistakenly believes that Roger is an undercover agent for the CIA. As Roger, incongruously attired in a natty business suit, stands on a deserted country road sweltering under the relentless rays of the noonday sun, a crop-dusting plane is engaged in spraying a nearby field that Roger suddenly realizes, is devoid of crops. Then, without warning, the aircraft swoops down on him like some brutal bird of prey and sprays him, first with machine-gun bullets and then with poison gas. In this single image of Roger frantically running for cover is distilled the essence of the Hitchcock touch. Here is the Hitchcock hero, isolated and totally vulnerable, being pursued across a parched, desolate prairie by an evil force that at first seemed to him harmless and unthreatening.

Another celebrated sequence in *North by Northwest* is the cliff-hanging scene on the colossal Mount Rushmore monument. Once again Hitchcock employs a traditional symbol of culture and stability as the background against which the hero undergoes a death-defying confrontation with hostile forces, just as he did in *Blackmail* and other films. In this instance Roger and his girl Eve (Eva Marie Saint) are nearly forced by one of the enemy agents to fall down the mountainside, but government agents arrive just in time to save them.

The wide public acceptance of *North by Northwest* was exceeded by *Psycho* (1960). Although *Psycho*, Hitchcock's masterpiece, was to become his biggest blockbuster, it was made on a relatively tight budget. This prompted the director to make the movie with the smaller unit of technicians and with the same modest technical facilities that were employed to turn out the weekly television series he was supervising at the time, rather than to employ the more elaborate and more expensive crew and facilities a big movie studio would have provided for him. The finished film, consequently, has a stark simplicity, to which Bernard Herrmann's spare musical background, scored solely for strings, is the perfect complement.

As the film opens, Marion Crane (Janet Leigh) seems to be a typical secretary until, on an impulse, she steals from her boss a large sum of cash with which to finance her marriage with her impecunious fiancé, Sam Loomis. Thereupon she immediately sets out to elope with Sam, who lives some distance away. After driving all day and managing to elude the suspicious highway patrolman who had been trailing her, Marion opts to seek shelter from the rainy night in a modest but immaculately kept motel just off the main road.

Norman Bates (Anthony Perkins), the shy, lanky, likable proprietor of the motel, easily arouses Marion's sympathies when the lonely young man sheepishly admits to her in the course of a chat that he is dominated by his elderly mother, who lives in the sinister mansion nearby. During the evening Marion resolves to go back home the following morning and return the stolen money.

Before retiring for the night, she takes a cleansing shower, permitting the water to wash away the guilt of larceny she now repents having committed. At this moment the shower curtain is whipped aside, and Marion is savagely stabbed to death by what appears to be a maniacal women inexplicably possessed of enormous physical strength. All the while the sound track emits a burst of shrill, high-strung music, with the notes of the slicing string instruments sounding like the piercing shrieks of some carnivorous bird, clawing at its prey.

This is, of course, the film's celebrated shower murder. Although it takes less than a minute of screen time, Hitchcock spent about a week filming the stabbing, which is composed of more than sixty individual shots. One of the reasons that he chose to shoot *Psycho* in black and white, at a time when feature films were increasingly being done in color, was that the slaying, if photographed in living color, would have simply been too gruesome for many moviegoers. As he put it, he wanted to scare his audience, not nauseate them. In any case, by unexpectedly killing off his heroine so early in the picture, Hitchcock managed to startle his audience into an unsettled state that lasts right up to the finish.

In the end Norman Bates is revealed to be the fiendishly deranged villain. It transpires that Norman, who had an incestuously possessive love for his mother, poisoned both her and her lover after he discovered them together. To obliterate the intolerable crime of matricide from his conscience, Norman took to nurturing a split personality. In making believe that his mother's personality at times had displaced his own, he was able to maintain the illusion that she was still very much alive. To reinforce this conviction, he employed his otherwise harmless hobby of taxidermy to stuff his mother's corpse with sawdust and preserve it in a state of quasi-permanence.

Furthermore, Norman would invariably don her clothing before he stabbed to death a woman to whom he was attracted, fantasizing all the while that it was his mother who perpetrated these crimes and not he, because in his own diseased imagination he assumed, quite gratuitously, that she was as incestuously jealous of him as he was of her. In addition, because Norman was pathologically shy with women, each of these killings took on the nature of a symbolic rape, giving the dripping knife and the gushing shower nozzle a definite phallic significance.

As one critic has written, Norman begins by enjoying his fantasies, and ends up with his fantasies enjoying him. For, by film's end, Norman's frail self-identity has been totally absorbed by the "mother" side of his schizophrenic personality. As he sits staring into space in a jail cell following his arrest, his complete withdrawal from reality is signaled by the blanket in which he has wrapped himself in order to

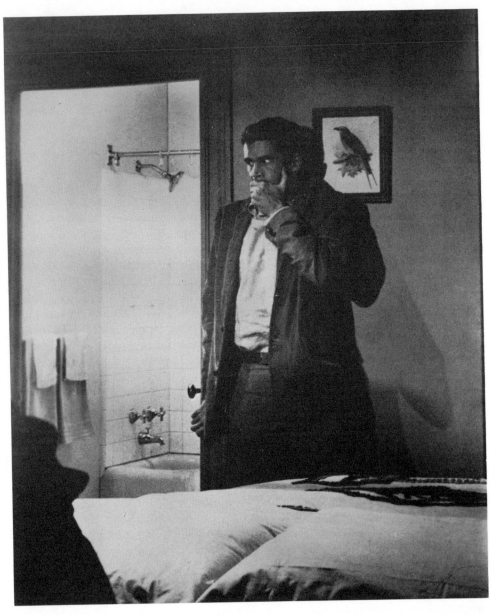

Anthony Perkins in the shower scene of *Psycho* (1960). (Museum of Modern Art/Film Stills Archive)

insulate himself completely from any further contact with the outside world. A smile gradually creeps over Norman's face, on which for a moment the grinning skull of his mother's corpse is superimposed. Through Norman's "puckered, mobile features," Peter Cowie comments, "Hitchcock projects an image of humanity clamped in its private trap of frustration and anguish. *Psycho* is not only Hitchcock's greatest film; it is the most intelligent and disturbing horror movie ever made."[5] No doubt about it.

Hitchcock's next venture was *The Birds* (1963), which portrays a full-scale attack by mankind's erstwhile fine-feathered friends on the population of a small California coastal town. No explanation is offered in the film for the sudden and unexpected hostility toward humanity that prompts flocks of ordinarily pacific creatures to lay seige to this village, but then one is not really required. Hitchcock wishes to examine how human beings react when thrown together in a crisis, regardless of its cause. If the upheaval that the characters have to contend with in *The Birds* had been an air raid, he said, with planes instead of birds raining havoc from the heavens, the theme of the movie would have remained the same.

One of the key visual images in the film occurs in the scene in which Melanie, the heroine (Tippi Hedren), is trapped in a telephone booth, while a flock of birds assaults it from all directions in a frenzied attempt to shatter the glass and break in. As Hitchcock himself has commented, this scene sums up the plight of the entire populace: it represents a reversal of the age-old conflict between man and bird, since in this instance human beings are in the cage and the birds are outside.

Hitchcock's last vintage thriller was *Frenzy* (1972), which *Variety* hailed as one of his "major achievements."[6] The story line of *Frenzy* recapitulates the Jack-the-Ripper plot of Hitchcock's first major motion picture, *The Lodger*, made almost a half century before. Hence, with *Frenzy*, Hitchcock's professional life in a sense had come full circle. Here once again is the archetypal Hitchcock hero intrepidly chasing down the criminal of whose crimes he is himself falsely accused. Meanwhile the police pursue him because, as one character acridly comments, the cops, as usual, are on the wrong track.

Richard Blaney (Jon Finch) is thought to be the "necktie murderer," a sexual psychopath terrorizing London, because both his estranged wife, Brenda Blaney (Barbara Leigh-Hunt), and his girl friend, Babs Milligan (Anna Massey), have fallen victim to the slayer. The real maniac, however, is none other than Richard's old mate Bob Rusk (Barry Foster), whose amiability marks him as another one of Hitchcock's superficially attractive psychotics—a long line of lunatics that reaches back to Bruno Anthony of *Strangers on a Train*, Charles Oakley of *Shadow of a Doubt*, and beyond.

Hitchcock wisely depicts only one of Rusk's hideous rape-murders in detail— that of Brenda—since, once the filmgoer has witnessed one of these atrocities, the director need only suggest thereafter that another is taking place off screen. Thus, when Rusk leads the unsuspecting Babs into his flat, the camera stops at the doorway and does not venture to follow them inside. Instead it slowly retreats down the shadowy staircase and out into the bright sunshine of the busy street, as if recoiling from the unspeakable act that is taking place behind curtained windows. Once outside, the camera pauses for a moment to survey the pedestrians going about their business, unaware of what is transpiring inside the building. By means of this brilliantly executed shot, Hitchcock once more reminds his audience, perhaps more effectively than ever before, of his disturbing conviction that catastrophe surrounds us all and can strike when we least expect it.

Hitchcock's last completed film, *Family Plot* (1976), a tale about the pursuit and capture of a master kidnapper, was a good film, but not on a par with *Frenzy*. Nevertheless, like every Hitchcock film before it, *Family Plot* reflects the provocative personal vision of the creative artist who made it. Indeed, may filmgoers have come away from his movies, *Newsweek* once noted, with some sobering thoughts about human nature as Hitchcock viewed it: that people are not always what they seem, neither as good nor as bad as they might perhaps at first appear; that good and evil can bundle together, like sly lovers, in the same personality. Further, the more perceptive viewers might just realize that these same truths also apply in some degree to themselves and not just to others. In Hitchcock's own words, if one has been brought up by the Jesuits, "as I was, these elements are bound to intrude."[7]

Although Hitchcock was nominated five times for an Academy Award as best director, it was never conferred upon him. The Motion Picture Academy did, however, somewhat belatedly vote him a special award, which he received at that Oscar ceremonies in 1967, in recognition for his lifetime achievement as a film maker. He was also knighted by Queen Elizabeth II in 1980. Surely his body of work richly deserved the accolades he received in later years, for his movies continue to fascinate audiences around the world. As Andrew Sarris has observed, some films age; some films date. Hitchcock's movies belong to the first category.

4

George Cukor
A Touch of Class

"When I came to Hollywood it was just at the time the talkies were coming in," George Cukor recalled. "Everyone thought I was a New York sophisticate. They immediately typed me." Critics and historians of the cinema have been trying to type Cukor ever since. Because he came to Hollywood from the Broadway theater, he was said to have made "theatrical" films; because some of Hollywood's finest actresses have excelled under his direction, he has been called a woman's director. The truth is that Cukor and his work defy facile classification because, like Howard Hawks, he directed a wide variety of films.

In classifying this director as an *auteur*, Andrew Sarris has written, "Cukor's filmography is his most eloquent defense. When a director has provided tasteful entertainment of a high order consistently, over a period of half a century, it is clear that said director is much more than a mere entertainer. . . . He is a genuine artist." Although many of Cukor's films are adaptations of literary works, particularly plays, the sum of his films reflects the personality of the man who directed them all. "The thematic consistency of Cukor's career has been achieved through a judicious mixture of selection and emphasis," Sarris continues. Cukor has always sought to choose material congenial to his personal interests and talents. Often he has explored the lives of the upper class with wry wit, thereby turning out films about sophistication done with sophistication. That these people are sometimes actors and actresses suggests that a major Cukor theme is the conflict of illusion and reality in people's lives; an actor, after all, runs the risk of making the world of illusion with which he is constantly involved his reality.

This theme is most obvious in three of Cukor's best motion pictures, all of which deal with show people—*A Double Life*, *A Star Is Born*, and *Les Girls*—and it appears in various transmutations in many of his other movies. In *Les Girls* the same events are told from four different points of view, each version differing markedly from the others. Because he allows each narrator "equal time," it seems that Cukor is sympathetic to the way each of them has subconsciously revised their common experiences in a manner that enables them to cope with the past in the present. As Sarris puts it, Cukor does not imply that people are liars, but rather that they tell the truth in their own fashion. This pattern is consistent in Cukor's work: "Cukor," he concludes, "is committed to the dreamer, if not to the content of the dream."[1]

George Cukor, who was born in New York City in 1899, began his professional

George Cukor with the author on the set of *Rich and Famous* (1981). (The George Cukor collection)

career as a stage manager in Chicago in 1919, and went to New York thereafter to direct for the Broadway theater during the 1920s. When the movies learned to talk, Cukor, like other stage directors, was summoned to Hollywood in the early 1930s. He became a dialogue director, a position usually filled by someone with theatrical experience who was hired to help silent film directors make the transition to talking pictures more smoothly. One of the films on which Cukor worked in this capacity was *All Quiet on the Western Front* (1930), in which Fred Zinnemann, another aspiring director, got his first job in pictures as an extra.

While he was still a dialogue director, Cukor's skill in handling actors was becoming apparent. Indeed, in the years ahead, several actors were to win Academy Awards under his direction: James Stewart in *The Philadelphia Story*, Ingrid Bergman in *Gaslight*, Ronald Colman in *A Double Life*, Judy Holliday in *Born Yesterday*, and Rex Harrison in *My Fair Lady*. Although producers could not have guessed in 1931 that all of this lay ahead of the young director, they eventually decided that he was ready to direct on his own and assigned him to *Tarnished Lady* (1931), with Tallulah Bankhead. The film was noteworthy only because it marked the first collaboration of Cukor and screenwriter Donald Ogden Stewart, who was to write six more films for Cukor, including *Holiday* and *The Philadelphia Story*.

"When I moved up from dialogue director to directing my own films," Cukor remembered, "it still took me three or four years to cotton on to the screen directing after coming from the theater. In films, for example, you are working with the actors and the camera and the microphone in very close quarters, whereas in the theatre the actors have to project to the back of the house. When making a movie, therefore, the director has to keep in mind that what is a good performance for the stage would be overacting on the screen."

When he got to Hollywood, Cukor went on, "the studios were all petrified about the coming of sound to motion pictures. Directors lost their heads and began to abandon everything they had learned about camera movement in the silent days. The camera was locked in a soundproof booth, so that its mechanical noises would not be picked up on the sound track. As a result, the director had to use a different stationary camera for long shots, for medium shots, and for close-ups," after the manner of live television shows some years later.

Confusion reigned, said Cukor. The so-called sound technicians had been recruited from the ranks of shipboard radio operators, who knew nothing about film making; yet they were dictating to actors and directors alike. "But gradually the techniques of making sound films were perfected," he concluded, "and everyone got used to them."

For one thing, noiseless cameras were developed, so that the camera no longer had to be quarantined in a soundproof booth during shooting but could move around freely among the actors once more. For another, actors began feeling more at home in the new medium of talking pictures, so that their performances became less stilted, just as directors like Cukor were beginning to feel more comfortable behind the camera.

Cukor's first important film during his early years as a director was *What Price Hollywood?* (1932), which later served as the basis of the 1937 film *A Star Is Born* directed by William Wellman, which Cukor in turn remade as a musical with Judy Garland in 1954. There are some differences between *What Price Hollywood?* and its two later incarnations as *A Star Is Born* in 1937 and 1954, but the plot is fundamentally the same in all three versions.

In *What Price Hollywood?* Constance Bennett is Mary Evans, a young hopeful who achieves stardom with the help of Max Carey (Lowell Sherman), an alcoholic director (the corresponding character in A Star Is Born is an alcoholic actor). Ironically, Max's career is going into a nosedive at the same rapid pace that Mary's is taking off. From this material Cukor created a sophisticated comedy-drama and drew fine performances from the leads, particularly Lowell Sherman, who made Max Carey a likeable as well as a tragic figure.

When Cukor began directing films, the studio system was firmly entrenched in Hollywood. Although the front office exercised a great deal of control over the directors and actors they held under contract, Cukor felt that studio executives nonetheless seriously sought to develop the talents of the artists in their employ. "It's true that an unintelligent producer could interfere in a director's work and make himself a nuisance," said Cukor. "But a lot of interesting screen personalities were developed and a lot of interesting films were made under the big studio system; so someone must have been doing something right." At Metro-Goldwyn-Mayer, for example, where Cukor worked for many years, "executives like Louis B. Mayer and Irving Thalberg collected a great roster of players, and helped to make the American film industry known throughout the world. They had vitality and conviction, qualities that have since been lost in the industry to a great extent." Cukor later underscored his esteem for Thalberg in particular in a letter when he said that Thalberg was "the most brilliant, the most creative producer that I ever worked with."[2]

Three of the films that Cukor made at MGM in the thirties took particular advantage of that studio's dazzling collection of stars: *Dinner at Eight*, *Romeo and Juliet*, and *The Women*. In the first of these, *Dinner at Eight* (1933), Cukor gave full rein to the theme that was to characterize so much of his later work, the attempt of individuals to reconcile their cherished dreams with the realities of their lives. The source of *Dinner at Eight* is the play by George S. Kaufmann and Edna Ferber. The plot revolves around a dinner party being given by the social climbing Millicent Jordon (Billie Burke), who is unaware that the steamship business run by her husband Oliver (Lionel Barrymore) is on the rocks and that Oliver himself is slowly dying of a heart condition.

As we meet each of the guests in his own proper milieu before he comes to the party, we discover that each of them in turn is nursing pretentions and illusions that are peculiarly his own. Dan and Kitty Packard (Wallace Beery and Jean Harlow) are vulgar nouveaux riches, who are trying to achieve a respectability that ill befits either of them. Larry Renault (John Barrymore) is a has-been actor whose alcoholism has ruined his career but who still insists that he can make a comeback.

Of Barrymore's performance, Cukor recalled, "Jack played a fourth-rate actor who commits suicide when he loses his last chance for a big part. I told Jack that since the actor had bungled everything in his life, something should go wrong even with his suicide, which the actor wanted to be very dramatic and tragic. As Jack walked across the room to plug up the chimney before turning on the gas, he tripped over a footstool and sprawled ignominiously on the floor. It was just the right pathetic touch." Another ironic touch occurs just before Renault dies, when he automatically adjusts the lamp shade above the chair in which he is to expire, so that the light will properly illuminate his handsome profile.

If Cukor is unsympathetic to the unreal dreams of wealth and respectability that so many of the characters in the film cherish, he nevertheless treats those dreams with compassion, as with Renault, or at least with indulgent good humor, as in the case of the Packards.

By the time the dinner party begins, one by one each of the central characters is made to face up to reality. Mrs. Jordon, for instance, recognizes the worthlessness of her pretensions to social preferment when she learns of her husband's illness and business crisis. When Kitty Packard meets Oliver Jordon, she realizes what a decent person he is and forces her husband to help Jordon save his business instead of taking advantage of Jordon's financial plight, as Packard had originally intended to do.

Nevertheless, Kitty, a former hatcheck girl, is still not above continuing to try to make a good impression on her social betters as the party goes on; and her last attempt provides the witty closing lines of the film. Kitty is talking with Carlotta Vance (Marie Dressler), a has-been actress who has accepted the eclipse of her career in a way that Larry Renault could not. Says Kitty to Carlotta as they go to dinner, "I was reading a book the other day. It's all about civilization or something. Do you know the guy said machinery is going to take the place of every profession?" Carlotta, by now slightly tipsy, retorts, "Oh my dear, that's something you need never worry about."

Cukor's *Romeo and Juliet* (1936), in contrast to *Dinner at Eight*, is something of a disappointment. The basic drawback of Cukor's intelligent rendering of Shakespeare's play is that the title roles were played by competent actors, Leslie Howard and Norma Shearer, who were, unfortunately, too old to enact credibly the young star-crossed lovers.

But Cukor was not crossed by the rest of the galaxy of stars in his cast. John Barrymore in particular stands out memorably as Mercutio and delivers Mercutio's tongue-twisting "Queen Mab" speech with a poetic lilt that amounts to one of the finest Shakespearean vignettes ever committed to film. Barrymore's performance more than repaid Cukor's efforts to keep him from being fired by MGM's production chief, Irving Thalberg, when Barrymore's drinking problem began to interfere with his work. With tragic irony Barrymore was in real life beginning to resemble Larry Renault, and Cukor was later to draw on his experiences with Barrymore during the making of *Romeo and Juliet* in delineating the character of the alcoholic actor in *A Star Is Born*.

Prior to making *The Women* (1939), Cukor's third major MGM film with a spectacular cast, he was engaged to direct David O. Selznick's mammoth Civil War epic, *Gone with the Wind* (1939), but was replaced by another director. "I was engaged by David Selznick a year before shooting began," said Cukor, who did background research for the film, held script conferences, conferred with the production designer, and directed the screen tests. "I shot the film for three weeks and then was replaced by Victor Fleming," Cukor added laconically. "Selznick was very nervous about the film and also replaced Lee Garmes, one of the best cinematographers in the business."

Cutting through the gossip and speculation that have surrounded Cukor's removal from the film, one can say that it seems most likely that Victor Fleming was substituted for Cukor because Clark Gable, aware of Cukor's reputation for being a good director of actresses, was concerned that the director was favoring Vivien Leigh and Olivia de Havilland in the scenes they were playing together and that ultimately their performances would eclipse his. Gable preferred Fleming to Cukor, since Fleming had earlier directed Gable opposite Jean Harlow in *Red Dust*, one of Gable's best films to that date.

Gentleman that he was, Cukor always courteously denied reports that he secretly coached Vivien Leigh and Olivia de Havilland in their roles in *Gone with the Wind* after he left the picture, since he did not want to take any credit away from Victor Fleming. Olivia de Havilland, however, told me: "When George Cukor was replaced, Vivien and I were beside ourselves because he had helped us to establish the characters that we were playing. During the subsequent months of shooting, whenever I would get nervous about how to play a scene that was coming up the following week, I would call George and ask him if I could go and see him over the weekend when we weren't shooting. I felt so treacherous about Vivien not receiving the same help that I was getting. Afterwards I found that she had done the same thing!"

Besides privately coaching Leigh and de Havilland in their parts, Cukor also left his mark on *Gone with the Wind* most especially by the very fact that nearly everything he shot was used in the final cut of the movie. Recalling Cukor's efforts to make the scenes he filmed come to life, de Havilland said, "No other scenes in the film have the richness of detail that one finds in those which George Cukor directed."

It was evident that MGM had not lost confidence in Cukor's talents as a result of his losing the director's post on *Gone with the Wind*. For he was immediately assigned to direct *The Women*, in which the studio's top actresses were to appear, including Norma Shearer, Joan Crawford, and Rosalind Russell. *The Women* was based on Claire Booth Luce's smash Broadway play about a group of wealthy women whose principal occupation seemed to be exchanging gossip about each other. Their flighty existence is nicely keynoted in the opening scene in which the camera tours a beauty salon, allowing us to catch snatches of the ladies' conversation. It finally comes to rest on Sylvia Fowler (Rosalind Russell), just as she hears a choice bit of gossip that sets the plot in motion. It seems that the husband of Mary Haines (Norma Shearer) is seeing Crystal Allen (Joan Crawford), a salesgirl in a department store, and Mary's friends lose no time in spreading the news.

In filming *The Women* Cukor rightly emphasized the clever dialogue of the script, since that was the play's main forte and remains the principal asset of the film. Rosalind Russell is at her best as the chief gossip in her tribe of friends; but

Joan Crawford's cool, slick portrayal of the determined gold digger is a classic of its kind.

By the late 1930s Cukor had reached the point where he was able to select the subjects which he wanted to film. When he was asked to direct a film with Greta Garbo, for example, he selected *Camille*, and made the film in which Garbo gave the best performance of her career. In *Camille* (1937) Garbo plays Marguerite Gauthier, a French courtesan dying of tuberculosis, who falls in love with the young diplomat Armand Duval (Robert Taylor). Marguerite desperately wants to make the most of the love that she shares with Armand for as long as she can, and so she gives up the nightlife of Paris to live in a country cottage with him. But their idyllic interlude is doomed to be short-lived; and, like many another Cukor hero and heroine, she is made to face this reality. Armand's father (Lionel Barrymore) persuades her that her affair with his son is ruining Armand's career, and she agrees to give him up.

Thinking that she is fickle, Armand denounces her publicly at a ball when next they meet. But they are reunited when he later learns of her fatal illness, and she dies in his arms. This last scene proves beyond a doubt that Garbo was a consummate acress, as well as a legendary beauty. As Armand lifts Marguerite from her sickbed in an embrace, life already seems to be slipping away from her. When he tells her that they will return to the country where her health will revive, we know that Marguerite can no longer hold on to this illusion, much as she would like to. "Perhaps it's better if I live in your heart, where you can't see me," she says; and a radiant smile fills her face as she dies. "Thus does this classic romance conclude precisely as it should," comments Bosley Crowther, "with the ideal, illusory woman, still lovely and imperishable, in a bereft man's arms."[3]

"Garbo went through a great deal to get a scene right," said Cukor; "and I once said to her that she seemed to act a role so easily. She laughed and said that she would kill me for saying that. You have to know how much to rehearse and not overdo it, so that the finished performance in the film will look spontaneous. Garbo knew how to do this. The proper amount of rehearsing does not diminish the spontaneity of a scene, however. When the moment of creation comes on the set, if it has been carefully prepared for, things will happen."

Cukor also directed Garbo in her last picture, *Two-Faced Woman* (1941). "It was a novel idea to have her play twins," he remarked, "but we started shooting before the script was really finished. We went along as best we could, but the picture was bad." Another reason that the film failed was that Garbo's personality was not attuned to playing a role that really called for the light touch of a comedienne, something she could never be.

If Cukor's creative association with Greta Garbo came late in the actress's career, his professional alliance with Katharine Hepburn began with her first film and endured through more than forty years.

Hepburn's first appearance in a Cukor film was in *A Bill of Divorcement* (1932), in which she played a young woman who gives up her own plans for marriage to take care of her insane father (John Barrymore). That Cukor was able to convince the front office at RKO to allow her to take a starring role in her very first picture is an indication of the respect that studio officials had for Cukor's judgment so early in his own career. Adela Rogers St. Johns, the journalist on whom Howard Hawks probably modeled the Rosalind Russell character in *His Girl Friday*, wrote in an article on Katharine Hepburn about being accosted by Cukor on the RKO lot one hot afternoon in 1932. "I've just seen a test of the girl I want for *Bill of Divorcement*," he said. "She looks like a boa constrictor on a fast, but she's great!"[4] Hollywood technicians had not yet learned how to photograph Miss Hepburn to best advantage or to record her clipped, metallic New England accent properly; so her screen test was not impressive. But Cukor had sensed her potential as a screen actress, and the years proved how right he was.

Among the many films in which Cukor directed Miss Hepburn are three in which she was teamed with Cary Grant. The first of these, *Sylvia Scarlett* (1935), was a flop. "That picture had something gallant and foolhardy about it," Cukor commented. "It had interesting and diverting things in it which an audience seems to enjoy today; but that was not the case when it was released. We all had a good time making it, but somehow I never got that picture to work. Perhaps the story line became too complicated as it unfolded." At any rate the movie marked the first time that Cary Grant played a unconventional rogue, instead of a conventional romantic screen hero, Cukor pointed out. "He gave a wonderful performance, but that didn't save the picture at the time."

Perhaps because the film begins as a frivolous farce and then takes a relatively serious turn as it nears the end, audiences were baffled by it at the time it was originally released. In any event, the theme of the film is very much allied to Cukor's personal vision. The picture opens with this preface: "To the adventurer, to all who stray from the beaten track, life is an extravagance in which laughter and luck and love come in odd ways; but they are nonetheless sweet for that." This preface is a toast to those who seek to fulfill their romantic illusions in life, and the first part of the film is in harmony with these sentiments.

At the beginning we follow the adventures of Sylvia (Katharine Hepburn), her father (Edmund Gwenn), and their companion in skullduggery, Jimmie Monkley (Cary Grant), as they swindle and con their way around England. Since Sylvia's father already had a police record in France before coming to England, Sylvia dresses as a boy in order that they might escape detection. But her disguise also betokens the unreal existence that she is living with the other two. The trio becomes further enmeshed in illusion when they become strolling players after they have tired of a life of petty crime.

A crisis arises when Sylvia begins to fall in love, first with Jimmie and then with Michael Fane, an artist (Brian Aherne). In effect, she has to choose between living in the real world with Michael or continuing to live in the world of fantasy with Jimmie. Sylvia finally faces reality, drops her disguise, and admits her feelings for Michael. She has, however reluctantly, turned her back on Jimmie and the madcap existence that he represents. Cukor seems to harbor some degree of affection for the world of romantic illusion; for there is usually a hint of regret in his films when reality inevitably impinges itself on the world of one of his dreamers, a world in which "life is an extravagance in which laughter, and luck, and love come in odd ways; but they are nonetheless sweet for that."

Katharine Hepburn and Cary Grant made *Bringing up Baby* for Howard Hawks in 1938 and then rejoined Cukor for the screen versions of two Philip Barry plays: *Holiday* and *The Philadelphia Story*. Miss Hepburn had done a scene from *Holiday* for her screen test, the one that had so impressed Cukor back in 1932; so it was no surprise that he chose her to play Linda Seton in his film of *Holiday* (1938), a role that she had understudied on Broadway a decade earlier.

Linda is bored and frustrated by the insulated life of luxury that her stuffy family leads, and she often takes refuge in the nursery room where she grew up in order to get away from them all. Linda's behavior represents an obvious retreat from reality into a never-never land, where she is free to indulge her youthful fantasies and longings. But she is shaken out of her lethargic existence when she is moved to endorse her sister's fiancé, Johnny Case (Cary Grant), in his refusal to join the family firm, entering which he sees as the price of his acceptance into the Seton clan. Johnny does not want to be dominated by the Setons, and his independent spirit inspires Linda to elope with him. Linda's resolve is strengthened by her awareness that her brother Ned (Lew Ayres) has ruined his life by constantly knuckling under to the family's demands on him, for he has retreated into alcoholism as his form of escape.

Ned's predicament lends a serious note to the comedy, making *Holiday* the kind of play that Gary Carey contends in his book on Cukor the director does best: "There is a strong human situation at its center and strong characters that can be developed," and are worth the time the camera spends lingering over them. "There is not a single misplaced camera set-up or ill-judged cut in the film."[5]

With *The Philadelphia Story* (1940), Cukor and Hepburn scored their biggest mutual triumph, with Cary Grant on hand once more to add luster to the proceedings. As Tracy Lord, Miss Hepburn gives her definitive performance as a strong-willed, supersophisticated young socialite who nonetheless retains an undeniable charm and elegance. In the opening scene Tracy throws her husband, Dexter Haven (Cary Grant), out of the Lord mansion after a quarrel, breaking one of his golf clubs over her knee for good measure. Dexter later gets even with Tracy for rejecting him in favor of George Kittredge, an insipid social climber, by inviting himself to the wedding and bringing along with him Mike Connor (James Stewart), a reporter from a tacky gossip magazine, just to embarrass his former spouse.

Stewart won an Oscar for his easygoing performance as the man who is finally able to melt Tracy's icy exterior and reveal a warm human being underneath. Then he gallantly turns her over to her ex-husband Dexter, whom she is at last prepared to accept as he really is, now that she has abandoned her unrealistic search for the ideal husband and has gotten rid of Kittredge.

As in *The Women*, the chief virtue of *The Philadelphia Story* is its sparkling dialogue; and Cukor wisely emphasizes the witty repartee as his camera moves about among the characters gathered for the wedding festivities. Cukor's accomplishment in making *The Philadelphia Story* a delightful farce stands out in relief when one compares it to the musical remake of his film, done by another director in 1956. The later movie, which boasted Bing Crosby, Grace Kelly, and Frank Sinatra in the roles played in Cukor's film by Cary Grant, Katharine Hepburn, and James Stewart, plodded along listlessly because the director lacked Cukor's flair for imparting a brisk pace and a light touch to a sophisticated comedy of this kind.

After the trio of films for Cukor in which Miss Hepburn costarred with Cary Grant, she later appeared in three Cukor films in which she was paired with Spencer Tracy: *Keeper of the Flame* (1943), *Adam's Rib* (1949), and *Pat and Mike* (1952). The best of the three is undoubtedly *Adam's Rib*, which was written to order for the team by Garson Kanin and Ruth Gordon, who together or separately were involved in one way or another in creating seven scripts for Cukor. Along with Donald Ogden Stewart, who worked on eight Cukor films, these writers constitute the talents to whom Cukor most frequently turned for material, an indication that he found their work congenial to his directorial style and outlook. For a director, the next best thing to writing his own scripts is to be able to work with writers who can provide him with scripts with which he is in emotional and intellectual sympathy. As Cukor himself put it, " If you select material that attracts you and touches your imagination, as I always have tried to do, your originality will come out in the handling of it, if you *have* any originality. I trust my intuition whenever possible."

Cukor illustrated his custom of trusting his intuition by recalling a scene which was done early in the shooting of *Adam's Rib*. Judy Holliday was playing her first major movie role as Doris Attinger, a young wife accused of the attempted murder of her husband Warren (Tom Ewell), whom she has discovered with another woman. Holliday's most important scene was the long and difficult one in which her lawyer, Amanda Bonner (Katharine Hepburn), interviews Doris for the first time in the women's house of detention. Although Holliday had no previous screen experience, Cukor decided to shoot the interview scene in one seven-minute take. Miss Holliday faced the camera the whole time and delivered a beautifully sustained performance. Many a more experienced actress would have hesitated to attempt singlehandedly to hold a movie audience's attention for so long a span of screen time; but Cukor had a hunch that she could carry it off, and she did.

While Amanda is serving as lawyer for Doris, her husband Adam (Spencer Tracy) is the attorney for Doris's husband Warren. Adam steadfastly tries to keep Amanda from escalating the case into a crusade for women's rights, and this proves to be quite a challenge. Finally Adam convinces Amanda by a ruse that Doris was not justified in shooting her husband. He threatens to shoot Amanda when he finds her in the company of another man. After she insists that he has no right to shoot her, Adam nonchalantly puts the gun into his mouth and bends the barrel with his teeth: it is made of licorice. This is the perfect conclusion to an inventive, inspired farce.

One of the fringe benefits of Cukor's making *Adam's Rib* was his discovery of Judy Holliday, who was to star in three films for Cukor: *Born Yesterday* (1950), *The Marrying Kind* (1952), and *It Should Happen to You* (1954). In *Born Yesterday* Miss Holliday recreated her stage role of Billie Dawn, for which she won an

Academy Award. As Billie, Miss Holliday rendered the definitive portrait of a beautiful but dumb blonde, just as Katharine Hepburn had given the definitive portrait of a sophisticated young socialite in *The Philadelphia Story* a decade earlier.

Billie is the mistress of a wealthy junk dealer, Harry Brock (Broderick Crawford), who is determined to bribe his way into Washington power politics. Harry engages Paul Verrall (William Holden) to give the scantily educated Billie an elementary course in political science, so that she will not embarrass him when he is entertaining the politicians he hopes to bribe. Billie learns enough from Paul to know that what Harry is doing is wrong, and she threatens to expose his plans unless he abandons them—a situation which closely parallels the way that Kitty Packard handles her husband in *Dinner at Eight* when she learns about his unsavory business deals.

In the role of Billie, Judy Holliday demonstrates her ability to make us laugh at Billie's dim-witted remarks, at the same time that she is stirring our compassion for Billie's vulnerable stupidity. In one scene the apelike Harry becomes exasperated with Billie and strikes her across the face. As she whimpers and cries softly, we realize just how deeply the actress has made us care for Billie.

In *The Marrying Kind* Miss Holliday gives another sympathetic yet humorous portrayal, this time of Florence Keefer, who wants to divorce her husband Chet (Aldo Ray). When the understanding divorce judge (Madge Kennedy) asks Florence and Chet the reason for their imcompatibility, Florence answers without hesitation,"Because we're married to each other." The real problem is that Florence and Chet have harbored unrealistic expectations of each other, and this becomes clear in the flashbacks in which each of them tells about their life together. Often we hear the voice of one of them narrating a past incident on the sound track, while we simultaneously see the same episode acted out before us on the screen as it is remembered quite differently by the other party. As the judge points out to them, "It's all in what you remember and in your point of view."

Their romantic illusions are totally shattered by the tragic death of their small son during a picnic. The judge suggests to them that this crisis, which initially has driven them further apart, can be the source of their reconciliation as they seek to give emotional support to one another.

The Marrying Kind has an affinity to *Sylvia Scarlett*, in that it begins as pure comedy and moves closer to serious drama as the romantic notions of the central characters are stripped away. It is interesting to note that by the 1950s audiences were more ready to accept a blend of comedy and drama than they were when Cukor served up the same combination fifteen years earlier.

We come now to the trilogy of film in which Cukor treats most explicitly his ongoing theme about the need to distinguish between illusion and reality in life: *A Double Life*, *A Star Is Born*, and *Les Girls*. Like many of Cukor's films, all three are about show-business types, people who make it their profession to create a world of illusion for others. But Cukor implies in these films that, in one sense, all of us lead this double life that moves between illusion and reality, as we seek to sort out fantasy from fact in our lives in order to deal realistically with our problems.

Signe Hasso and Ronald Colman in his Oscar-winning role in *A Double Life* **(1947). (The George Cukor collection)**

Ronald Colman earned an Oscar for his performance as Anthony John in *A Double Life* (1947). John is an actor who becomes so identified with the roles he plays that he develops a murderous streak of jealousy while playing Othello. With increasing difficulty he tries to divorce himself from the role when he is offstage; but he ultimately fails to do so. In the film's strongest scene the personality of Othello slowly possesses the actor while he is spending the evening with his mistress, a cheap waitress (Shelley Winters). When he becomes obsessed with the idea that she is still seeing other men, he strangles her just as Othello kills Desdemona in the play.

After the police have discovered that John is the murderer, they go to the theater and wait for him backstage while he finishes what is to be his last performance. Once more merging illusion with reality, John plays Othello's suicide scene with a real dagger and ends his life as he ends the play. The film's final, unforgettable image is that of the curtains parting to allow the star to take his bows, while the spotlight reveals an empty stage.

The character that links *A Star Is Born* (1954) with *A Double Life* is not singer Vicki Lester (Judy Garland), to whom the title refers, but her husband, actor Norman Maine (James Mason), whose star is descending at the same rapid pace that Vicki's is rising. Norman is not consciously jealous of his wife's success in films, but her career does serve to underscore his own decline as a movie idol. He tries to soften the bitterness of this reality by living most of the time in an alcoholic haze, from which Vicki is finally powerless to rescue him. Nonetheless she never ceases to love him.

After his suicide she introduces herself proudly, with tears welling up in her eyes, to a packed auditorium that has come to hear Vicki Lester sing, as "Mrs. Norman Maine"—as if to emphasize that she has no intention of dissociating herself from Norman in death any more than she did in life. This is undoubtedly the most moving finale of any Cukor film; and it puts the finishing touch to Judy Garland's superb portrayal of Vicki, a girl who keeps herself firmly rooted in reality even while caught up in the fantasy world of motion-picture making, but who is unable to help her husband do the same.

A Star Is Born, as mentioned, is Cukor's musical remake of his earlier film *What Price Hollywood?*; and it is interesting to note how incidents that are referred to in *What Price Hollywood?* are developed in depth in *A Star Is Born*. For example, in *Hollywood* a newspaper headline announces that the heroine has won an Academy Award. In *A Star Is Born* this item is expanded into a major sequence, in which the event is spoiled by the appearance at the ceremonies of the star's drunken actor-husband, proclaiming that he made the worst picture of the year.

A Star Is Born was one of the first films in which the wide screen was used intelligently. Cukor made no attempt to keep the action centered symmetrically in mid-screen, as had been customary in wide screen films at that time. Rather he allowed the action to move from one side of the screen to the other, thus using to best advantage the increased space available in the new format. When Judy Garland sings "The Man that Got Away" in a small nightclub after hours, Cukor has the camera follow her as she roams around, sometimes almost disappearing out of

**Judy Garland in *A Star Is Born* (1954), George Cukor's musical remake of his earlier film
What Price Hollywood? (The George Cukor collection)**

the frame. Garland is rarely in the center of the screen during the number; and this
very lack of perfect pictorial composition made the scene more dynamic and spontaneous, Cukor felt.

A Star Is Born is among the best movie musicals ever made, with the Harold
Arlen-Ira Gershwin songs carefully integrated into the plot in a way that keeps the
film from being an episodic "backstage musical." When Vicki sings "It's a New
World I See" after Norman's suicide, for example, the context adds an extra
dimension to the pathos already inherent in the number.

Even a veteran director like Cukor was unable to keep studio officials from trimming nearly half an hour out of the three-hour film. This was done in order to make
possible an additional daily screening of the picture wherever it played, thereby
increasing the film's revenue. In later years Cukor was philosophical about this
tampering with his film, since *A Star Is Born* earned a secure reputation as a classic
musical. But he still felt that he and the script writer, Moss Hart, would have done a
smoother job of shortening the film. "Had we been allowed, Moss Hart and I could
have shaved away twenty or so minutes from the film which would have been im-
perceptible to the audience," said Cukor. Instead the studio took out whole scenes

to bring the running time of the film down to two and a half hours. One scene in particular is a special loss. In it Norman proposes to Vicky in the recording studio where the dubbing of the songs for one of Vicki's films is in progress. When the recording of one of her songs is played back, Norman's tender proposal to Vicki, made while the microphone was still on, comes booming over the loudspeaker, to the delight and embarrassment of both of them.[6] Nevertheless, in the last analysis, *A Star Is Born* was not marred in any essential way by the studio's meddling with the movie.

One has only to consider the inferior 1976 remake of *A Star Is Born*, recast this time as a rock musical for Barbra Streisand, to confirm the fact that Cukor's musical version of this oft-told tale is unquestionably the most enduring of them all. As mentioned earlier, when a movie directed by a major director like a Hitchcock or a Cukor has been remade by other hands, the remake almost invariably suffers by comparison with the original.[7]

Cukor's second major musical, *Les Girls* (1957), is the most explicit of all his films in dealing with his theme of the conflict of fact and fantasy. In *The Marrying Kind* the viewer was often shown two versions of past events, as remembered by Florence and her husband Chet. In *Les Girls* the audience is given not two but four versions of the common past shared by showgirls Sibyl Wren (Kay Kendall), Joy Henderson (Mitzi Gaynor), and Angele Duclos (Tania Elg), and their lead dancer Barry Nichols (Gene Kelly). When Sibyl writes a book about their experiences together as troupers, Angele sues her for libel; and all four of them have to appear in court to give their rendition of the facts.

Each of the girls "remembers" their mutual past in a way that projects a somewhat romanticized self-image of the individual recounting the story. It remains for Barry to give a relatively unvarnished account of the various romantic entanglements the girls had during the period in which they all toured Europe together. The trial ends with Angele dropping her charges and Barry winning Joy, the least glamorous but most sensible girl of the group. In choosing Joy, Barry is plumping for a down-to-earth individual who represents the superiority of reality over illusion; and this note nicely rounds out the trilogy of films in which Cukor treats this theme.

Although Cukor claimed that he never felt completely at home making musicals, during the 1960's he made two more eye-filling musicals: *Let's Make Love* (1960) , a backstage musical with Marilyn Monroe, and *My Fair Lady* (1964). As a matter of fact, the peak of Cukor's career came with the latter musical, which won him the Academy Award as best director and which was also named best picture of the year. "Even though I received an Oscar for the picture," Cukor said, "I have never really felt at home in making musicals. I don't know enough about music to put songs in the proper places within the action of the story. Of course, in the case of *My Fair Lady* we had the original stage version to go by."

Nonetheless, he continued, "the transition from stage to screen is tricky. On the one hand, you can't turn out a photographed stage play; on the other hand, you can't rend the original stage version apart. If you don't know what was good about the original play, you pull it apart to make a different version for the screen; and you have nothing left. George Bernard Shaw had worked on the script for the

Audrey Hepburn and Rex Harrison in *My Fair Lady* (1964), for which both George Cukor and Harrison won Academy Awards. (The George Cukor collection)

screen version of his *Pygmalion* (1938), on which *My Fair Lady* was based. In it he allowed the ending of his original play, in which the hero and the heroine did not get back together, to be changed so that the story ended happily. Lerner and Loewe used this ending for *My Fair Lady* on the stage, and we kept it for the film."

Although there are several sumptuous production numbers in Cukor's film of *My Fair Lady*, the movie comes most fully to life in the final scene. Henry Higgins, the egotistical speech professor (Rex Harrison), finds himself alone; he is bemoaning the fact that in spite of himself he has fallen in love with Eliza Doolittle (Audrey Hepburn), the cockney flower girl whom he turned into the belle of a society ball to win a bet. Harrison half sings, half talks "I've Grown Accustomed to Her Face," which is as close to a declaration of love as the reserved professor would ever permit himself to utter. There is something deeply touching about a man who had fancied himself a loner having to admit his need for another human being.

This scene alone would have qualified Harrison for the Academy Award he garnered for his portrayal of Higgins. Here too the directorial hand of Cukor is most evident, helping Harrison not only to tone down his stage performance for the closeness of the camera, but also to give a fresh reading of a scene that he had already done more than a thousand times on the stage. In this scene Harrison admirably achieved the kind of controlled spontaneity that Cukor says he so respected in Garbo and that he has striven to bring to all of his films.

In 1969 Cukor finished *Justine*, a project on which two other directors had worked before he took over the picture, so that the film is really marginal to his career. Then, in 1972, Cukor undertook the direction of *Travels with My Aunt*, based on the Graham Greene novel. Maggie Smith plays the title role of Aunt Augusta, a dotty old lady with a delightfully wicked past. She takes it upon herself to initiate her inhibited middle-aged nephew Henry (Alec McCowen) into the more exciting side of life by taking him on a world tour that includes people and places not described in a guide book.

"We were dealing with the work of a very talented novelist," Cukor said; "so we tried to incorporate every important episode and incident from the novel into the film; above all we wanted to preserve the spirit of Greene's very amusing novel. Greene has created some very rich and marvelous characters in the story; the warmth and range of both the elderly aunt and her middle-aged nephew attracted me to the story. We hope we have preserved the essence of the novel on the screen."

During the 1970s Cukor was reunited with Katharine Hepburn to make two notable telefilms, *Love among the Ruins* (1975) and *The Corn is Green* (1979)—in addition to the eight theatrical features they had made together. Then, in 1980, at the age of eighty-one, he undertook the direction of *Rich and Famous*, an updated, streamlined version of John Van Druten's play *Old Acquaintance*, which had been filmed in 1943 by Vincent Sherman under the play's original title, When I visited the set of *Rich and Famous* (1981), Cukor remarked that it was the quality of Gerald Ayres's screenplay that drew him to direct the picture. "I still find a witty, intelligent script irresistible," he explained.

In the film Jacqueline Bisset and Candice Bergen costar, respectively, as Liz and

Merry, two college coeds who become bitter rivals in both their personal and professional lives as the years go on. In one clever scene Merry, now a successful commercial novelist, shares a moment of truth with Liz. Referring to the fact that Liz is a respected writer who has never had a bestseller, Merry comments in a rare moment of generous candor that, instead of being rich and famous like herself, Liz is "only famous—which is harder to do."

But the script had visual as well as verbal gems for Cukor to mine. One visual symbol that pervades the film is the teddy bear that Liz and Merry have both cherished since they were college roommates. In a fit of mutual bitchiness during a climactic quarrel late in the movie, each claims the bear as her own; and they literally tear the stuffing out of this treasured souvenir of their youth so that neither of them can keep it, thereby destroying the last vestige of the happy college days they had shared together.

In the final sequence of the film they are once more reconciled to each other, as they spend New Year's Eve alone together, since neither has a husband to share the occasion with. Appropriately enough, they toast the New Year with champagne that has gone flat, sadly symbolic of the way their personal lives have likewise gone stale. They are two lonely, abandoned females, both well into their thirties, aware that all that is left of their broken lives is their relationship with each other: a lovely, elegiac note on which to conclude the film.

Directing *Rich and Famous* merited the octogenarian film maker the distinction of being very likely then the oldest director ever to make a major motion picture, and likewise marked him as enjoying one of the longest continuous careers in movies and TV of any director ever. As we concluded over conversation about the film, it was obvious that Cukor had lost none of the enthusiasm for the movie business that he brought with him to Hollywood in 1929. "I look upon every picture that I have made as the first one I've ever done—and the last," he reflected. "I love each film I have directed, and I have tried to make each one as good as I possibly could. Mind you, making movies is no bed for roses. Every day isn't Christmas. It's been a hard life, but also a joyous one."

It could be said that Cukor was the prototype of the ideal Hollywood *auteur*, for he was a skilled craftsman who recognized that a good film is the product of many talents. He was therefore able to work successfully within the Hollywood system and at the same time add a personal touch to the films he directed.

Perhaps Cukor best explained his attitude toward the collaborative nature of movie making when he said, "I don't say that I personally write or edit a picture. But I do try to influence everyone who works with me on a film, in order to get the best out of them that they have to give. I see what every individual can accomplish on their own, and then I make suggestions; and together we work out each step of the production. I let each of them know that I need every scrap of assistance they can give me." Nevertheless, Cukor also recognized in practice the principle of the *auteur* theory, elaborated in the Prologue of this study, that only the director can forge the finished picture into a unified whole. He added that he was most pleased when the resulting film showed no obvious signs of "direction" at all, because he as director had integrated as smoothly as possible into the completed movie the contributions of everyone associated with the production.

Cukor received his share of accolades, including the prestigious D. W. Griffith Award from the Directors Guild of America in 1981. Yet some of the satisfaction which he derived from his long career was no doubt grounded in the fact that he brought so much enjoyment to so many. Richard Schickel perhaps said it all when he wrote of Cukor, "His movies can be appreciated—no, liked—at one level or another by just about everyone."[8]

George Stevens on location for *The Greatest Story Ever Told* **(1965). (Cinemabilia)**

5
George Stevens
In Search of a Hero

When Graham Greene was a film critic back in the 1930s, he developed his concept of poetic cinema. A poetic film is a movie that, while it entertains the viewer, also challenges him, not only by depicting life as it is, but also by implying life as it ought to be. The films of George Stevens come close to verifying Greene's notion of poetic cinema, for Stevens often presents a hero who is dissatisfied with society at large and strives in so far as he can to diminish the gap between life as it is and life as it ought to be.

Such a character is not the same as the dreamer with whom George Cukor's films frequently deal, for the Cukor character is often an individual who prefers to retreat into a world of private illusion and who must instead be made to face his problems squarely. By contrast, the typical Stevens character is enough of a realist to view this imperfect world for what it is, but he is also enough of a romantic to want to help make that world approximate a little more closely what it ought to be. As an idealist, he stands apart from his fellow men who do not share his aspirations; he is, therefore, an outsider.

"I am aware that I deal with outsiders," Stevens said when the topic was broached to him; "I suppose it is because I myself have always felt more at home as an observer than a participant in various situations. One can trace this theme in my work back to a film like *Alice Adams* (1935), in which Katharine Hepburn plays a girl who is basically an outsider."

In his book on Stevens, Donald Ritchie traces the development in Stevens's films of the director's personal vision from an idealism that is unduly romantic and optimistic to one that is relatively more practical and realistic. In his early films, according to Ritchie, Stevens allows his chief characters to bring their problems to a happy resolution, thereby implying that a better world is already in the offing. "Until World War II," Ritchie writes, "Stevens remained a full romantic, one of Hollywood's finest examples."[1] The war brought the disillusioning realization that a better world was not just around the corner, however. Accordingly, Stevens's postwar films took on a more sober tone and carried the inference that the individual, however resourceful, would have to struggle even harder than before to realize his personal ideals in a world that seemed farther than ever from accepting him or his values.

As his career progressed, Stevens chose from the projects he was offered subjects that struck a chord not only in his consciousness but in the consciousness of the mass audience as well. This is because Stevens's fellow Americans had shared his journey from prewar optimism to postwar disillusionment and could therefore intimately understand and respond to his motion pictures.

Stevens was born in Oakland, California, in 1904 and began his career in the film industry in 1921 as a cameraman at the Hal Roach Studios. There he worked on several Laurel and Hardy two-reelers, most notably *The Battle of the Century* (1927), *Two Tars* (1928), and *Big Business* (1929). "I learned to like comedy by working with Laurel and Hardy, even though I come from a family of serious actors," he told me. "Those early silent comedies gave me a comic sense which I was able to draw upon later in the comedies that I directed myself. Even when I have made serious films, I have always tried to include a legitimate comic turn in the plot somewhere."

Stevens stayed on with Roach as a cameraman when sound pictures came in and therefore gained experience in making talking pictures right from the beginning. One day he was photographing a two-reel comedy for Roach when the latter suggested that it was time for Stevens to try his hand at directing. Roach wanted Stevens to take over the direction of a comedy short that was already in progress, but Stevens declined. "If you want me to direct a picture, let me get my own story, so I'll know what I'm doing," he said. This procedure of finding a story to direct that appealed to him is one that Stevens followed throughout his career and accounts for the continuity in his work.

Stevens directed some of the short comedies in the *Boy Friends* series in 1930, such as *Call a Cop!* and *The Kick-Off*. By 1933 he was ready to move up to feature production, and he began making full-length comedies of the same type as the farcical short films he had been doing up to this point. In 1935 Stevens got the chance to direct his first film of substance, *Alice Adams*. It was also the first of his three films with Katharine Hepburn, who by this time had already won recognition for her work with George Cukor in *A Bill of Divorcement* (1932) and *Little Women* (1933).

Alice Adams is based on Booth Tarkington's Pulitzer Prize–winning novel about a girl in a prosperous Midwestern town whose family has not been able to "keep up with the Joneses." Since her father is only a clerk, Alice is never invited to any of the social functions given by young people her own age. Her mother feels this more keenly than Alice herself, and points out to Alice that these youngsters are the children of men who grew up with her father. "It is clear that in her indignation over the coldness shown her daughter by the town's newly organized first families," writes Elliott Sirkin, "she is the spokeswoman for Stevens and for the film."[2] Stevens would satirize an equally materialistic community in *Giant* two decades later.

Alice is Stevens's first outsider, as he himself said; and he visualizes her status symbolically in the scene in which she attends a party to which she has managed to wangle an invitation. As the other guests begin to move toward the dance floor, Alice, painfully obtrusive in her white gown but nonetheless ignored, stands moping beneath a staircase. Then, unexpectedly, she is asked to dance by handsome and wealthy Arthur Russell (Fred MacMurray).

Very much on the defensive, Alice spins a series of fabrications about her family's social status for Arthur, not realizing that it is her wit and spirit that have beguiled him, not her stories. Deciding to impress him further, she invites him to dinner with her family, an event that turns out to be an unmitigated disaster. Alice and her parents desperately try to impress Arthur, but their pretentiousness is only too obvious. The dinner sequence is skillfully directed by Stevens to be both funny and touching. The Adams' failure to be something that they are not is epitomized by their maid (Hattie McDaniel), who trundles around the dining room in an ill-fitting maid's outfit that has been borrowed for the occasion, her little lace cap all askew.

Finally Alice has the courage to admit to Arthur the deceptions with which she has crippled their relationship, and she sends him away. This first step toward self-knowledge and maturity is shortly followed by another. She faces her brother Walter's employer and persuades him to allow her to pay back the money which Walter has embezzled from the company in his misguided attempts to better the family's social position. To do this Alice decides to become a secretary, a decision that spells the end of her ambitions to break into the town's elite social circle. Admittedly, by going this route, "she'll never be able to wipe out the snobbery and materialism that have been oppressing her," Sirkin comments. "But she will be able to ignore them, and that's a triumph in itself."[3]

At this point the film disconcertingly changes direction, and Alice finds Arthur waiting for her on the front porch, ready to forgive her dishonesty and to be reconciled with her. This synthetic happy ending is the film's only substantial departure from Tarkington's novel. The latter ends with Arthur and Alice parting for good, with the implication that Alice has grown in maturity as a result of the experience. This is the ending Stevens has prepared us for in film, but it is not the ending that he delivers.

It is unlikely that the ending of the picture as it stands was studio-imposed, since Stevens rejected the original script of the film and had it totally revised according to his specifications before shooting began. Donald Ritchie is nearer the truth in saying that the film's ending was in harmony with Stevens's personal vision as far as it had developed at the time he made *Alice Adams*. In that period of his career Stevens's attitude toward life as reflected in his films implied a much more romantic optimism than would mark his postwar work.

The happy ending of Alice Adams, which suggests that Alice and Arthur will soon marry, seems to come as an instant reward to Alice for her willingness to own up to her past mistakes and to profit by them. As the poor girl now turned rich, Ritchie concludes, "she reconciles within herself the unfortunate social schism that prevented the world from being the place it should have been. From now on, for her at least, it will be."[4] This is the kind of facile happy ending that Stevens will later reject, notably in *A Place in the Sun*, in which George Eastman will learn the same lesson as Alice about social climbing, but only after he has made more serious mistakes than she did, for which he will pay with his life.

Stevens made two other films with Katharine Hepburn, *Quality Street* (1937), which costarred Franchot Tone, and *Woman of the Year* (1942), the first of the nine films in which she was to costar with Spencer Tracy. *Woman of the Year* featured a

Spencer Tracy and Katharine Hepburn, stars of *Woman of the Year* **(1942). (Author's collection)**

slapstick sequence in which Stevens drew on his days with Laurel and Hardy. The career-girl heroine (Hepburn) tries to prove to her sweetheart (Tracy) that she has her domestic side by making him his breakfast. In the ensuing scene, however, she succeeds only in hilariously reducing the kitchen to a shambles.

Like Hawks and Cukor, Stevens has been able to make films in several different genres with equal dexterity. Besides comedies, melodramas, and Westerns, Stevens also tried his hand at musicals: *Swing Time* (1936), which is generally considered one of the best of the nine musicals that Fred Astaire and Ginger Rogers made as a team, as well as *A Damsel in Distress* (1937), with Astaire and Joan Fontaine.

The Astaire musicals, of course, are completely compatible with the generally optimistic and romantic mood of the films Stevens made in the 1930s. In *Swing Time* Astaire plays Lucky Garnett, a professional dancer, who is attracted to Penny Carrol (Ginger Rogers). He enrolls in the dancing school where she works in order to get to know her better. The plot is pleasantly forgettable, since it is calculated solely to provide opportunities for the musical numbers composed for the film by Jerome Kern and Dorothy Fields. For example, when Lucky deliberately stumbles around during his first lesson with Penny and feigns discouragement, she sings to him, "Pick Yourself Up, Dust Yourself Off, and Start All Over Again."

This story line is a long way from the meaty plots of later screen musicals like Cukor's *A Star Is Born* and *Les Girls*. Nevertheless, Astaire's musicals have other virtues, and the two films he made with Stevens illustrate this. Astaire customarily worked out his dance routines with the camera in mind and would cooperate with the director of the picture to make the camera an integral part of the number. For instance, Astaire and Stevens utilized trick photography in the "Bojangles of Harlem" number in *Swing Time*, in which Astaire dances with three huge shadows of himself projected on the wall behind him, counterpointing his dance routine with steps of their own. In *A Damsel in Distress* Astaire worked out with Stevens a perfect blend of music and camera movement for the George and Ira Gershwin song "A Foggy Day." Astaire glides through a forest lit by the shimmering moonbeams that are streaming through the trees, with Stevens's fluid camera staying with him throughout the number.

The time-honored problem, examined in this book's Prologue—how an *auteur* director could maintain creative control of his films in an expanding industry—often confronted Stevens during his early years as a director. By 1938 he realized that the only way for a director to gain artistic independence was to act as his own producer, and he was among the first to do so. "When the movie industry was young," he said, "the film maker was its core and the man who handled the money was his partner. When the director finally looked around, he found his partner's name on the door. Thus the film maker became the employee, and the man who had time to attend to the business details became head of the studio." In producing as well as directing his films, Stevens would himself be responsible for making the decisions that would enable him to finish a film within the time and budget he had been alloted by the front office, and he would not have to answer to someone else concerning these factors of film production while he was shooting a picture.

One of the first films Stevens both produced and directed was *Gunga Din* (1939). It starred Cary Grant, who would soon appear in two more films for Stevens, *Penny Serenade* (1941) and *The Talk of the Town* (1942). During this period the ubiquitous Mr. Grant was making films like *Only Angels Have Wings* and *His Girl Friday* for Howard Hawks, and *Holiday* and *The Philadelphia Story* for George Cukor. In *Gunga Din* he plays Cutter, a sergeant in the British army in India. Along with his buddies (Douglas Fairbanks, Jr., and Victor McLaglen), Cutter spends his spare time getting into brawls in the local bars when not engaged in battling the enemy.

Stevens was dissatisfied with the original scenario for *Gunga Din*, which had been developed by Ben Hecht and Charles MacArthur from Rudyard Kipling's poem. Hecht and MacArthur had written the famous comedy about the newspaper business, *The Front Page*, which Howard Hawks filmed as *His Girl Friday*. "When they prepared a script for *Gunga Din*," Stevens recalled, "it turned out to be *The Front Page* in India, with most of the scenes taking place in offices. I wanted to make an outdoor film, so I worked over their script with some other writers and added the material on the Eastern cult that had formed a secret society to upset the British rule in India. But when we started the film, the new script wasn't finished. I remember sitting in the back of a truck on location writing dialogue, while the soldiers were being drilled on the parade ground nearby for another scene."

Stevens incorporated some slapstick into the fight scenes of the film; but he was careful, he said, not to let these comic sequences interfere with the overall serious tone of the film. Thus the climax of *Gunga Din* is played straight, for all of the action and suspense that Stevens can mine from the situation. Cutter and the Indian water boy Gunga Din (Sam Jaffe) have been captured by the secret society and have learned that the outnumbered British troops are riding into an ambush in which they will surely be slaughtered by the band of terrorists. Gunga Din manages to slip away and warn the advancing British troops by blowing a bugle call that puts them on their guard. Just at that moment he is shot by one of his captors; but he continues to blow the bugle as long as he has strength to do so, and the sound of the horn poignantly dies out as Din's own life ebbs away. In the ensuing battle Cutter escapes; but the film nevertheless ends on a somber note, as the British army holds a military funeral for Din, who had always wanted to be a British soldier, and he is posthumously given the rank of corporal.

Pauline Kael has called *Gunga Din* "a model of the action genre, so exuberant and high-spirited that it both exalted and mocked a school boy's version of heroism."[5] True, Cutter, the hero, escapes death and helps the British win the day. Nevertheless, in emphasizing Gunga Din's death, the film makes the point that no victory is achieved without sacrifice, a reflection that definitely takes *Gunga Din* out of the class of mindless adventure yarns. With this film Stevens, then, was already mitigating the romantic idealism of his previous films, something that is also evident in *The Talk of the Town* and in *Penny Serenade*.

In the latter film Julie Adams (Irene Dunne), who is thinking about divorcing her husband Roger (Cary Grant), listens to some old records which serenade her with a number of tunes that are implicitly associated with various incidents in her married life. It seems that, after their own baby was stillborn, Julie and Roger adopted a little girl, who subsequently succumbed to a fatal disease.

One reviewer smirked that for the couple to lose one child is understandable; for them to lose a second seems like carelessness. On the contrary, surely Stevens's purpose is to contrast the response of Roger and Julie to the loss of their first child with their reaction to the loss of the second: The death of their unborn child brings them closer together, as they strive to lend each other the mutual support they both need to go on with their married life. The demise of their adopted child, however, temporarily drives them apart; since, by the time of the little girl's death, she has grown to be the very center of their lives.

In the end Julie and Roger adopt yet another child, as they courageously determine to make a go of their marriage once more. This bittersweet love story, altogether, makes for an endearing film, which is both ably directed and skillfully played.

The Talk of the Town casts Cary Grant as Leopold Dilg, a suspected arsonist who has broken out of jail. He is temporarily seeking sanctuary in the home of Judge Michael Lightcap (Ronald Colman), with the collusion of Lightcap's housekeeper, Nora Shelley (Jean Arthur). Nora's initial attempts to keep Leopold's true identity a secret from the judge provide Stevens with the opportunity for some delightful comic vignettes. In one scene Nora keeps Michael from seeing Leopold's picture on the front page of the morning paper lying on the breakfast table by adroitly sliding a fried egg over the photograph.

As an escaped prisoner, Leopold is clearly one of Stevens's outsiders. In addition, he is by nature an independent individual; and he frequently discusses with Michael the clash between individual freedom and the law. Leopold is ultimately able to inspire Michael with a fresh respect for the freedom of the individual, since Michael's theoretical studies of the law had threatened to stifle his awareness that human rights are at stake in every case. By the time that Michael discovers Leopold's true identity, he is fully prepared to risk his own career by defending Leopold, who accuses crooked business interests in the town of having framed him with the arson charge.

Leopold is eventually acquitted, and Michael is appointed to the Supreme Court. Like *Alice Adams*, Michael receives an almost instant reward for risking his own personal welfare for another. Nonetheless, Michael is aware that he must conscientiously strive to champion a more humane application of the law in his newly attained, exalted position. With privilege, he realizes, goes obligation. Michael's refined sense of justice will make him a loner like Leopold, for he will have to stick to his convictions whether they are popular or not; and he is fully aware of this as he goes into his first session of the court. In the later films of his prewar period, Stevens seems to be saying that the idealist who is dissatisfied with life as it is and wants to do his part to build a better world is not going to have an easy time of it. Leopold has not; nor will Michael.

Cary Grant did not appear in Stevens's next film, *The More the Merrier* (1943), but did star in the remake, *Walk, Don't Run* (1966). As directed by Stevens, *The More the Merrier* is a delightful picture of the housing problem in wartime Washington. The later version transplanted the story to Tokyo during the 1964 Olympics, and somehow lost a lot of the verve of the original along the way. Stevens, whose *Gunga Din* was remade disappointingly as *Sergeants Three* in 1962 with Frank Sinatra in the Grant role, believed that remakes are often foredoomed to fall short of the originals on which they are based.

"I saw *Sergeants Three* on television," he commented. "The actors went through the motions of the original story of *Gunga Din*, but missed the real feeling of the film. I feel the same way about *Walk, Don't Run*. For a film to come off well you have to feel the risk of trying to make something work. When I saw *Gunga Din* again recently, I thought I would be disappointed in it; but I wasn't. It worked; it had that combination of love and doubt that makes a film come off. That is something that remakes usually don't have. It is true that I made *A Place in the Sun* (1951) from Theodore Dreiser's novel *An American Tragedy*, which Josef Von Sternberg had already filmed in 1931 under the novel's title. But I went back to Dreiser's original novel, not to Von Sternberg's film version, when I prepared my film. Also, *An American Tragedy* was not one of Von Sternberg's better films because it was one of his first efforts in the sound medium. I thought the novel deserved another chance."

In 1943 Stevens joined the Signal Corps as a combat photographer. On his return to civilian life he joined fellow directors Frank Capra (*It's a Wonderful Life*) and William Wyler (*The Best Years of Our Lives*) in implementing their joint conviction that they could help build a better postwar world by making films with throught-provoking themes which reflected the critical times. The three directors formed Liberty Films, an independent production company; and Stevens accordingly determined not to resume making the relatively light type of films that had become associated with his name before the war. His first contribution to this movement toward motion pictures that would give audiences something to think about was *I Remember Mama* (1948), with Irene Dunne in the role of Mama.

"A great deal of the credit for *Mama* belongs to producer-director Stevens," wrote James Agee. "Always one of Hollywood's better directors, he developed while he was away at war like few other talented picture makers. In *Mama*, his first movie since his return, he felt no timidity about tackling a script that lacked action and a strong plot. He concentrated, with confidence and resourcefulness, on character, mood, and abundant detail."[6]

In seeking to help his audience cope with the postwar world of the present, Stevens took them into the past for a look at a family of immigrants trying to adjust to their new environment in turn-of-the-century San Francisco. The immigrant, of course, is the quintessential outsider, as I mentioned in treating Chaplin's film *The Immigrant*; and it is therefore understandable that Stevens was attracted to this subject, since his films so often focus on the outsider.

Mama is one of the most practical of Stevens's idealists, and she encourages her family to train themselves to make the most of whatever talents they have. Her daughter Katrin (Barbara Bel Geddes) becomes a writer, and the story of the family as told in the film is the source of her first successful book. *I Remember Mama* implies that America remains a land of opportunity for the resourceful. In this sense, it serves as a prologue to the three best films that Stevens directed: *A Place in the Sun*, *Shane*, and *Giant*. In this trilogy of films Stevens almost seems to be testing the practical idealism, which had evolved in his postwar movies out of the more romantic brand that permeated his prewar films, in order to see how it works out in practice.

I Remember Mama was the only film that Stevens made for Liberty Films, for his partnership with Capra and Wyler had been dissolved by the time he was ready to make another movie. Liberty Films was an interesting experiment; but the 1940s were still a bit too early for Hollywood to accept fully the concept of independent production companies, since the studio system would remain in its heyday until the early 1950s. Nevertheless, Liberty Films was not all that premature, for it would only be a few years before Hollywood executives would begin to turn to the independents to help them try to save the audience they were losing to television. In any event, in making the successful *I Remember Mama* independently, Stevens had proved his capabilities as a producer-director; and he therefore returned to work for the major studios with the artistic control of his films guaranteed.

George Eastman (Montgomery Clift), the hero of his next film, *A Place in the Sun* (1951), is not a practical idealist, for he is not interested in making the world a better place in which everyone can live. His preoccupation is to better his own personal status, regardless of what it might cost himself or others. Stevens contrasts George, the selfish opportunist, with his mother, Hannah Eastman (Ann Revere), who is the true practical idealist in the movie. She is a woman very much like Mama in Stevens's previous film, who runs a mission to help the poor.

George leaves his impecunious home to go to work in his uncle's factory, in the hope that he can impress his uncle with his initiative and advance quickly within the company's structure. His personal life becomes complicated when he falls in love with two girls: Alice Tripp (Shelley Winters), another factory worker, who represents the familiar working-class world in which George grew up, and wealthy Angela Vickers (Elizabeth Taylor), who represents the world to which George aspires. George's complex personal life reaches a crisis when Alice becomes pregnant. George decides to drown her in order to keep her from ruining his chances of marrying Angela. He takes Alice rowing on a lake; they argue, and in the ensuing scuffle Alice falls into the lake and drowns. George is convicted of murder, although he goes to his death still wondering whether or not he deliberatly allowed Alice to die.

A Place in the Sun was a great box-office hit, despite the unhappy ending that Stevens retained from the novel, for happy endings were still the order of the day in Hollywood movies in the early 1950s. The film was an artistic success as well, winning Stevens the Academy Award as best director and also the Screen Directors' Guild Award.

When the film had its television premiere in 1966 Stevens instigated a lawsuit to ensure that the TV network would show the film in its entirety without cuts. His concern was understandable, for *A Place in the Sun* builds slowly toward its climax. Earlier scenes, apparently unimportant, contribute to the gradual development of characterization, atmosphere, and the impact of the film as a whole. "The network

Montgomery Clift and Shelley Winters in *A Place in the Sun* (1951), for which George Stevens won an Oscar. (Museum of Modern Art/Film Stills Archive)

wanted to delete all of the overlapping dissolves throughout the film, and I prevented them from doing this," Stevens explained. "For example, there is a slow dissolve from the mansion in which Angela Vickers lives to the drab little flat where Alice Tripp lives; and for a moment the two places are on the screen together in an overlap dissolve, indicating the difference between the two worlds in which George Eastman is simultaneously moving." Later in the film there is a shot of the lake, which slowly dissolves to a shot of Alice waiting for George. For an instant the face of Alice and the image of the lake are on the screen together, ominously prefiguring Alice's death by drowning.

The scenes just described indicate the care that Stevens lavished on his films. Yet he avoided the sort of cinematic effects that draw attention to themselves. "In general I use the camera as a witness to what is happening in the scene, and don't attempt to comment on the action," Stevens explained. It was his purpose "to keep the director from being in evidence in a film. He should give the audience the privilege of seeing people at a time when they are exposing themselves to others, without being aware that they are doing so. When the camera moves too much or when the director in some other way makes his presence felt in the scene, I get the feeling that I can see his shadow falling across the screen."

Stevens understood the visual dimension of the cinema as only a cameraman could, and he was able to make audiences see and feel as he did. In *Shane* (1953) he captures the animal fury of a fight by shooting it between the legs of a panicking horse. He represents the isolation of the little community of settlers in the same film by photographing a funeral scene in long shots that show the mourners dwarfed by the mountains on the horizon, and then panning to the watching cattlemen nearby, with whom the farmers are engaged in a range war.

Shane is a classic Western that shows how an expert director can infuse a hackneyed plot with a new vitality. *Shane* (Alan Ladd), though a loner by nature, is drawn into sympathy with the homesteaders when one of them, Joe Starrett (Van Heflin), takes him home to meet his wife (Jean Arthur) and son Joey (Brandon de Wilde). Unlike George Eastman, Shane wants to do his part to help make a better world for others, specifically for these farmers who have earned his respect. Shane consequently finds himself pitted against Wilson (Jack Palance) the sinister gunman whom the cattlemen have hired to terrorize the homesteaders.

In the final confrontation between Shane and Wilson, both protagonists appear to be larger-than-life human beings who represent forces greater than themselves. Shane is the epitome of the mythical Western hero, the man who comes from nowhere, accomplishes some selfless task for others, and then rides off alone. Wilson, who is garbed in black, is, in Pauline Kael's phrase, a "prince of darkness" who symbolizes the forces of evil that Shane must face unflinchingly.[7]

Shane kills Wilson in the shootout, and as he rides out of town Stevens uses his color camera to photograph the stunning vistas of mountain ranges that will swallow him up. Joey cries plaintively, "Come back, Shane," as his voice echoes and reverberates through the canyons. But Shane, of course, will not come back. In fact in *Shane* Stevens gave the mythical Western hero his last true incarnation on film. In other Westerns, such as Fred Zinnemann's *High Noon* (1952), the Western hero was already being presented as an ordinary human being, rather than as larger than life; and Howard Hawks would continue this trend in his trio of Westerns: *Rio Bravo*, *El Dorado*, and *Rio Lobo*.

Stevens continued to be attracted by epic subject matter and in 1956 made a monumental film of Edna Ferber's novel *Giant*, which again won him the Academy Award as best director and the Screen Directors' Guild Award. *Giant* is made with the same precision and skilled craftsmanship that marks every film Stevens directed, even though it runs for 200 minutes—only twenty minutes shorter than *Gone with the Wind*.

Stevens's painstaking care seemed to inspire his actors to give performances that often surpass their work for other directors. As Bick and Leslie Benedict, a married couple maturing into middle age on a huge ranch in modern Texas, Rock Hudson and Elizabeth Taylor have never been better. Stevens said that he would prepare his actors for a particularly difficult scene, in which there must be a great deal of interaction between characters, by rehearsing the scene on a set enclosed within four walls. He used this method several times while making *Giant*. "I rehearsed on a four-walled set," he said, "because otherwise the actors would get the feeling that they were performing on a stage with a proscenium arch, and would arrange themselves as if for an audience. Then, when I took away the fourth wall, I would tell the

James Dean and Elizabeth Taylor in *Giant* **(1956), for which George Stevens won a second Academy Award. (Movie Star News)**

actors to do the scene the way that we rehearsed it, as if the fourth wall was still there. As a result, the actors created a more genuine feeling of reality and inter-action among themselves when the scene was shot. That gives the audience the impression that they are watching something that could really be happening."

James Dean died in an auto accident just after finishing *Giant* and received a posthumous Academy Award nomination for his role as Jett Rink, the cowhand on the Benedict ranch who becomes a Texas oil magnate. Jett is an outsider from the start and is as remote from the other cowhands on the Benedict ranch as he is from the Benedict clan. Nevertheless, he secretly loves Leslie from a distance, which is the only way he could really love anybody. Like George Eastman, Jett is the kind of outsider who is ambitious and self-centered; he is bent on gaining the money and prestige that will win him acceptance by his social betters. By striking oil Jett does become rich, but he remains an outsider.

Even after he becomes wealthy, Jett is not accepted by the Texas "aristocracy," who patronize him for his inability to adopt the pretensions of the nouveaux riches. Although Jett has grown calloused and selfish in his rise to power, he continues to win our sympathy; for we are able to perceive in Jett right to the end the same lonely and vulnerable cowboy that he always has been, despite all of his bravado. This is emphasized in his last scene in the picture, when he appears at a banquet in his honor blind drunk and passes out at the speakers' table. By the time he awakens, the embarrassed guests have all departed. In a stupor he delivers his speech to an empty dining room.

Stevens photographs Jett during his speech in looming long shots that encompass the hugh banquet hall and dwarf Jett in his isolation. The harmonica theme, associated earlier in the film with Jett when he was a cowhand, accompanies Jett's speech. The music adds another pathetic note to the scene because it reminds us that, underneath, Jett remains the man he has always been. Jett finally collapses, overturning the whole speakers' table, as his bid for status comes crashing down with him.

By reflecting on the tragedy of Jett's life, Bick seems to have finally realized the truth of a comment made earlier in the film by his son-in-law, a remark that serves as an ironic reference to the film's title. The acquisitive Texas millionaires have confused bigness with greatness, said the young man, and have become less human in the bargain.

That Bick is becoming more concerned for others is reflected in the last sequence of the film, in which he gets into a fight with the proprietor of a highway luncheonette who refuses service first to his son's Mexican-American wife and child and then to a Mexican family in a nearby booth. To his great credit Bick goes down swinging and for the first time in his life loses a fight. Now that he has been roused to action, the implication is that he will be more concerned for the needs and welfare of the Mexican-Americans who work on his ranch; previously, he had thought of them as a mere source of manpower for his work force.

The better world that Bick, the practical idealist in the movie, hopes to help build with his considerable resources is symbolized in embryo in the last image of *Giant*: his daughter's white child playing contentedly in a playpen with his son's half-breed baby. For the first time in a Stevens film, the practical idealist is not an outsider, but an insider who wants to help the outsiders. In Bick's case, bigness may at last come to mean greatness.

One of Stevens's last assignments as a Signal Corps photographer was to photograph the gas ovens at Dachau.[8] This experience very likely drew him to want to film *The Diary of Anne Frank* (1959), the story of a young Jewish girl who was to die in a concentration camp. After hiding out for most of the war in an attic, she and her family are inevitably captured by the Nazis. But the film does not conclude on a negative note; instead we hear over the sound track Ann's own words from her diary, in which she affirms her continued belief in the basic goodness of man, even in the face of the inconceivable atrocities of the Nazi regime. And her affirmation, one infers, is also the director's.

When the wide-screen process was introduced in the early 1950s, Stevens had quipped that the dimensions of the wide screen were better suited to photographing a boa constrictor than a human being. His misgivings about the new format were justified, at least in the case of *Anne Frank*. Since the family spends the greater part of the film living in the stifling atmosphere of an attic, the dominant feeling of the film is one of claustrophobia. The wide-screen ratio in which the movie was shot, therefore, militates against communicating this suffocating atmosphere to the audience.

The Greatest Story Ever Told (1965) was a subject much better suited to the expanse of the wide screen. In it Stevens turned to the ultimate and transcendent example of the practical idealist determined on improving a fallen world: Jesus Christ. Although Stevens's reverent film avoids all of the sacrosanct clichés of other Hollywood biblical epics, it is too much of a slow-moving, solemn pageant to engage the viewer's emotions in the way that Stevens's best work does.

With *The Only Game in Town* (1970) Stevens returned to the genre of romantic comedy that he mined so satisfyingly in the 1930s and early 1940s. The film treats the love affair of Fran, a Las Vegas dancer (Elizabeth Taylor), and Joe (Warren Beatty), a compulsive gambler who supports his habit by playing the piano in a cocktail lounge. The two move from a mere sexual attraction toward each other to true love and finally to marriage. Yet at the final fadeout neither has any illusions about the problems inherent in their maintaining a lasting relationship. Therefore the movie does not represent a return to the more romantic optimism that marked Stevens's earlier comedies, for the maturing of Stevens's vision kept pace with the development of his artistic capacity to express that vision. It is the examination of this double process of development that makes the study of the films of George Stevens, and directors like him, so rewarding.

6
Fred Zinnemann
Darkness at Noon

In the 1930s and 1940s, short subjects frequently augmented the bill of the average movie house. Of the studios that produced them only Metro-Goldwyn-Mayer was wise enough to use its short-subjects department extensively as a workshop to train new talent for feature production. "I think the best thing that ever happened to me," Fred Zinnemann said, "was my contract to make shorts for MGM. You had to make a fast, good-looking picture within a limited budget and time schedule, and it was marvelous training. That meant you had to invent cinematic ways of telling your story quickly and effectively. That was the best school a director could have."

Born in Vienna in 1907, Zinnemann grew up wanting to be a musician but turned to law when he discovered that he had little musical talent. "When I received my master's degree in law in 1927, I felt that I would be bored stiff working in law the rest of my life," Zinnemann remembered. "So I decided to try a career that would be more adventurous. But when I told my family that I wanted to go into motion pictures, the roof fell in. Movies in those days were not considered to be a serious career. My relatives took turns trying to talk me out of it. When I finally persuaded them that I was serious about it, my parents agreed that I should go to Paris to a technical school where I could learn to be a cameraman. I attended the Technical School for Cinematography in Paris."

When Zinnemann finished his work at the film school, he became an assistant cameraman in one of the studios in Berlin, where he was fortunate enough to work with several good German cinematographers, such as Eugene Schufftan. In 1929 Zinnemann was Schufftan's assistant on a film called *Menschen am Sontag* (*People on Sunday*), a semidocumentary about four young people spending a weekend in the country. The film was directed by Robert Siodmak and written by Billy Wilder, both of whom, like Zinnemann, would later migrate to Hollywood and become directors there.

At this time sound pictures were being introduced in America, and Zinnemann decided to go to Hollywood to find out what they were all about. He carried with him a letter of introduction to Carl Laemmle, the head of Universal Pictures, who made Zinnemann an extra in one of the first major sound films, *All Quiet on the Western Front* (1930). Zinnemann doubled as a German soldier and a French ambulance driver. "When I talked back to the assistant director one day, I was fired," he recalled. This was a minor incident in Zinnemann's career, but a significant one, since it indicated the spirit of independence he maintained throughout his whole career in pictures.

Fred Zinnemann on location for *The Day of the Jackal*. (The Fred Zinnemann collection)

Zinnemann then became an assistant to the German director Berthold Viertel, who was working in Hollywood. Through Viertel he met Robert Flaherty (*Nanook of the North*), the distinguished pioneer of documentary film making, whose realistic techniques would influence Zinnemann's own films. Zinnemann was impressed by Flaherty's independent spirit, and so he temporarily abandoned his hopes to establish himself in Hollywood and went with Flaherty to Berlin in 1931 in order to plan a documentary about an obscure nomadic tribe in central Asia, a region belonging to the USSR. But the film was never made.

"Bob was a romantic," Zinnemann explained. "He wanted the film to be a monument to a lost culture, whereas the Russians wanted him to make a propaganda picture showing how miserable these people were before the Russian Revolution. Although nothing came of the project, it was a valuable experience for me. In fact, Robert Flaherty is probably the greatest single influence on my work as a film maker, particularly because he was always his own man. If he believed in a project, he stayed with it. This made it impossible for him to work in Hollywood, however, where you had to know how to bend."

Zinnemann returned to Hollywood and was hired to work with the famous dance director Busby Berkeley, selecting camera angles for the dance numbers in the Eddie Cantor vehicle *The Kid from Spain* (1932). He was able to utilize the experience gained in his association with Flaherty on his next assignment, directing a documentary called *The Wave* (1935), about the life of the fishermen in the Gulf of Vera Cruz. Zinnemann became deeply involved with his subject and spent a year in the jungle making the film. This picture confirmed Zinnemann in his decision never to make a film in which he was not personally interested—an attitude that has not endeared him to the front office of the studios where he has worked.

On the strength of *The Wave* Zinnemann was hired by the short-subjects department at MGM in 1937. From this reservoir of talent the studio chose writers, actors, and directors who had the potential to go into feature film making. Directors like George Sidney (*Anchors Aweigh*) and Jules Dassin (*The Naked City*) got their start making shorts at MGM, as did Zinnemann.

At first Zinnemann made one-reelers, which entailed telling a story in ten minutes. This meant he had to develop an economy in storytelling that would prove valuable to him in his subsequent career. "I remember doing the life of Dr. George Washington Carver, from the time he was kidnapped by slave traders as a baby until he was ninety-five, in ten minutes," says Zinnemann. "The one-reelers were shot silent because they were narrated. Then I was promoted to two-reelers, which used dialogue and were shot as regular sound films."

Thus Zinnemann compressed the whole early history of motion picture making in the span of time that he spent making shorts at MGM: from one-reelers to two-reelers, from silent films to sound pictures. Among his two-reelers were films made for the *Crime Does Not Pay* series, a group of crisply cut realistic films that were to strengthen Zinnemann's propensity for realism—an inclination already nurtured by his work with Flaherty and by making *The Wave*.

Zinnemann recalled a scene in one of the *Crime Does Not Pay* series that well illustrates the ingenuity and imagination a director had to have in order to make shorts with little time and less money: "I had to do a crowd scene outside a hospital at night and was given ten extras for the crowd. So I dressed one of them as a policeman and had him push the other nine extras back toward the camera. This gave the impression that a great number of people were milling around."

In 1941 Zinnemann was at last promoted to making features at MGM, and he started off by making two low-budget thrillers. The first was *The Kid Glove Killer* (1942), a better-than-average whodunit about a criminologist uncovering the murderer of a mayor, featuring Marsha Hunt, Van Heflin, and Lee Bowman. Then he made *Eyes in the Night* (1942), a routine private-eye yarn with Edward Arnold as a blind detective. "While I was making my first full-length films at Metro," Zinnemann commented, "I had a strong feeling of going backwards; it was frustrating to do donkey work because I felt that I had done my apprenticeship in the shorts department. But I did get to do one interesting film during that time, *The Seventh Cross* (1944). Perhaps because I knew Europe well, this film about the Second World War seemed to have an authentic look about it, and was well received."

Spencer Tracy starred as an anti-Nazi who tries to flee Germany in 1936, after escaping from a concentration camp. The documentary flavor of the film is established in the opening shot of a row of crosses that stand out against the bleak landscape of the camp compound. The camera pans down the row of crosses and then stops at the seventh. This is the one reserved for George Heisler (Spencer Tracy) when he is recaptured. During the movie Zinnemann created the tense atmosphere of foreboding in which a hunted man moves by a variety of means: shots of long shadows looming down dark, twisted streets; the murky fog that envelops Heisler when he sinks to the ground in exhaustion. When the picture was completed, Tracy predicted that the film's young director was going places.

After making a significant film like *The Seventh Cross*, Zinnemann was deeply disappointed to be given inferior scripts to direct, such as the one for an uninspired racetrack farce entitled *My Brother Talks to Horses* (1946). "It is true that I had learned my trade at Metro, and that therefore the studio was justified to some extent in expecting me to cooperate," Zinnemann conceded. "Nevertheless, the front office exercised a total kind of power over its employees in those days. I was under a seven-year contract to MGM, which meant that in a sense I was considered studio property."

Some of the assignments he was given he declined to accept; and when he had turned down three scripts in a row, Zinnemann became the first director in studio history to be suspended for being uncooperative. Even though the suspension lasted only three weeks, it was enough to give Zinnemann the reputation of being a director who was difficult to deal with. "There was a kind of jungle telegraph in Hollywood," said Zinnemann, "by which one studio notified all of the others in town about a troublesome employee; so that it was difficult for him to get a job anywhere." A European producer named Lazar Wechsler saved the day. Having been impressed by *The Seventh Cross*, Wechsler asked Zinnemann to make a film for a Swiss motion picture company about displaced European children after World War II. MGM was delighted to let Zinnemann go to Europe to make *The Search* (1948) on location there and even helped finance the picture.

Zinnemann chose a promising young actor named Montgomery Clift to play Ralph Stevenson, an American GI who tries to help a Czech boy find his mother, from whom the lad was separated in a concentration camp. Clift was still an unknown when *The Search* was made, even though he had already finished Howard Hawks's *Red River*, because *Red River* had not yet been released. It is as much a tribute to Zinnemann's direction as to Clift's performance in *The Search* that someone asked Zinnemann after seeing the film, "Where did you find a soldier who could act?"

Zinnemann's favorite scene in *The Search* is the one in which the boy (Ivan Jandl) is afraid to trust Ralph, because the lad has learned from his days in the camp to fear anyone in uniform. In despair of reaching the boy, Ralph throws open the front door of the house where they are staying and tells the youngster that he can leave anytime he wants to. Zinnemann keeps his camera inside the house and photographs the boy going out of the door and crossing the street. We see him in the distance as he pauses, stands looking back for a moment, and then hesitatingly comes back into the house. "Here is a human being who has been living in a wilderness," Zinnemann commented; "and now he is finally willing to gamble on the fact that this man in uniform is really a decent person."

Without Zinnemann's knowledge, the producers of *The Search* added some spoken narration at the beginning of the film, which explains the situation in postwar Europe at the time. The commentary is totally unnecessary since the situation is obvious from the images on the screen. As James Agee wrote, "While starving children grab for bread, a lady commentator informs one that they are hungry, and that the bread is bread."[1] Zinnemann tried to have the narration removed from the soundtrack when he found out about it, but by then it was too late to eradicate it without destroying that part of the sound track. This incident increased Zinnemann's vigilance in guiding a film through the postproduction stage, and it represents the last serious interference that Zinnemann experienced in making a film.

The Search was a great success; MGM was pleased; and "the bush telegraph" in Hollywood spread the word that Zinnemann was once more in the studio's good graces.

The release of *The Search* coincided with the movement toward greater realism in the cinema that followed World War II. During the war, audiences had gotten used to the documentary realism employed in making even fiction films about the war. They continued to demand this kind of naturalism in postwar films, not only in war films like *The Search*, but in other kinds of pictures too, such as crime melodramas. Now movies were frequently shot on location in order to lend them a stronger sense of realism. Hence postwar films were often acted out in realistic surroundings, which dictated that the actors give performances for the most part free of theatrical mannerisms and that the camera employ a newsreellike style to photograph the action. As Roger Manvell has written, these films "gave screen fiction a new kind of verisimilitude which was to be developed later to great advantage in more ambitious productions than these initial, mostly low-budget films.[2]

Zinnemann was in the front rank of directors using the new naturalism, as evidenced by his next film. *Act of Violence* (1948) is a psychological thriller about Frank Enley, an ex-GI (Van Heflin) who is stalked by another ex-soldier, Joe Park-

Van Heflin and Robert Ryan in *Act of Violence* **(1948). (The John Baxter collection)**

son (Robert Ryan), who bears him a grudge that goes back to their days in a Nazi prison camp. At that time Frank had apparently betrayed Joe's escape attempt to the camp commandant. Since the war Frank has been trying to bury the past by becoming a responsible member of his small town community, but the presence of Joe, of course, precludes this.

In passing from *The Search* to *Act of Violence*, we see emerging the pervasive theme that was taking shape in Zinnemann's work. The thematic note found repeatedly in his film is initially sounded in the very title of his first major success, *The Search*. In that film the search is aimed at establishing the identity of a lad who has lost touch with his family through the cruelly impersonal events of war. *Act of Violence* represents the search of an ex-GI branded as a coward during the war, who wants to recover his self-identity in the postwar world. This search by an individual for his self-image is the principal motif in all of Zinnemann's subsequent films. The individual achieves personal self-awareness by meeting a crisis; and once he has genuinely come to know himself, he is capable of establishing a place for himself in society.

Zinnemann agreed that this theme is embedded in his films. It was best expressed, he told me, by Hillel two thousand years ago: "If I am not for myself, who will be for me? And if I am only for myself, what am I? And if not now, when?" Zinnemann often develops this theme in his films by focusing on an individual who wants to achieve his self-identity while trying to function within a large institution such as the army.

It is logical that this theme of the individual preserving his self-identity in an institutional context should appeal to Zinnemann. For throughout his career he sought to maintain that degree of independence within the studio system which would allow him to express his personal vision in terms of his own cinematic style.

Understandably, therefore, Zinnemann took a great interest in the burgeoning, after World War II, of small independent production companies aimed at making films free from the oppressive overhead and control of the large studios. One of the first such companies was Liberty Films, which George Stevens formed with two other film directors, as noted in chapter 5. Others formed independent production companies as well. One of these, producer Stanley Kramer, signed Zinnemann to a three-picture contract. Each of these three films, *The Men*, *High Noon*, and *Member of the Wedding*, develops Zinnemann's theme of the individual achieving a self-knowledge that enables him to find his place in the community in which he lives.

In *The Men* (1950), Ken (Marlon Brando) is a paraplegic veteran who at first is unable to accept the fact that he is destined to spend the rest of his life in a wheelchair. Through the understanding help, first of his fellow patients in a veterans' hospital, and then of his fiancée (Teresa Wright), he is able to adjust to the situation. The semidocumentary quality of the picture was helped immeasurably by the fact that *The Men* was shot on location in the Birmingham Veterans' Hospital, with several of the patients playing themselves.

Zinnemann's next film, *High Noon* (1952), along with George Stevens's *Shane*, is one of the true classic Westerns of the screen. Gary Cooper won an Oscar as Will

Kane, the ex-marshal of small community Hadleyville. Kane is about to leave town with his Quaker bride Amy (Grace Kelly) when he learns that Frank Miller, a paroled desperado, is returning to town on the noon train to revenge himself on Kane for sending him to prison. Since the new marshal is not due to arrive until the next day, Kane realizes that if he leaves Hadleyville without a marshal, even for twenty-four hours, Miller and his gang will quickly re-establish it as a wide-open frontier town.

Kane decides, over the protests of his wife, to remain and fight Miller. If he runs away, he tells her, he will never again be able to face himself. He solicits the aid of the townspeople to help him defend their town against Miller and gang. But they staunchly maintain that Kane's is a private quarrel with Miller, and they leave him to meet the noon train alone. The camera follows Kane down the deserted main street of the town, then pulls back and rises above him to show the solitary figure of Kane, a man deserted by those who should have helped him, going to face his destiny.

Kane wins the gun battle with Miller and his men aided—surprisingly—by his Quaker wife. Afterwards he throws his tin star in the dust, not only to indicate that he is giving up his job, but also to imply his disdain for the fear-ridden community that failed to back him up in his attempt to protect them.

Zinnemann felt that *High Noon* was such an enormous hit because it was the product of the cooperation of several talented people, each expert in his own area of film making: writer Carl Foreman, editor Elmo Williams, composer Dimitri Tiomkin, and cinematographer Floyd Crosby. "The cameraman, Floyd Crosby, had the courage to give it the style that we had agreed upon," said Zinnemann. "Floyd and I thought that *High Noon* should look like a newsreel would have looked, if they had had newsreels in those days; and we studied Matthew Brady's photographs of the Civil War as an aid. Crosby used flat lighting that gave the film a grainy quality."

Up to that time, Zinnemann continued, "there was almost a religious ritual about the way that Westerns were made. There was always a lovely sky with pretty clouds in the background. Instead Crosby gave the sky a white, cloudless, burnt-out look. From the first day the front office complained about the poor photography. Most cameramen might have struck their colors, but Floyd went ahead anyway. Subliminally the photography created the effect we wanted; it made the film look more real. We also dressed Gary Cooper in black, so that when his lonely figure came forth into the stark, bright stillness, his destiny seemed even more poignant."

Zinnemann's customary care for detail has never been so much in evidence as in his direction of *High Noon*. The picture runs approximately the same length of time as the action of the plot—about eighty-five minutes—or, in story terms, from about 10:40 AM to shortly after noon. So, as the film built towards its climax Zinnemann gradually increased the tempo of the clock pendulums that were visible in various scenes, to heighten the effect of time running out.

Howard Hawks, as noted in chapter 2, said that he made *Rio Bravo* as a kind of "answer" to *High Noon* because he did not believe that a good marshal would go around town asking for other people's help to do his job. "I'm rather surprised at this kind of thinking," Zinnemann said in response. "Marshals are people, and no two people are alike. The story of *High Noon* takes place in the Old West, but it is really a story about a man's conflict of conscience, and the lengths to which he must go to defend his own convictions.

At the time *High Noon* was made, the anti-Communist witch-hunt encouraged by Senator Joseph McCarthy and carried on by the House Unamerican Activities Committee was in full swing in Hollywood; and men like Charlie Chaplin, Joseph Losey, and Carl Foreman, the script writer of *High Noon*, were being blacklisted from working in Hollywood. Foreman was able to finish his work on *High Noon* before the ax fell on him, and he has said that, in writing the script for the film, he made reference to the contemporary situation; "I used a Western background to tell a story of a community corrupted by fear, with implications that I hoped would be obvious to everyone who saw the film, at least in America."[3]

Primarily, however, audiences reacted to *High Noon* as an exciting Western melodrama, one of the best of its kind. The movie set a precedent in Western films by showing a hero who is in no way superhuman, but who is instead quite capable of feeling fear while he is executing his duty. The film also set another screen precedent in the use of a title song to establish the mood of a film. In this case it is a plaintive melody sung by Tex Ritter, the Western balladeer.

Zinnemann's third and last film for Kramer was *The Member of the Wedding* (1952), based on Carson McCullers's stage version of her own novel. With extraordinary skill Julie Harris recreated her stage role of the tomboy Frankie, a girl half Harris's age at the time she made the film. Frankie is uneasy about embarking on her teens. She no longer wants to be a child like her friend John Henry (Brandon de Wilde); and yet she realizes that she is not yet prepared to enter the adult world of her other friend, Berenice (Ethel Waters), who keeps house for Frankie's widowed father. She futilely tries to force her brother to take her along on his honeymoon as a "member of the wedding," because she desperately wants to belong somewhere. At the end of the picture, John Henry unexpectedly dies, and with him Frankie's childhood. As she makes friends with a girl her own age, she is taking her first steps toward growing up.

Zinnemann was criticized for confining the movie mostly to the single kitchen setting of the play, but this helps to define the narrow horizons of the world in which Frankie seeks to discover herself. As Alan Stranbrook puts it, "Membership of society is won only by first painfully carving out one's own identity—this is the motto which Zinnemann extracts from the tale."[4]

In reflecting on his association with Stanley Kramer during the period in which he made the above three films with him, Zinnemann said, "Kramer is a creative personality. He is not like those producers who know nothing about how a picture is made, but nevertheless tell you what to do. Kramer has good ideas; but then so do I." Putting the matter less diplomatically, another director, Edward Dmytryk, who worked for Kramer on films like *The Caine Mutiny* at about the same time as Zinnemann, told me that during the period that Kramer was producing films, he was really itching to become a director himself. This often led him to interfere with the direction of a film he was producing, which inevitably caused clashes between producer and director. Kramer eventually became a director in his own right, and Zinnemann returned to working for the large Hollywood studios. But he brought with him a reputation further enhanced by the films he had made for Kramer, and this allowed him to obtain a large measure of creative control over the films he was now to make.

That Zinnemann used his artistic independence wisely is clear from the high quality of *From Here to Eternity* (1953). By the end of the credit sequence of the picture, Zinnemann has already sketched his theme for the audience. In the foreground is a squad of soldiers drilling to a sergeant's commands at Hawaii's Schofield Barracks in 1941. From the distance Private Robert E. Lee Prewitt (Montgomery Clift) is seen coming out of the shadows with a barracks bag slung over his shoulder, indicating that he is new to the camp. He is a loner who is trying to cope with an organization that does not encourage individuality, which is reflected in the soldiers who are being drilled into uniformity on the parade ground. All of this is presented to the audience within the first few moments of the film, while the credits are unrolling.

Prewitt is a good boxer, but he now refuses to fight because he accidentally blinded his last opponent. His commanding officer tries to pressure him into winning the army trophy for his company; and a tug of war ensues between the nonconformist Prewitt and the equally stubborn officer, who intends to make him knuckle under. Prewitt seems capable of stoically withstanding pressures of any kind, until he learns that his buddy Maggio (Frank Sinatra), another nonconformist, has been beaten to death in the stockade by the sadistic Sergeant Judson (Ernest Borgnine).

Prewitt seeks out Judson, kills him in a knife fight, and hides out in the apartment of his mistress (Donna Reed). When the Japanese attack on Pearl Harbor is announced, however, he tries to return to his company but is shot and killed by a panicky sentry at the camp.

Earlier Prewitt had told his girl, "I love the army. When a man loves a thing, that doesn't mean it has to love him back. I left home at seventeen; I didn't belong no place until I joined the army." Since Prewitt had always defined his self-image in terms of his membership in the army, he could not have remained away from it for long in any case.

From Here to Eternity was showered with Academy Awards, including the best picture of the year; best supporting actor, Frank Sinatra; best supporting actress, Donna Reed; and best director. Zinnemann also received the Screen Directors' Guild Award for the film. He deserved these honors; for in filming *From Here to Eternity* he produced a ruggedly realistic, tightly constructed version of James Jones's sprawling novel. It is indicative of the sense of realism Zinnemann created in the film that the newsreel footage of the Japanese bombing of Pearl Harbor which he worked into the picture meshed perfectly with the material he had shot himself for these same scenes.

Zinnemann accomplished a similar feat in his later film, *Behold a Pale Horse* (1963). The background of the story is the Spanish Civil War; Manuel (Gregory Peck), who has fought for the losing side, becomes a fugitive and anarchist after the war is over. The film opens with newsreel shots of the Civil War, followed by the first scene in which Manuel appears. The transition from the newsreel footage to the fictional narrative is so smooth that one hardly notices it, until Peck comes on screen. "We duped the negative of this scene," said Zimmerman, "to make it look grainier and grainier; so that it blended right in with the newsreel material." This smooth elision of the historical situation with the story served to give the film as a whole an authentic, naturalistic aura.

The stark realism of Zinnemann's clean black-and-white photography also helped to give *A Hatful of Rain* (1957) a documentary air, especially in the location scenes shot around New York City. This film is a compassionate study of ex-serviceman John Pope (Don Murray), who must summon the courage to admit to his wife that he is a drug addict and accept her help in overcoming his habit. Zinnemann's vivid realism is especially evident in the sequence in which Johnny roams the streets late at night, intent on robbing someone to obtain the money he needs to pay off a pusher. The black wintry landscape, framed by leafless trees, is the perfect atmosphere for this grim scene.

The location work in *The Sundowners* (1960) is even more impressive. Zinnemann took his cast and crew to Australia to film the story of Paddy Carmody (Robert Mitchum), his wife Ida (Deborah Kerr), and their son Sean (Mitchell Anderson, Jr.), an itinerant family that wanders the countryside taking work where they can find it. At the point we meet them, however, Ida and Sean are beginning to weary of the kind of life and want to settle down. Unfortunately for them, Paddy is not ready to curb his wanderlust by becoming part of a community.

As the tension mounts in the family, Sean suggests to his mother that they let Paddy move on without them. In one of the film's finest moments, Ida says to her son, " There is someone waiting for you to spend your life with; there's no one waiting for your dad and me but each other. Don't ever ask me to choose between your father and you, because I'll choose him every time." And so, once more, they pack up and move on together.

Zinnemann himself described *The Sundowners* as a film about "people who can be in love after fifteen years of marriage, and can feel secure as long as they are together, even though all that they own are the clothes on their backs." The film really mirrors Zinnemann's admiration for all of the people who live a pioneer existence in the Australian "outback." As the proprietor of a tavern in the movie puts it, "These people battle all their lives to keep this part of the country alive."

Ed Fischer comments that *The Sundowners* is that most uncommon of films, one peopled entirely with good-natured characters, among whom there really are no "bad guys." "In *The Sundowners*," he writes, "the main conflict is between the wanderlust in Paddy's soul and the desire to settle down that tugs at his wife and son. But Paddy is not a villain, the wife is not a shrew. They are, in the main, good people and believable people. . . . All of which suggests that Fred Zinnemann, the director, is a rare human being."[5]

The Nun's Story and *A Man for All Seasons* are among Zinnemann's finest achievements. Moreover, they also come closest to articulating fully the central theme of his work. Sister Luke in *The Nun's Story* wants to follow her own personal conscience, while at the same time adapting to the demands made on her by the religious institution to which she belongs. Thomas More in *A Man for All Seasons* also has a conflict to conscience, for he must seek to reconcile his personal commitments to God with those he has made to his king.

"This theme," Zinnemann said, "applies to the—sometimes tragic—clash of an individual with the community to which he belongs; an individual who is trying to follow his own personal conscience against all kinds of odds (*From Here to Eternity* and *The Nun's Story*); it applies equally to a purely interior dilemma, where the conflict of conscience is not so much directed against an opponent, but rages within the soul of the individual himself (*High Noon* and *Man for All Seasons*)."

Zinnemann had great difficulty in interesting a studio in producing *The Nun's Story* (1959). As one executive said, "Who wants to see a documentary about how to become a nun?" Consequently Zinnemann formed his own production company to make the picture. When Audrey Hepburn decided to accept the lead, Warner Brothers agreed to distribute the film.

The nun of the title is Gabrielle Van Der Mal (Audrey Hepburn), the daughter of a Belgian physician, who enters an order of nursing sisters who work as missionaries in the Belgian Congo. "I really wanted to photograph the scenes in the European convent in an austere black-and-white and the scenes in the Congo in color," Zinnemann remembered. "But I felt that coming back to black-and-white at the end, when Sister Luke returns to Belgium, would be too self-conscious. Instead I tried to get the European scenes to look as close to black-and-white as possible." He accomplished this by photograping the scenes in the Belgian convent mostly in greys and pastels, a sharp contrast to the lush colors he employed for the scenes in the Congo.

Zinnemann was fascinated by the opportunity to do a study of a nun in the contemporary world: "It was a whole new world to me. I had always thought of the entire institution of convent life as a refuge for people who didn't have strength enough to stay in the world. Only after I read Kathryn Hulme's book about Sister Luke did I realize the amount of force and vitality this whole institution has. This made it a voyage of discovery; you could open the door of a convent and be in a new world."

The director does just that at the beginning of *The Nun's Story*. As the door of the convent swings open to admit Gabrielle, the audience has the feeling of being permitted to go inside with her. "The following hour or so," writes John Howard Reid, "covering the girls' instruction, their acceptance into the Congregation of Postulants, and their taking of final vows, is one of the most moving and engrossing hours in contemporary cinema."[6]

Once Gabrielle has become Sister Luke, she goes to work in the sisters' hospital in the Belgian Congo as a nursing sister. Because of ill health, however, she is later forced to return to Belgium. Having grown used to the greater opportunities for initiative that she enjoyed while working in the Congo mission hospital, she finds the more structured life of the European convent intolerable. Sister Luke finally resolves her inner conflict by deciding to leave the convent, to continue in the nursing profession as a laywoman.

In the last scene we see her once more dressed in the same garb in which she had entered the convent fifteen years before. The door that had opened to admit her at the beginning of the film now swings open once more, this time to allow her to leave. She walks through the door, away from the camera, toward the world that waits beyond. The only sounds heard are those of her footsteps retreating into the distance as the convent bell, that once summoned her, chimes for those who remain within.

It was rather exceptional at the time for a major studio to end a picture without the customary musical finale. Asked why he decided to dispense with the usual closing music for the film, Zinnemann replied: "While Franz Waxman was scoring the picture I discovered that he had a deep dislike for the Catholic Church, and this was coming across in his music. The theme he wrote for the convent scenes would have been more appropriate for scenes set in a dungeon, so I got him to write another. For the final scene he wrote an exultant theme to end the film, and I removed it from the sound track. When Jack Warner asked me why I had done so, I answered his question with another: 'What kind of music do you want at the end of the picture? If the music expresses gloom, it will imply that it is too bad that Sister Luke left the convent. If it is joyful, people will think that Warner Brothers is encouraging nuns to leave the convent.' And so the movie ends in silence, the way I wanted it to."

A Man for All Seasons (1966) is Zinnemann's screen version of Robert Bolt's play about Thomas More's crisis of conscience over accepting Henry VIII as head of the Church of England as well as his king; and it is the other film in which Zinnemann's abiding theme is most clearly found. Robert Bolt wrote a disciplined script that, like his original play, is shot through with applications for our own day. More tells Cardinal Wolsey at one point, "When statesmen forswear their own consciences for the sake of their public duties, they are leading their country into chaos."

The transition from Sir Thomas More to Saint Thomas More is remarkably achieved in Paul Scofield's Academy Award–winning portrayal. Early in the film More tells his wife, "Set your mind at rest; this is not the stuff of which martyrs are made." Later on, however, More realizes that "to be human at all perhaps we must stand fast a little, even at the risk of being heroes." At his trial More sets his keen legal mind to defending himself, and even here he manages to preserve some of his celebrated wit. To a witness who has perjured himself in return for being made Attorney General for Wales, More says, "Why Richard, it profits a man nothing to give his soul for the whole world. But for Wales!"

Zinnemann made a film for the eye as well as for the ear. The badge of office of the Chancellor of the Realm functions as a visual symbol in the film in a way that recalls Zinnemann's use of the marshal's badge in *High Noon*. At the Beginning of *A Man for All Seasons* there is a close-up of the gold medallion of the Chancellor of the Realm set against the scarlet cassock of Cardinal Wolsey (Orson Welles). Later it is taken from Wolsey, who is dying in disgrace, and comes to rest on the breast of Thomas More. Eventually, when More resigns his post, his daughter Margaret (Susannah York) takes it tearfully from round his neck, as More relinquishes it to the Duke of Norfolk, the king's representative, prior to his trail.

Paul Scofield in *A Man for All Seasons* (1966), for which both Fred Zinnemann and Scofield won Oscars. (Author's collection)

"I have always been concerned with the problem of the individual who struggles to preserve his personal integrity and self-respect," said Zinnemann; and clearly the trial and execution of Thomas More represents such a struggle, masterfully rendered on film. *A Man for All Seasons* proved one of Zinnemann's greatest artistic and popular successes. It received the Academy Award as best picture of the year, and won for Zinnemann the Oscar as best director of the year, as well as the Screen Director's Guild award.

Judith Crist called the picture at the time of its release "a film for all times, a thinking man's spectacular, one whose depth of content is matched only by the artistry of its form. It is certainly the best film of the year, but it goes well beyond calendar confines."[7]

After *A Man for All Seasons* Zinnemann made *The Day of the Jackal* (1973), based on Frederick Forsyth's novel about an attempted assassination of Charles de Gaulle. "I shot it properly—like a newsreel, in France, Italy, and Austria," he said, "with a cast made up largely of unknowns." This film, therefore, marks a return to the spare semidocumentary style of earlier Zinnemann films like *Act of Violence* and *High Noon*; and he employed a similar approach in filming *Julia* (1977).

The plot of *Julia* stems from a chapter in the second volume of playwright Lillian Hellman's memoirs, which recalls the relationship of Lillian (Jane Fonda) and her

Fred Zinnemann directing Vanessa Redgrave in the title role of *Julia* (1977), for which the actress won an Oscar. (Fred Zinnemann collection)

close friend Julia (Vanessa Redgrave). The pair grew up together in New York City but were separated when Julia moved to Europe and in due time became a political activist in the turbulent years preceding World War II. The film deals primarily with Lillian's battle to be worthy of Julia's friendship, by living up to Julia's standard of values and her unconditional commitment to the fight for human rights. Lillian's friendship with Julia is tested to the utmost when Julia takes the occasion of a brief visit of Lillian's to Europe to ask her to smuggle a large sum of money into Nazi Germany to aid some political and religious refugees.

"I think it is important to point out that Julia never forced a challenge on Lillian at any time in their lives," said Zinnemann. "In the flashback to their girlhood, when Julia crosses a stream ahead of Lillian by negotiating her way over a log, she doesn't force Lillian to follow her example. She rather suggests that Lillian cross further down on the bank, where it would be easier for her. It is Lillian who insists on following Julia's lead and crossing at the more precarious point, trying to prove to herself that she can overcome her fear." Referring to this incident, Johann (Maximillian Schell), an ally of Julia's who contacts Lillian about the secret mission, says to her that Julia has told him Lillian never lets her fears stand in the way of her accepting a challenge.

It is true, Zinnemann continued, that, when Lillian agrees to carry out this dangerous mission at Julia's request, "she is full of fear; and the closer the train takes her to the German border, the greater her panic becomes. Therefore the suspense in this sequence comes not just from the external circumstances of Lillian's smuggling the money past the Nazis, but, more importantly, from her internal tension. Will she go to pieces under the pressure of the situation before she completes her task? And when she does pull herself together and meet the challenge successfully, the picture is really over." The balance of the movie, in which Lillian finds out about Julia's brutal murder at the hands of the Gestapo, the director concluded, "is really something of an epilogue."

Julia, which was lauded as a gripping, provocative drama, is yet another Zinnemann film that dramatizes his favorite theme: the conflict that results from an individual having to summon the courage to follow their personal convictions in the face of all sorts of obstacles.

Zinnemann followed *Julia* with *Five Days One Summer* (1982). Set in the Swiss Alps, the movie tells of a mountain climbing holiday involving Douglas, a middle-aged man (Sean Connery); Kate, his young mistress (Betsy Brantley); and Johann, their guide (Lambert Wilson), who gradually becomes attracted to Kate. The movie was filmed entirely on location in the Alpine region, Zinnemann pointed out; and there is an implicit contrast between the purity of the snow-white mountains, "and the messiness of the characters' private lives." Indeed, Zinnemann succeeded in rendering the mountainous landscape an imposing presence in the movie; and it is a tribute to his expert handling of his actors that the grandeur of the breathtaking mountain range does not dwarf the human conflict being played out by the trio of principal characters, as the rivalry of the two men for the girl slowly and subtly asserts itself.

Inevitably the friction between Douglas and Johann erupts into violence. Their encounter on a mountain slope ends with one of them falling to his death, while Kate is forced to wait down below to see which man will come back to her. As Zinnemann told me, "I was always intrigued by the situation of the girl not knowing until the last moment which of the two men in her life had been saved.'8 The moviegoer is likewise intrigued by the suspenseful ending of this well-wrought film.

Surveying his long career, Zinnemann mused, "The director has much more freedom today in making a film than he had during the anonymous days in Hollywood, when films were made on an assembly line." Nevertheless, like George Cukor, he was quick to point out that a number of outstanding pictures were made under the studio system. "I will always think of myself as a Hollywood director," he added, "not only because I grew up in the American film industry, but also because I believe in making films that will please a mass audience, not just in making films that will express my own personality or ideas. I have always tried to offer an audience something positive in a film, to leave them looking up rather than looking down. If I have managed to do that, and entertain the audience as well, I'm satisfied."

7
Stanley Kubrick
Stop the World

As a director Stanley Kubrick is virtually in a class by himself because he taught himself the various aspects of the film making process and became a director without serving the usual apprenticeship in a film studio, where he would have had to work his way up to the status of director by way of lesser jobs. By the time he began directing films for the major studios, he was able to do so with a degree of independence that few other directors have been able to match. Kubrick oversees every aspect of production when he makes a film: script writing, casting, shooting (often operating the camera himself), editing, and choosing the musical score. To that extent he is pre-eminently an *auteur*.

When asked why he thought the major film companies had decided to extend wide artistic freedom to directors like himself, Kubrick replied, "The invulnerability of the majors was based on their consistent success with virtually anything they made. When they stopped making money, they began to appreciate the importance of people who could make good films." Kubrick was one of the directors they turned to; and when they did, it was after he had learned the business of film making from the ground up and was ready to answer the call.

Kubrick was born in the Bronx section of New York City in July, 1928, and took his first step toward film making when he began selling pictures to *Look* magazine while he was still a student at Taft High School. He joined the staff after graduation and, while working there, decided to expand a picture story he had done on boxer Walter Cartier into a documentary short call *Day of the Fight* (1950). "I did everything from keeping an accounting book to dubbing in the punches on the soundtrack," Kubrick remembers. " I had no idea what I was doing, but I knew I could do better than most of the films that I was seeing at the time." Kubrick had spent his savings, $3,900, to make the film; and the RKO circuit bought it for $4,000. At the age of twenty Kubrick had made a film on his own that had shown a profit, however small. From that moment on he was a confirmed film maker.

RKO advanced him $1,500 for a second short, *Flying Padre* (1951), about a priest in New Mexico who flies to see his isolated parishioners in a Piper Cub. When he broke even on that one, Kubrick borrowed $10,000 from his father and his uncle and decided to take the plunge into feature film making. He went on location to the San Gabriel Mountains near Los Angeles to make *Fear and Desire* (1953), a movie dealing with a futile military patrol trapped behind enemy lines in an unnamed war.

Kubrick made the film almost singlehandedly, serving as his own cameraman,

Stanley Kubrick directing Keir Dullea and Gary Lockwood in *2001: A Space Odyssey* **(1968).**
(Movie Star News)

sound man and editor, as well as director. The film was shot silent, and he added the soundtrack afterward. The young director was pleasantly surprised when *Fear and Desire* received some rather good reviews and played the arthouse circuit. As a consequence he borrowed money, chiefly from another relative, a Bronx druggist, and made *Killer's Kiss* (1955), again handling most of the production chores himself. He moved another step closer to the big time when United Artists agreed to distribute it.

Kubrick shot the film on location in the shabbier sections of New York, which gave it a visual realism unmatched by the postsynchronized soundtrack. Money began running out during the post production work, and Kubrick was unable to afford an editing assistant. "I had to spend four months just laying in the sound effects, footstep by footstep," Kubrick says. Nevertheless he was able to inject some life into the routine story with the inclusion of two key fight sequences, one in the ring and one in a mannequin factory at the climax of the movie.

The hero of the story is a fighter named Davy (Jamie Smith), who is a loser in the ring but who is able to save his girl from being kidnapped by slugging it out with her abductor. In this scene Davy and Rapallo, the kidnapper (Frank Silvera), fight to the death amid the mannequins, using whatever blunt instruments they can lay their hands on. When Davy delivers the death blow, Rapallo falls backward with dummies crashing all around him. Kubrick ends the scene with a closeup of the smashed head of a mannequin, a metaphor for the dead Rapallo.

Later Davy and the girl meet in the congestion of Grand Central Station to leave New York for good, in favor of making a home on Davy's family's farm. In their departure from the brutal big city, which had proved a harsh and unpleasant place for both of them, we see the first indication of Kubrick's dark vision of contemporary society. In this and even more in his subsequent films, Kubrick shows us modern man gradually being dehumanized by living in a materialistic, mechanized world, in which one man exploits another in the mass effort to survive. Moreover, in his later motion pictures Kubrick extends his vision into the future to suggest that man's failure to cooperate with his fellow man in mastering the world of the present can only lead to man's being mastered by the world of tomorrow.

In 1955 Kubrick met James B. Harris, an aspiring producer, who put up more than a third of the $320,000 budget needed to finance *The Killing* (1956), with United Artists providing the rest. This was the first of the three-film partnership between Kubrick and Harris.

Based on Lionel White's novel *Clean Break*, Kubrick's tightly constructed script follows the preparations of a group of smalltime crooks bent on making a big killing by robbing a race track. They have planned the robbery to coincide with the actual running time of the seventh race; and Kubrick photographs the robbery in great detail, with all of its spilt-second timing. He builds suspense with great intensity by quickly cutting from one member of the gang to another, in a series of flashbacks that show how each has simultaneously carried out his part of the plan—all leading up to the climactic moment when they get away with the money.

The movie's real merit lies in the ensemble acting Kubrick elicited from a group of capable Hollywood supporting players, who rarely got a chance to give perfor-

mances of any substance. Sterling Hayden plays Johnny Clay, the tough organizer of
the caper; Jay C. Flippen is the cynical older member of the group; Elisha Cook,
Jr., is the timid husband who hopes to impress his voluptuous wife (Marie Windsor)
with stolen money, since presumably he cannot otherwise give her satisfaction.
Together they help Kubrick create the grim atmosphere of the film, which builds to
an ironic conclusion when Clay's suitcase blows open just as he and his girl friend
Fay are about to board a plane for the tropics; and the stolen money flutters all over
the windy airfield. Like Davy and his girl in *Killer's Kiss*, Johnny and Fay hoped to
escape the corrosive atmosphere of the big city by flight to a cleaner environment.
But for Johnny, brutalized by a life of crime, it is already too late.

The title of the story is a reference to Thomas Gray's "Elegy in a Country Church-
Kubrick next acquired the rights to Humphrey Cobb's 1935 novel *Paths of Glory*,
which he had read in high school, and set about writing a script. But no major
studio was interested in financing the film until Kirk Douglas agreed to star. Then
United Artists backed the project with $935,000. Despite the flood of antiwar films
over the years, *Paths of Glory* (1957) ranks with Joseph Losey's *King and Country*
as one of the most uncompromising examples of the genre.

The ghastly irresponsibility of officers toward their men is climaxed by the behavior of General Mireau (George Macready), who hopes to gain a promotion by
ordering his men to carry out a suicidal charge. When they falter, he madly orders
other troops to fire into the trenches on their own comrades. Afterwards, Colonel
Dax (Kirk Douglas) must stand by while three soldiers are picked almost at random
from the ranks to be court-martialed and executed for desertion of duty, as an
"example" to the rest of the men, for failing to attack the enemy stronghold as
Mireau had commanded.

The title of the story is a reference to Thomas Gray's "Elegy in a Country Church-
yard," in which the poet warns that the "paths of glory lead but to the grave." It
becomes increasingly clear as the film progresses that the paths of glory the generals
are following lead, not to their graves, but to the graves of the enlisted men, who
are ordered to die in battles fought according to a strategy manipulated by the
generals for their own self-advancement.

Peter Cowie has written that Kubrick uses his camera in the film "unflinchingly,
like a weapon": darting into close-up to capture the indignation on Dax's face,
sweeping across the slopes to record the wholesale slaughter of a division, or
advancing relentlessly at eye level toward the stakes against which the condemned
men will be shot.[1]

The film is filled with both visual and verbal ironies that reinforce its theme.
Toward the end of the central battle scene, Dax must attempt to lead yet another
hopeless charge on the impregnable German lines. As he climbs the ladder out of
the trench, exhorting his men all the while to renew their courage, he is thrown
backwards into the trench by the body of a French soldier rolling in on top of him.
In the scene in which the condemned await execution, one of them complains that
the cockroach which he sees on the wall of their cell will be alive after he is dead.
One of his comrades smashes the cockroach with his fist, saying, "Now you've got
the edge on *him*."

The epilogue to the film ends on a note of hope for humanity. Dax watches his men join in the singing of a song about love in wartime, led by a timid German girl prisoner (played by German actress Suzanne Christian, who is now Mrs. Stanley Kubrick). Dax walks away, convinced by the good-natured singing that his men have not lost their basic humanity, despite the inhuman conditions in which they live and die. The thematic implications of Kubrick's later films will not be quite so optimistic.

In *Paths of Glory* Kirk Douglas gave one of his best performances, and he therefore wanted to work with Kubrick again. He did so when Kubrick took over the direction of *Spartacus* (1960), a spectacle about slavery in pre-Christian Rome. But this time their association was less satisfactory than it had been on *Paths of Glory*. Douglas was not only the star of the film but its producer as well, and friction developed between producer and director.

"*Spartacus* is the only film over which I did not have absolute control," says Kubrick. "Anthony Mann began the picture and filmed the first sequence, but his disagreements with Kirk made him decide to leave after the first week of shooting. The film came after two years in which I had not directed a picture. When Kirk offered me the job of directing *Spartacus*, I thought that I might be able to make something of it if the script could be changed. But my experience proved that if it is not explicitly stipulated in the contract that your decisions will be respected, there's a very good chance that they won't be. The script could have been improved in the course of shooting, but it wasn't. Kirk was the producer. He and Dalton Trumbo, the scriptwriter, and Edward Lewis, the executive producer, had everything their way." Kubrick's experience with the making of *Spartacus* served to strengthen his resolve to safeguard his artistic independence on future films, a resolution that he has kept.

With the collapse in the 1950s of Hollywood as the center of world film making, some of America's independent film makers moved to Europe, where they could make films more economically and hence more easily obtain the backing of American capital. Kubrick went to England to make *Lolita* (1962) and remained to make all of his subsequent films there. Nonetheless, he has not ceased to consider himself an American director, for only two of these films, *A Clockwork Orange* and *Barry Lyndon*, were set in Britain and had predominantly British casts. In this respect Kubrick can be sharply contrasted with Joseph Losey, another American director who migrated to England. Losey's films became so thoroughly British in concept and character that he has been placed among the directors in the section of this book devoted to the British cinema.

In *Lolita* Peter Sellers plays Clare Quilty, a television personality who is the rival of middle-aged Humbert Humbert (James Mason) for the affections of twelve-year-old Dolores Haze (Sue Lyon), known to her friends as Lolita. Because, at the time that Kubrick made *Lolita*, the freedom of the screen had not advanced to the point it has reached now, he had to be more subtle and indirect than Vladimir Nabokov had been in his novel about suggesting the sexual obsession of an older man for a nymphet.

"I wasn't able to give any weight at all to the erotic aspect of Humbert's relationship with Lolita in the film," says Kubrick, "and because I could only hint at the

Peter Sellers and James Mason in *Lolita* **(1962). (Cinemabilia)**

true nature of his attraction to Lolita, it was assumed too quickly by filmgoers that Humbert was in love with her," as opposed to being merely attracted to her sexually. "In the novel this comes as a discovery at the end, when Lolita is no longer a nymphet but a pregnant housewife; and it's this encounter, and the sudden realization of his love for her, that is one of the most poignant elements of the story."

Even in the film as it stands, Kubrick has managed to suggest something of the erotic quality of Humbert's relationship with Lolita from the very beginning. The first image of the film, seen behind the credits, is Humbert's hand reaching across the wide screen to caress Lolita's foot as he begins to paint her toenails, thus indicating the subservient nature of his infatuation for Lolita.

In order to avoid giving the plot too serious a treatment, Kubrick decided to emphasize the black comedy inherent in the story. Pauline Kael writes, "The surprise of *Lolita* is how enjoyable it is; it's the first new American comedy since those great days in the forties when Preston Sturges recreated comedy with verbal slapstick. *Lolita* is black slapstick and at times it's so far out that you gasp as you laugh."[2] Kubrick strikes this note of black comedy at the outset in the prologue that follows the credits.

Humbert Humbert threatens Clare Quilty with a gun as the latter stumbles about among the cluttered rooms of his grotesque mansion, not taking too seriously Humbert's threats to kill him, until it is too late. Quilty seeks refuge behind a painting that is propped up against a piece of furniture, and we watch the painting become filled with bullet holes as Humbert empties his gun into it. As the plot unfolds in flashback, we discover that Humbert shot Quilty, not just because Quilty had lured Lolita away from him, but because, after he had done so, Quilty merely used her for a while and then coldly discarded her.

In the difficult role of Humbert, James Mason gives a perfect portrayal of a man who has been victimized by his own obsession, but who strives nevertheless to maintain an air of surface propriety in his relationship with Lolita. There is, for example, the look of consternation that steals across his face when Lolita's dowdy mother (Shelley Winters), whom Humbert only married to be near Lolita, tells him that she has packed her daughter off to summer camp so that *they* can be alone. Peter Sellers is equally good as Clare Quilty, especially in the scenes in which Quilty dons a variety of disguises in his efforts to badger Humbert by a succession of ruses into giving up Lolita. Because of Sellers's brilliant flair for impersonation, these scenes are among the best in the film.

For those who appreciate the black comedy of *Lolita*, it is not hard to see that it was just a short step from that film to Kubrick's masterpiece in that genre, *Dr. Strangelove, or: How I Learned to Stop Worrying and Love the Bomb* (1964), the first of Kubrick's science-fiction trilogy. He had originally planned the film as a serious adaptation of Peter George's *Red Alert*, which is concerned with the insane General Jack D. Ripper (Sterling Hayden) and his decision to order a troup of B-52 bombers to launch an attack inside Russia. But gradually Kubrick's attitude toward his material changed: "My idea of doing it as a nightmare comedy came in the early weeks of working on the screenplay. I found that in trying to put meat on the bones and to imagine the scenes fully, one had to keep leaving things out of it which were either absurd or paradoxical in order to keep it from being funny; and these things seems to be close to the heart of the scenes in question."

Kubrick kept revising the script right through the production period, he says. "During shooting many substantial changes were made in the script, sometimes together with the cast during improvisations. Some of the best dialogue was created by Peter Sellers himself." Sellers played, not only the title role of the eccentric scientist, but also Merken Muffley, the president of the United States, as well as Captain Mandrake, a British officer who fails to dissuade General Ripper from his set purpose.

General Ripper's mad motivation for initiating a nuclear attack is his paranoid conviction that his diminishing sexual potency can be traced to an international Communist conspiracy to poison the drinking water. Kubrick subtly reminds us of the General's obsession by a series of sexual metaphors that occur in the course of the film. The very opening image of the film shows a nuclear bomber being refueled in mid-flight by another aircraft, with "Try a Little Tenderness" on the sound track to accompany their symbolic coupling. As Ripper describes to Mandrake his concern about preserving his potency, which he refers to as his "precious bodily essence," Kubrick photographs him in close-up from below, with a huge phallic cigar jutting from between his lips all the time he is talking.

Ironies abound throughout the picture. During an emergency conference called by President Muffley, a disagreement between General Buck Turgidson (George C. Scott) and the Russian ambassador (Peter Bull) threatens to turn into a brawl, and the president intervenes by reminding them, "Please, gentlemen, you can't fight here; this is the War Room."

Later, when Mandrake tries to reach the president in order to warn him about the imminent attack on Russia, he finds that he lacks the correct change for the coin telephone—and that the White House will not accept a collect call! He demands that Colonel Guano (Keenan Wynn) fire into a Coca-Cola machine in order to obtain the necessary money. Guano reluctantly agrees, ruefully reminding Mandrake that it is he who will have to answer to the Coca-Cola Company. Guano blasts the machine, bends down to scoop up the cascading coins, and is squirted full in the face with Coke by the vindictive machine.

Kubrick had originally included a scene in the film in which the War Room personnel engage in a free-for-all with pastry from a buffet table. But he deleted it from the final print of the film when he decided that "it was too farcical and not consistent with the satiric tone of the rest of the film." Very much in keeping with the satiric mood of the picture is the figure of Dr. Strangelove himself, who is Kubrick's vision of man's final capitulation to the machine. He is more a robot than a human being: his mechanical arm spontaneously salutes Hitler, his former employer; his mechanical hand, gloved in black, at one point even tries to strangle the flesh and blood that still remain in him.

In the end a single U.S. plane reaches its Russian target. Major "King" Kong (Slim Pickens), the skipper of the bomber, manages to dislodge a bomb that has been stuck in its chamber as he sits astride it and to unleash it on its target. As the bomb hurtles toward the earth, it looks like a mighty symbol of potency clamped

Sterling Hayden and Peter Sellers in *Dr. Strangelove* (1964). (Bennett's Book Store)

between his flanks, thus rounding out the sexual metaphors that permeate the film. The bomb hits its target, setting off the Russians' retaliatory Doomsday machine. There follows a series of blinding explosions, while on the sound track we hear a popular ditty Kubrick resurrected from the Second World War: "We'll meet again, don't know where, don't know when." Kubrick used the original World War II recording by Vera Lynn, which served to bring back to popularity not only the song but Miss Lynn as well.

One critic summed up the film by saying that the humor Kubrick had originally thought to exclude from *Dr. Strangelove* provides some of its most meaningful moments. These are made up of the incongruities and misunderstandings we are constantly aware of in our lives. But on the brink of annihilation they become irresistibly absurd.

In essence, *Dr. Strangelove* depicts the plight of fallible man putting himself at the mercy of his infallible machines and bringing about by this abdication of moral responsibility his own destruction. These sentiments are very close to those which Chaplin expressed in his closing speech in *The Great Dictator*: "We think too much and feel too little. More than machinery we need humanity. More than cleverness we need kindness and gentleness. Without these qualities, life will be violent and all will be lost."

Kubrick further explored his dark vision of man in a mechanistic age in *2001: A Space Odyssey* (1968). In explaining how the original idea for the film came to him, he says, "Most astronomers, and other scientists interested in the whole question, are strongly convinced that the universe is crawling with life; much of it, since the numbers are so staggering, equal to us in intelligence, or superior, simply because human intelligence has existed for so relatively short a period." He got in touch with Arthur C. Clarke, whose science-fiction short story "The Sentinel" Kubrick thought could be made the basis of a screenplay; and the rest is motion picture history. They first turned the short story into a novel, in order to develop completely its potentialities, and then turned that into a screenplay. MGM bought their package and financed the film for six million dollars, a budget that, after four years of work on the film, eventually rose to ten million. *2001* opened to indifferent and even hostile reviews, which subsequent critical opinion has completely overwhelmed, and went on to win a large audience.

The film begins at the dawn of civilization, with an ape-man who learns to employ a bone as a weapon in order to destroy a rival. In learning to extend his own physical powers through the use of a tool-weapon to kill one of his own kind, the ape-man has ironically taken a step toward humanity. As the victorious ape-man throws his weapon spiralling into the air, there is a dissolve to a spaceship soaring through space in the year 2001. "It's simply an observable fact," Kubrick has commented, "that all of man's technology grew out of his discovery of the tool-weapon. There's no doubt that there is a deep emotional relationship between man and his machine-weapons, which are his children. The machine is beginning to assert itself in a very profound way, even attracting affection and obsession."[3]

This concept is dramatized in the film when astronauts Dave Bowman (Keir Dullea) and Frank Poole (Gary Lockwood) find themselves at the mercy of computer HAL 9000 (voice by Douglas Rain), which controls their spaceship. There are repeated juxtapositions in the film of man, with his human failings and fallibility, alongside machinery—beautiful, functional, but heartless. When Hal the computer makes an error, he refuses to admit the evidence of his own fallibility and proceeds to destroy the occupants of the spaceship to cover it up. Kubrick, as always, is on the side of man, and he indicates here as in *Strangelove* that human fallibility is less likely to destroy man than the abdication of his moral responsibilities to supposedly infallible machines.

Kubrick believes man must also strive to gain mastery over himself and not just over his machines. "Somebody said that man is the missing link between primitive apes and civilized human beings. You might say that the idea is inherent in the story of *2001* too. We are semicivilized, capable of cooperation and affection, but needing some sort of transfiguration into a higher form of life. Since the means to obliterate life on earth exist, it will take more than just careful planning and reasonable cooperation to avoid some eventual catastrophe. The problem exists as long as the potential exists, and the problem is essentially a moral and spiritual one."

Hence the film ends with Bowman, the only survivor of the mission, being reborn as "an enhanced human being, a star child, a superhuman, if you like," says Kubrick, "returning to earth prepared for the next leap forward of man's evolutionary destiny." Kubrick feels that "the God concept is at the heart of the film" since, if any of the superior beings that inhabit the universe beyond earth were to manifest itself to a man, the latter would immediately assume that it was God or an emissary of God. When an artifact of these extraterrestrial intelligences does appear in the film, it is represented as a black monolithic slab. Kubrick thought it better not to try to be too specific in depicting these beings. "You have to leave something to the audience's imagination," he explains.

It is significant that Kubrick set the film in the year 2001, because Fritz Lang's groundbreaking silent film *Metropolis* (1927) takes place in the year 2000. This reference to Lang's film is a homage to the earlier master's accomplishment in science fiction, an achievement that Kubrick's film has built on and surpassed.

The overall implications of *2001* seem to suggest a more optimistic tinge to Kubrick's view of life than had been previously detected in his work. For in *2001* he presents man's creative encounters with the universe and his unfathomed potential for the future. In the third film of the trilogy, *A Clockwork Orange* (1972), the future appears to be less promising than it was in *2001*. If in *2001* Kubrick showed the machine becoming human, in *A Clockwork Orange* he shows man becoming a machine. Ultimately, however, the latter film only reiterates in somewhat darker terms the theme of all of Kubrick's previous work, namely, that man must retain his humanity if he is to survive in a dehumanized, materialistic world. Moreover, *A Clockwork Orange* echoes the warning of *Strangelove* and *2001* that man must strive to gain mastery over himself if he is to master his machines.

A Clockwork Orange is adapted from Anthony Burgess's novel of the same name, a nightmarish fantasy about England in the near future. It concerns a young hoodlum named Alex (Malcolm McDowell), whose only salutary characteristic seems to be his predilection for Beethoven, whom he refers to affectionately as "Ludwig Van." In order to keep Alex from committing any more crimes, the state deprives him of his free will; and he therefore becomes "a clockwork orange," someone who appears to be fully human but is basically mechanical in all of his responses. (Burgess borrowed the term from the old cockney phrase, "as queer as a clockwork orange.")

Just as *2001* ended with a close-up of the star child staring into the camera as it journeys back to earth in anticipation of the next step in man's evolution, so *A Clockwork Orange* begins with a close-up of Alex staring into the camera with a smirk on his face, as he looks forward to the coming night of sexual escapades and "ultra-violence" with his gang. Since the brutal Alex is a long way from the evolutionary progress that the star child represents, one might infer that Kubrick is saying in this film that the world will get worse before it gets better.

Alex's world as it is projected in the picture has a basis in reality, in that it reflects in an exaggerated form tendencies which already exist in contemporary society. Antiutopian novels like Waugh's *Love Among the Ruins*, Orwell's *1984*, and Burgess's *A Clockwork Orange* are not so much predictions of the future as parodies of the materialism, sexual indulgence, and mindless violence of the present. That is why Mr. Alexander, the writer in *A Clockwork Orange*, whose wife eventually dies of a vicious assault by Alex and his henchmen, remarks late in the film that his wife was really a victim of the Modern Age.

In essence, the ugly and erratic behavior of Alex and his clan is their way of asserting themselves against the depersonalized regimentation of the socialized state in which they live. Alex, for example, lives with his family in Municipal Flat Block 18A, a sterile and characterless apartment building. Later on, when his crimes catch up with him and he is sent to prison, he is referred to as 655321. But one wonders if he can be any more anonymous in jail than he was when he was a member of the regimented society that lies beyond the prison walls.

In an effort to get his jail term shortened, Alex volunteers to undergo "the Ludovico treatment." This is a brainwashing technique that renders him nauseous when confronted with opportunities for indulging in sex and violence, the very experiences that once gave him delight. Only the prison chaplain speaks up against the treatment. "Goodness comes from within," he insists. "Goodness must be chosen; when a man can no longer choose he ceases to be a man."

Upon his release Alex is totally unprepared to cope with the calloused and corrupt society that awaits him. He is beaten senseless by two of his old gang members, now policemen of a state that is becoming more and more fascist in its efforts to impose law and order on the populace. After he attempts suicide, however, Alex realizes with great joy during his convalescence in the hospital that the effects of the brainwashing are wearing off; indeed, he is returning to his old self, complete with all of his former proclivities. In brief Alex has regained his free will.

Because Kubrick has been unsparing in detailing Alex's depraved behavior in *A Clockwork Orange*, the film was a source of great controversy when first released. In defending his film and the philosophy that underlies it, Kubrick countered, "The essential moral of the story hinges on the question of choice; and the question of whether man can be good without having the choice to be evil; and whether a creature who no longer has this choice is still a man."

The fact that Alex is evil personified is important, Kubrick continues, to clarify the point that the film is making about human freedom. "If Alex were a lesser villain, then you would dilute the point of the film. It would then be like one of those Westerns which purports to be against lynching, and deals with the lynching of innocent people. The point of such a film would seem to be, 'You shouldn't lynch people because you might lynch innocent people'; rather than, 'You shouldn't lynch anybody.' Obviously, if Alex were a lesser villain, it would be very easy to reject his 'treatment' as inhuman. But when you reject the treatment of even a character as wicked as Alex, the moral point is clear."[4] To restrain man is not to redeem him; redemption, as the prison chaplain points out in the film, must come from within.

"The film and the book are about the danger of reclaiming sinners through sapping their capacity to choose between good and evil," Anthony Burgess adds. "Most of all, I wanted to show in my story that God made man free to choose either good or evil; and that this is an astounding gift."[5] Malcolm McDowell's own feelings about Alex at the end of the film bear out Burgess's remarks, as well as Kubrick's: "Alex is free at the end; that's hopeful. Maybe in his freedom, he'll be able to find someone to help him without brainwashing. If his 'Ludwig van' can speak to him, perhaps others can."[6]

In analyzing *A Clockwork Orange*, one cannot overlook the musical score.

Kubrick has always taken an interest in the choice of music in his films, stemming from the early days when he performed every job in the film-making process by himself. He often likes to employ recordings of familiar melodies on the sound track as an ironic counterpoint to the action, as when "We'll Meet Again" served as the accompaniment to the nuclear holocaust in *Dr. Strangelove*.

His use of "Singing in the Rain" in *A Clockwork Orange* is another stroke of genius. Early in the film Alex sings this song while beating a writer and raping his wife with the help of his gang. Then, during the closing credits of the movie, as a final irony, Kubrick has Gene Kelly's original rendition of the song from the 1951 film *Singin' in the Rain* played on the soundtrack, just after Alex has jubilantly declared that he is cured—which means that he is fully able to go back to his previous vicious behavior. The words of the song in this context take on an ironic quality, as Kelly exults that it is "a glorious feeling" to be "happy again." As Kelly proclaims that "there's a smile on my face for the whole human race" and that he's "ready for love," one remembers the circumstances in which Alex sang the song earlier in the film and realizes that to Alex they would mean that he is ready to resume his "ultra-violence" and lustful behavior. One might go a step further in tying the song in with the film and say that anyone who is not concerned for mankind's future as depicted in *A Clockwork Orange* is indeed singing in the rain.

"It takes about a year to let an idea reach an obsessional state, so I know what I really want to do with it," Kubrick says of the way that he initiates a new project. After spending some time looking for a project to follow *A Clockwork Orange*, he finally decided to step back into the past and dramatize *Barry Lyndon*, a tale of an eighteenth-century rogue written by Victorian novelist William Makepeace Thackeray.

Barry Lyndon (1975), for which Kubrick wrote the screenplay, narrates the amorous adventures of a Don Juan who hops from bedchamber to gaming room with equal ease. Yet he never completely loses the engaging qualities of his youth, even when he gradually becomes more corrupt and dissipated as he gets older. Barry (Ryan O'Neal) spends much of his time roaming across Europe, bilking unsuspecting aristocrats in posh gambling salons, until he meets Lady Lyndon (Marisa Berenson), a rich young window, and marries her for her wealth and title. He then proceeds to dominate his wife and to exploit her fortune in a shameful fashion, until his stepson, Lord Bullingdon, who quite despises Barry, challenges him to a duel. The embittered young man wounds his stepfather in the leg, rendering him crippled for life, and sends him packing. As one reviewer correctly characterized Barry Lyndon, he turns out to be nothing more than a seedy soldier of fortune, who winds up with nothing to show for his wasted life but wounds and scars.

Even though *Barry Lyndon*'s running time of just over three hours makes it the longest movie Kubrick has made, it still reflects the kind of cinematic economy we have come to expect of his work. Frequently a single telling image can communicate more to the viewer than several lines of dialogue, and Kubrick has proved himself a master at creating such visual metaphors. In the scene in which Barry is engaged in courting Lady Lyndon by flirting with her across a gaming table, a candelabrum stands in the foreground of the shot. In this way Kubrick emphasizes the flame that has been kindled in the lady for Barry's youth and good looks, and the flame that has in turn been kindled in Barry for her wealth and status.

In photographing a scene lit solely by candles, Kubrick marked an advance in cinematography, since no scene in a motion picture had ever been lit with so little illumination before. He accomplished this by using an extremely sensitive lens originally developed by NASA for photographing the instrument panel of a spaceship. Even when making a costume picture, Kubrick is quick to adapt the latest technical developments in other fields to cinema.

In *Barry Lyndon* one finds resonances of a theme that has reasserted itself in much of Kubrick's best work, that the best laid plans often go awry. He has frequently shown in his films how human error and chance can thwart an individual's best efforts to achieve his goals, as in *The Killing* and his science-friction trilogy. In this list of movies about human failures, the story of Barry Lyndon easily finds a place, for Barry's lifelong schemes to become a wealthy nobleman in the end come to nothing. And the same can be said for the frustrated writing aspirations of the emotionally disturbed hero of Kubrick's horror film, *The Shining* (1980), derived from the novel by Stephen King.

Jack Torrence (Jack Nicholson), his wife Wendy (Shelley Duvall), and son Danny (Danny Lloyd) move into a resort hotel in the Colorado Rockies, which, as things turn out, is apparently haunted. Jack had signed on to be caretaker of the summer resort for the winter, feeling that the undemanding job would give him time to work on a writing project, so that he can finally realize his unfulfilled aspirations to become a successful author. Right from the day of his arrival Jack cannot shake the eerie feeling that he has lived in the hotel before, even though he cannot remember any prior visit; and, as the story develops, it appears that he has—in a previous incarnation, some fifty years before.

As time goes on, Jack begins to "shine" (experience visions which project him back in time to his former life). In the course of these extrasensory experiences Jack encounters a bartender and a waiter in the hotel's posh night club, the Gold Room, both of whom recognize him. Given the deference that both men show him, Jack, it appears, was obviously not a hotel employee during his former existence, but an honored guest—perhaps a successful author (in which case one can understand his drive to be a professional writer once again, in his present existence). The tip-off that Jack was not a mere caretaker in the establishment last time around is a photograph hanging unobtrusively in the hotel lobby among other pictures, which shows Jack posing with some other guests at a swanky party in the ballroom; the photo is dated July 4, 1921.

Coming back to the same luxury hotel in his present existence as a miserable menial becomes a subconscious source of resentment and frustration for Jack, as does the fact that he has gotten absolutely nowhere on his writing project. Moreover, when he and his family are snowbound in the hotel as a result of a fierce storm, Jack finds the ensuing isolation and loneliness attendant on being marooned in the hotel—coupled with his painful awareness of his failure to make anything of himself as a writer—too much for him to bear. As Thomas Nelson comments in his book on Kubrick, Jack begins to act "as if his life in the present time were a bad dream from the future (i.e., post-1921)."[7]

As Jack descends into madness, his trancelike states of shining degenerate into macabre visions of his previous life, although they had initially seemed so pleasant when he found himself chatting with the bartender and the waiter in the Gold Room and moving among the other guests. By contrast, in these later visions the charming party guests with whom he had once frolicked have now been transformed into blood-spattered ghouls, cackling crones with rotting flesh, and even skeletons covered with cobwebs.

Jack finally goes totally berserk, and seeks to take out his wild anguish and mental suffering on his hapless wife and son, whom he stalks throughout the hotel grounds, bent on mayhem, at the film's chilling climax. But they manage to escape his clutches, as he wanders in his madness through the maze of hedges on the grounds, until he dies of exposure in the snow.

The Shining is a stand-out example of the horror genre, because Kubrick frequently suggests, rather than spells out, the dark, disturbing implications of the grotesque happenings he depicts. For example, Jack learns in the course of the film that the hotel's previous caretaker killed his wife and child, and then shot himself. Kubrick leaves the viewer to infer that perhaps Jack has become so obsessed with this atrocity by film's end that he finally feels compelled, in the depths of his insanity, to repeat the savage crimes of the former caretaker by attempting to destroy his own family. In any event, it is he, and not his wife and son, who perishes at the conclusion of the movie.

Like Norman Bates in Alfred Hitchcock's *Psycho*, Jack started out enjoying his visions of the past and wound up with his visions enjoying him. For Jack ultimately became so haunted by the past that he lost his grip on the present, and finally withdrew into the state of madness that destroyed him. All in all, *The Shining* is the kind of film that continues to linger in the filmgoer's memory long after one has seen it.

Although movie reviewers were divided about the picture, the general public was fairly unanimous in accepting the film. As a matter of fact, it was his most commercially successful movie up to that time, as Kubrick noted in a letter at the time.[8]

Kubrick's following film was also a box office winner. For his next subject Kubrick made an antiwar movie in the tradition of *Paths of Glory*, entitled *Full Metal Jacket* (1987), from the book *The Short-Timers* by Gustav Hasford. The present film, which Kubrick cowrote with Michael Herr (*Apocalypse Now*) and Hasford, examines the experience of some marines during the Vietnam War. The movie's title refers to the copper casing of the rifle cartridge that is the standard ammunition used by the marines in the field—perhaps a metaphor for the hard shell a tough fighting man is supposed to develop in order to face combat. The movie is climaxed by an extended battle sequence in which a group of marines becomes engaged in street fighting with some diehard snipers in a fire-gutted, rubble-strewn enemy town.

"If I'm forced to suggest something about the deeper meaning of the story," says

Matthew Modine (right) in *Full Metal Jacket* (1987). (Collectors Book Store)

Kubrick, it would be that the film is built around the concept of man's fundamental capacity for both good and evil: "altruism and cooperation on the one hand, aggression and xenophobia on the other."[9] This idea is most clearly articulated in the movie when a hardbitten old colonel notices that the hero, who is nicknamed Private Joker (Matthew Modine), is wearing a helmet that bears the slogan, "Born to Kill," while he also sports a peace button on his battle fatigues. When the officer presses Joker for an explanation of this anomaly, he replies, "I suppose I was trying to say something about the duality of man."

Joker's own ambivalence about his attitude toward war is brought into relief in the battle scene just mentioned, when he gazes down upon a mortally wounded Vietnamese sniper, who has killed three of his buddies. When the sniper, who happens to be a young girl, begs him to finish her off, he at first hesitates and then complies. Is his act principally motivated by mercy or revenge? Joker does not seem to know for sure. Yet, one suspects, his conflicting emotions about the fate of the sniper are meant to represent once more the contrary inclinations in human nature toward altruism and agression, drives which, as already noted, are epitomized by the two emblems which Joker continues to wear throughout the movie.

Clearly *Full Metal Jacket* can be characterized as a thought-provoking war movie, a film that offers no ready answers to the painful political and moral issues it raises.

It is clear that Kubrick can make any source material fit comfortably into the fabric of his work as a whole, whether it be a remote and almost forgotten Thackeray novel like *Barry Lyndon* or a provocative thriller by a contemporary novelist such as *The Shining*. What's more, it is equally evident that Kubrick plans to continue to use his artistic independence to create films that will stimulate his audience to come to terms with serious human problems, as his pictures have done from the beginning.

Summing up his personal vision as it appears in his films, Kubrick has said, "The destruction of this planet would have no significance on a cosmic scale. Our extinction would be little more than a match flaring for a second in the heavens. And if that match does blaze in the darkness, there will be none to mourn a race that used a power that could have lit a beacon to the stars to light its own funeral pyre."

Francis Coppola, director of *Tucker* (1988), on location. (Larry Edmunds's Cinema Book-shop)

8
Francis Coppola
The Lower Depths

"The trouble with American film making is that producers don't allow the risk of failure. If a good film can't risk being a failure, it won't be really good." So said Francis Coppola when he spoke with me at the Cannes Film Festival, one of the international festivals at which a movie of his had won a prize. Add to that the five Academy Awards he has received during his career, and one can see that Coppola's penchant for making films which, in his words, "depart somewhat from the ordinary Hollywood fare," has often paid off.

Coppola also has the distinction of being the first major American motion picture director to emerge from a university-degree program in film making. Moreover, he has since helped other graduates get their start in the industry, including George Lucas (*Star Wars*) and John Milius (*The Wind and the Lion*).

Francis Ford Coppola was born in Detroit, Michigan, in 1939; he received his middle name because he was born in the capital of the American automobile industry, and in Henry Ford Hospital as well. He consistently used his full name professionally for some years, but has tended more and more to suppress his middle name, ever since he got to hear of the old adage which warns that people tend to dismiss as an upstart someone who calls himself by three names.

His high school years began at Cornwall-on-Hudson, a military academy in New York State; but when the script and lyrics he wrote for a school musical were revised without his consent, he angrily quit the academy and transferred to Great Neck High on Long Island, from which he graduated in 1956. He then attended Hofstra University, and, after graduating from college in 1960, he enrolled in the master's program in film at the University of California at Los Angeles.

Coppola gained invaluable practical experience in film making during this period by working for independent producer-director Roger Corman (*House of Usher*) in various capacities, from scriptwriting to film editing. Finally Corman gave Coppola the chance to write and direct his first feature, a low-budget effort called *Dementia 13* (1963), a horror film he shot quickly and cheaply on location in Ireland. The set designer for the movie was Eleanor Neil, who became Coppola's wife when the film unit returned to the States. He was subsequently hired as a scriptwriter by Seven Arts, an independent producing company; and he received a screen credit as co-writer on two 1966 films, on which he worked for Seven Arts: *This Property Is Condemned* and *Is Paris Burning?*. He also coscripted *Patton* for Twentieth Century–Fox around this time, although that picture, as it happened, did not reach the screen until 1970.

The experience that the neophyte film maker had gained from making *Dementia 13* and from collaborating on various other movies helped him convince Seven Arts to allow him to write and direct his first important film, *You're a Big Boy Now* (1967), which he shot on location in New York City. In due course, Coppola submitted the finished film to UCLA as his master's thesis and thereby gained his degree of Master of Cinema in 1968. The movie, which he adapted from a novel by David Benedictus, is a freewheeling comedy about a young fellow on the brink of manhood (Peter Kastner) who takes a giant step toward maturity when he finally gets out from under the control of his domineering parents (Geraldine Page and Rip Torn) and endeavors to make it on his own in the big city.

Although the film was not a financial success, it garnered some positive reviews. Consequently Seven Arts, which by this time had merged with Warner Brothers, was sufficiently impressed with Coppola's handling of *Big Boy* that the company asked the promising young director to make *Finian's Rainbow* (1968), a large-scale movie musical starring Fred Astaire. The studio was pleased with Coppola's direction of the picture, particularly his filming of the musical numbers; and the front office was therefore willing to finance the picture he wanted to make next, a modest production based on an original scenario of his own, entitled *The Rain People* (1969).

The plot of this tragic drama concerns Natalie Ravenna (Shirley Knight), a depressed young housewife with a child on the way who impulsively decides to walk out on her husband one rainy morning and to make a cross-country trek in her station wagon. She takes this rash course of action in the hope of getting some perspective on her life. Natalie at this juncture feels stifled by the responsibilities of married life, epitomized by the prospect of having a child. In the course of her journey she picks up a hitchhiker, an ex-football player named Jimmy "Killer" Kilgannon (James Caan), who turns out to be mentally retarded as a result of a head injury he suffered in his final game. In effect, Natalie now has yet another "child" on her hands, and, almost in spite of herself, she gradually comes to care for him more and more as they travel along together.

In a sense both Natalie and Jimmy qualify to be numbered among the rain people of the film's title. The rain people are tender, vulnerable types who, as Jimmy himself describes them at one point, are "people made of rain; when they cry they disappear, because they cry themselves away." Like the rain people, Natalie and Jimmy are easily hurt, and, sadly, they will both end up wounding each other deeply.

For her part, Natalie is touched by Jimmy's disarming vulnerability; but she is also wary of his growing emotional dependence on her and wants to break off their burgeoning relationship. She consequently secures him a job on an animal farm they happen to come across during their trip, in order to be able to move on without him. But the childlike Jimmy spoils everything by releasing all the animals from their cages, because he simply cannot stand to see them penned up. Jimmy is fired, of course, and Natalie is enraged at him for continuing to be attached to her. She accordingly abandons him on the road and forthwith takes up with Gordon, a state highway patrolman (Robert Duvall). Gordon, whose wife is dead, invites her back to the trailer park where he lives with his young daughter, Rosalie.

Jimmy surreptitiously follows Natalie to Gordon's trailer and furiously bursts in on them in order to save her from Gordon's advances. Rosalie also shows up unexpectedly; when she sees the hulking "Killer" Kilgannon attacking her father, she frantically grabs his patrolman's pistol and shoots Jimmy. The movie ends abruptly, with Natalie sobbing inconsolably as she cradles the mortally wounded Jimmy in her arms, futilely promising to care for him from now on. "I'll take you home and we'll be family," she murmurs as Jimmy expires.

For the first time, Coppola's overriding theme, which centers on the importance of the role of a family spirit in people's lives, is clearly delineated in one of his films. "I am fascinated by the whole idea of family," he says, adding that in his films this theme "is a constant." Thus, as Robert Johnson notes in his book on Coppola, Natalie takes to the open road to escape the responsibilities of family life, only to find that she has taken them with her. This fact is strikingly brought home to her when she reflects that her unborn child, the very emblem of her marriage, is always with her, accompanying her wherever she goes. And this reflection in turn ultimately leads her by the end of the picture to reconcile herself to her responsibilities as a wife and mother; for she realizes that in trying to escape the obligations of family life she has brought nothing but misery to herself and others. Hence the movie ends, Coppola emphasizes, with an implicit "plea to have a family."[1]

Coppola assembled a hand-picked cast and crew to make the movie, which he planned to shoot entirely on location. Together they formed a caravan consisting of five cars, as well as a Dodge bus that had been remodeled to carry their technical equipment. They travelled for four months through eighteen states, filming as they went. Coppola did not set out with a finished screenplay in hand but continued filling it out as shooting progressed. When he spied a setting that appealed to him along the way, the group would stop, and he would work out a scene for the actors to play.

Because the script for *The Rain People* was developed in this piecemeal fashion, the story does not hang together as coherently as one would like. As a matter of fact, Coppola is the first to concede that the killing that climaxes the movie is a kind of *deus ex machina* he concocted in order to resolve the movie's plot. The lack of a tightly constructed plot line made for a slow-moving film, and hence *The Rain People* did not win over the critics or the mass audience.

Still there are some fine things in the film, for example, the key scene in which Jimmy liberates the animals from their captivity is a symbolic reminder that Natalie at this point still feels cooped up by circumstances and likewise yearns to be set free from the emotional entanglements in her life. Another neat Coppola touch is having Gordon live in a mobile home, an indication of the transient nature of his life since he lost his wife and, by the same token, a foreshadowing of the sort of rootless existence Natalie is opening herself to if she opts to foresake her husband for good.

Because *The Rain People* did not fare well at the box office, Coppola experienced some difficulty in launching another film project—until the release of *Patton* (1970). Coppola won an Oscar for cowriting the screenplay for this epic World War II movie, which he had worked on just before he made *Big Boy*. Since Coppola's stock had now risen in the industry, Paramount decided to entrust him with the

Marlon Brando in the title role of *The Godfather* **(1972), for which both Francis Coppola and Brando won Academy Awards. (Musuem of Modern Art/Film Stills Archive)**

direction of a gangster picture about the Mafia they were going to make called *The Godfather*, based on the bestselling novel by Mario Puzo.

The Godfather (1972) begins in 1945, on the wedding day of Connie Corleone (Talia Shire, Coppola's sister), who is the daughter of Don Vito Corleone (Marlon Brando), the chieftain of one of the most powerful of the New York Mafia "families." The jubilant wedding reception in the sunny garden of the don's estate offers a sharp contrast to the somber scene in his study, where the godfather sits in semi-darkness, stroking his cat and listening to the petitions being presented to him by his associates. He is following a custom which dictates that a godfather must seriously consider any request for help made to him on such a festive occasion.

Vito Corleone is a calculating man who has always run his empire of crime with the efficiency of a business executive. Whenever he encountered resistance from someone with whom he wanted to make a deal, the don simply extended to him what he ominously terms "an offer he couldn't refuse," and he got what he wanted. The awesome Don Vito is, therefore, the object of the envy and the hatred of some other Mafiosi, who fear that he is becoming too powerful. Accordingly an assassination attempt is made on his life, which leaves him incapacitated for some time. Sonny, his oldest son (James Caan), rules in his stead for the duration of his illness. Michael, Don Vito's youngest son (Al Pacino), just home from serving in the army during World War II, is anxious to prove himself to his father. He gets the chance to do so when he convinces Sonny to let him even the score with the family's enemies by killing the two individuals responsible for the attempt on their father's life: a leading mobster and a corrupt cop.

In one of the most riveting scenes in the picture, Michael successfully carries out his plan to gun down both men in a Bronx restaurant. He then escapes into temporary exile in Sicily, in order to be out of the reach of reprisals. While in Sicily Michael meets and marries Apollonia, a beautiful peasant girl. Despite the bodyguards that surround Michael and his new bride, Apollonia dies in an explosion that had been intended to kill Michael. Embittered and brutalized by this never-ending spiral of revenge, Michael returns to America, where his tough methods of dealing with other Mafiosi continue to impress his father; and he gradually emerges as the heir apparent of the aging Don Vito.

Friction between the Corleones and the other Mafia clans continues to mount; and the volatile Sonny is gunned down as the result of a clever ruse. Then, when the ailing Don Vito dies as well, the Corleone family closes ranks under Michael's leadership, and the new don effects the simultaneous liquidation of their most powerful rivals by having them all killed on the same day and at the same hour. Coppola intercuts these murders with shots of Michael acting as godfather at the baptism of his little niece. The ironic parallel between Michael's solemn role as godfather in the baptismal ceremony and the stunning "baptism of blood" he has engineered to confirm his position as godfather of one of the most formidable Mafia clans in the country is unmistakable.

By this time Michael has married again; and the movie ends with his second wife Kay (Diane Keaton) standing in the doorway of the study where Don Vito once ruled, watching the members of the Corleone Mafia family kissing Michael's hand as a sign of their loyalty to him. The camera draws away and the huge door of Don Michael's study closes on the scene, shutting out Kay—and the filmgoer—from any further look at the inner workings of the Mafia.

Coppola's continuing preoccupation with the importance of family in modern society is once again brought into relief in the present picture. As a matter of fact, the thing that most attracted Coppola to the project in the first place was that the book is really the story of a family. It is about "this father and his sons," he says, "and questions of power and succession." In essence, *The Godfather* offers a chilling depiction of the way in which Michael's loyalty to his flesh-and-blood family gradually turns into an allegiance to the larger Mafia family to which they in turn belong, a devotion that in the end renders him a cruel and ruthless mass killer.

With this film Coppola definitely hit his stride as a film maker. He tells the story in a straightforward, fast-paced fashion that holds the viewer's attention for close to three hours. Under his direction the cast members without exception give flawless performances, highlighted by Brando's Oscar-winning performance in the title role. *The Godfather* also received Academy Awards for the best picture of the year and for the screenplay, which Coppola coauthored with Puzo. Furthermore, the picture was an enormous critical and popular success.

Nevertheless, a few reviewers expressed some reservations about the film. The movie was criticized in some quarters for subtly encouraging the audience to admire the breathtaking efficiency with which organized crime operates. Coppola counters that such was never his intent. He feels that he was making an especially harsh statement about the Mafia at the end of *The Godfather*, when Michael makes a savage purge of all of the Corleone clan's known foes. If some reviewers and moviegoers missed the point he was trying to make, however, he looked upon the sequel, which Paramount had asked him to make, as "an opportunity to rectify that."[2] For in the sequel Coppola would see to it that Michael was shown to be manifestly more cold-blooded and cruel than his father ever was.

The Godfather-Part II (1974), which was once again coauthored by Coppola and Puzo, treats events that happened before and after the action covered in the first film. The second *Godfather* movie not only chronicles Michael's subsequent career as head of the "family business," but also presents, in flashback, Don Vito's early life in Sicily, as well as his rise to power in the Mafia in New York City's "Little Italy" after his immigration to the United States. As Pauline Kael says, "We only saw the middle of the story in the first film; now we have the beginning and the end"[3]

Godfather-II begins where the previous picture left off: with the scene in which Don Michael's lieutenants pay him homage as his father's rightful successor. Then the movie switches to a scene from the childhood of Michael's father, when young Vito's own father was murdered for defying the local Mafia don back in the Sicilian village where Vito was born. Vito's mother and older brother were also killed shortly afterward for attempting to take vengeance on the Mafia chief; and Vito, now an orphan, escaped to America. Back in the present, the film focuses on another youngster, Michael's son Anthony, who is enjoying a big celebration in honor of his first Communion. The party is being held on his father's estate at Lake

Tahoe, which is now the center of Michael's business operations. Michael, like his father before him, privately conducts his business affairs while the festivities are in full swing.

The story continues to shift back and forth between past and present, as we watch Vito (Robert DeNiro) return to Sicily briefly in order to gun down the old Mafia chieftain responsible for the deaths of his parents and his brother. In a parallel act of vengeance Michael arranges for the assassination of rival mobster Hyman Roth (Lee Strasberg), who had plotted to have Michael slain. Michael also has his weak and ineffectual older brother Fredo (John Cazale) shot when he learns that Fredo, who all along had been jealous of his kid brother Michael for superseding him as head of the Corleone family, had coperated with Roth's scheme to kill Michael.

Throughout the picture Coppola makes it clear that the higher Michael rises in the hierarchy of Mafia chiefs, the lower he sinks into the depths of moral degradation. His wife Kay is appalled by what he has become and finally comes to the bitter conclusion that Michael will never change his ways and phase out his unlawful business interests, as he has promised her so often that he would. Indeed, it is far too late in the day for Michael to become a legitimate businessman, even if he wanted to. "He can never go back to the time before that moment in the restaurant when he shot his father's enemies," Pauline Kael writes. "Michael's act, which preserved his family's power," ruined his own life by setting him on the road to a life of crime.[4]

Because Kay is now as aware of this painful reality as Michael himself is, she finally informs him that she is going to leave him and take their little boy and girl with her. At the climax of their dreadful quarrel, Kay reveals that the miscarriage she had told Michael she had suffered earlier was actually an abortion. She killed their unborn son, she explains, because she would not bring another child into the vicious Corleone world. Michael is shocked to learn of the loss of a second son, who would have helped to keep the Corleone name alive; and he angrily slaps his wife across the face. But, Robert Johnson comments, it is Kay who has delivered the severest blow. Michael orders Kay to get out, but she must leave their children behind.

Once Michael has become permanently alienated from his wife, he is left a lonely, disconsolate man, living in virtual isolation in his heavily guarded compound at Lake Tahoe. Michael may have built the Corleone family into one of the strongest Mafia clans in America, but he has at the same time lost most of his own immediate family: he murdered his only remaining brother, his first wife was killed by his enemies, and his second wife has been banished. In brief, the vile family business has invaded his home and all but destroyed it.

In making *Godfather-II*, "I wanted to take Michael to what I felt was the logical conclusion," says Coppola. "There's no doubt that, by the end of this picture, Michael Corleone, having beaten everyone, is sitting there alone, a living corpse." The final image of Michael, sitting in a thronelike chair, brooding over the loss of so many of his family, recalls the shot in the film's first flashback in which the sickly young Vito Corleone sits in an enormous chair in a lonely hospital room at Ellis

Island, right after his arrival in the New World. The lad, we know, came to America because of a vendetta against his family in his own country, and he will grow up to wreak vengeance on the man who slaughtered his loved ones back home.

Years later his son Michael will in turn take it upon himself to avenge the murderous attack on his father's life; by so doing he will inevitably become an integral part of the ongoing pattern of vengeance that began with the massacre of his ancestors long before he was ever born. Hence, Johnson perceptively observes, there is a direct connection between the frail little boy sitting alone in the oversized chair early in the movie and his grown son sitting alone in a majestic chair late in the movie. Coppola articulates that connection when he remarks that in *Godfather-II* his purpose was "to show how two men, father and son, were . . . corrupted by this Sicilian waltz of vengeance."[5]

The second *Godfather* film, like the first, was awarded Oscars for best picture of the year and for the best screenplay. In addition, Coppola also won the best director Oscar; and Carmine Coppola, his father, received an award, as did Nino Rota, for the film's musical score, while Robert DeNiro was named best supporting actor. Moreover, *Godfather-II*, like *Godfather-I*, was also favorably received by both critics and moviegoers. What's more, the two films, taken together, represent one of the supreme achievements of the cinematic art. In covering a span of some seventy years, from the childhood of Vito Corleone to the adult life of his son Michael, *Godfather I* and *II* are, as Rob Edelman rightly asserts, "equal in scope and majesty to *Gone with the Wind*."[6]

Although both of the *Godfather* films were productions originated by Paramount Pictures, Coppola continued to maintain his own independent production company, through which he initiated projects that he arranged to finance, shoot, and release in cooperation with various major studios. He initially named this operation, which he established in San Francisco in 1969, American Zoetrope, after the primitive mechanism that was a forerunner of the motion picture projector.

In 1980 he purchased the old Hollywood General Studios in the heart of the film colony, which had all the elaborate technical facilities necessary for shooting a motion picture that his San Francisco setup did not have. He christened his new acquisition Zoetrope Studios and envisioned it as similar to a repertory theater company, where a group of artists and technicians would collaborate in making movies together. But after the commercial failure of two major films produced there, an expensive musical entitled *One from the Heart* (1982), which he directed, and a detective movie made by another director, Coppola was ultimately forced to sell the studio facilities in 1982. Nevertheless, the Zoetrope name still survives as the title of Coppola's production company, which is once again based in San Francisco. Under the Zoetrope Studios emblem he continues to develop projects for filming, which he then carries through in association with some major film studio, just as he did before he owned a studio of his own for a time.

The first film he directed after shutting down his own studio in Hollywood was conceived on a smaller scale than the big-budget movies he had made during the previous decade. *The Outsiders* (1983) was derived from a novel by S. E. (Susan Eloise) Hinton that her devoted teenaged readers had turned into a bestseller. The story revolves around the ongoing feud between two gangs of teenage boys living in Tulsa, Oklahoma, in the Sixties: One group is made up of underprivileged lads known as greasers, the other group is comprised of upperclass youngsters.

The movie opens with Ponyboy (C. Thomas Howell), the film's narrator, beginning to write a composition for his teacher about some recent events in which he has figured. We hear him recount what happened, voice-over on the sound track, as the plot unfolds. Ponyboy belongs to the greasers, most of whom are orphans like himself, boys who have consequently formed a surrogate family of their own. The gang member Ponyboy looks up to as a father figure is Dallas (Matt Dillon), a street-wise young fellow who has just gotten out of jail.

One night Ponyboy and his other chum, Johnny (Ralph Macchio), are accosted by some members of the rival gang who are drunk. When the other boys attack Ponyboy, Johnny panics and pulls a knife, stabbing one of them to death. Johnny and Ponyboy run to Dallas for help, and he advises them to hide out in an abandoned country church for the time being. Dallas comes to their hideout later on to tell them that a witness to the fatal stabbing is willing to testify in their behalf, and they decide to give themselves up. Before they can start back to town, however, a fire breaks out in the dilapidated church, and the trio are suddenly called upon to save the lives of some children who happen to be in the old building when the blaze starts. Tragically, Johnny is severely burned during the course of the courageous rescue effort, and he dies shortly afterward.

Later on Dallas, the ex-convict, lapses into his old ways, attempts to hold up a store, and is killed in a reckless scuffle with the police. Reflecting on the loss of his two best friends, Ponyboy hopes to come to terms with this double tragedy by writing down what happened in a composition for his teacher. After all, one of his brothers tells him, "Your life isn't over because you lose someone." And so the movie ends where it began, with Ponyboy writing the essay that forms the content of the film's spoken narration.

The Outsiders was a bona fide blockbuster, despite the fact that some critics dismissed the movie as a minor melodrama unworthy of Coppola's directorial talents. On the contrary, the picture deserves a respected place in the Coppola cannon for various reasons, not the least of which is the host of consistently excellent performances he drew from his youthful cast, most notably Matt Dillon, C. Thomas Howell, Ralph Macchio, Tom Cruise, Emilio Estevez, and Rob Lowe as the greasers.

On the technical side, the camera work in the movie, which was filmed entirely on location in Tulsa, Oklahoma, is superb. Coppola employs shots of some incandescently beautiful sunsets throughout the movie to symbolize the brevity of youth. "When you watch the sun set, you realize it is already dying," he explains. "The same applies to youth. When youth reaches its highest level of perfection, you can already sense the forces that will destroy it."[7] Coppola's remark becomes still more meaningful when one relates the golden sunsets pictured in the movie to a poem by Robert Frost that Ponyboy recites to Johnny, in which the poet likens the innocence of childhood to gold. Johnny picks up on the poem's theme by offering his pal this advice: "Stay gold, Ponyboy; stay gold." This is Johnny's way of encouraging

Ponyboy not to lose the fundamental wholesomeness of youth as he grows older and is forced to face more and more of the grim realities of the adult world.

After filming *Rumble Fish* (1983), adapted from another Hinton novel, Coppola was brought in at the eleventh hour to collaborate on a picture called *The Cotton Club* (1984). By the time he signed on to rewrite the script and to direct the movie, the project was plagued with a variety of production problems, as well as with an unviable screenplay; Coppola did his best to improve matters.

The Cotton Club was designed as a musical about the famed Harlem nightspot that flourished in the Prohibition Era, where the entertainers were black and the customers were white. Because the club was run by a racketeer named Owney Madden (Bob Hoskins) and his cohorts, the plot at times takes on the dimensions of a gangster picture, thereby recalling the director's *Godfather* films. The concept of blending the format of the movie musical with that of the gangster movie—the two most popular film genres during the period of the early talkies—seemed like a dandy idea in theory; but it did not work out satisfactorily in practice. Admittedly, *The Cotton Club* has its share of eye-filling musical numbers, featuring the celebrated dancer Gregory Hines, plus some exciting action sequences built around harrowing gangland shootouts between rival mobs of bootleggers. Nevertheless, despite Coppola's conscientious efforts to whip the movie into shape, *The Cotton Club* remains a hybrid, a mixture of two disparate screen genres that, in the last analysis, never quite coalesce into a unified work of art.

In any event, Coppola had much better luck with his next venture, *Peggy Sue Got Married* (1986), a remarkable fantasy warmly applauded both by the critics and the general public. The title character is a woman approaching middle age (Kathleen Turner), who passes out at the twenty-fifth anniversary reunion of her high school graduating class and wakes up back at old Buchanan High in 1960, her senior year. But she has brought with her on her trip down memory lane her forty-two-year-old mind, and hence she views things from a more mature perspective than she possessed the first time around. Thus, when Peggy Sue tells her younger sister that she would like to get to know her better, she adds a perceptive remark that could only have come from her older self: "I have too many unresolved relationships."

One relationship she has failed to resolve in her later life is that with her estranged husband, Charlie Bodell (Nicholas Cage, Coppola's nephew), who, of course, is still a teenager when Peggy Sue meets him in the course of her return visit to her youth. She and Charlie married right after high school but have since split up because Peggy Sue discovered that he was cheating on her with a younger woman.

Early in the movie, before she was transported backward in time, Peggy Sue had mused to herself during the reunion celebration, "If I knew then I know now, I'd do a lot of things differently." But the question is, now that she appears to have the chance of a lifetime to change her destiny by altering her past, will she?

In Charlie's case, when he comes to court Peggy Sue in the course of her return trip to her adolescent years, her sour experiences with him in later life prompt her to break their engagement. "I'm not going to marry you a second time," she tells the uncomprehending Charlie, who cannot foresee the future as she can. Their lovers' quarrel comes to an end when they kiss and make up—and make love; and

Kathleen Turner in the title role of *Peggy Sue Got Married* (1986). (The Author's collection)

this occasion turns out to be the time Charlie gets Peggy Sue pregnant, with the result that she does in fact decide once again to marry Charlie. In short, she winds up not doing things any differently the second time around after all, although she promised herself she would!

Back in present time, Peggy Sue had been taken to the hospital in the wake of her fainting spell at the reunion. Charlie is at her bedside when she awakens, and begs her to take him back. Their daughter is there too, and the three of them embrace. For Peggy Sue the high school reunion has proved to be the occasion of a family reunion as well. The reconciliation of Peggy Sue and her husband at the fadeout challenges the viewer with the notion that, as Gene Siskel puts it, "it is a generous and proper idea for us to accept the whole package, faults and all, of the people we care about."[8] *Peggy Sue Got Married* thus reaffirms the need we all have to preserve strong family ties in life, a perennial Coppola theme.

In reworking the screenplay along with the scriptwriters prior to filming, Coppola says that the model he kept in mind was Thornton Wilder's endearing play *Our Town*, in which the heroine "goes back and sees ... her youth." He wanted to invest the movie with "that kind of small-town charm and emotion."[9] And so he did, for he managed to turn out a touching, sensitive film that ranks high on the list of his best movies.

From the film's opening sequence onward, Coppola demonstrates that he is in total control of his material. The picture begins with a shot of a TV set on which Charlie can be seen doing a commercial for his hardware store. Coppola's camera pulls back to reveal Peggy Sue primping at her dressing table before departing for the high school anniversary party. Her back is to the television set, indicating that she has, at this junction, turned her back on her philandering spouse. When she arrives at the party, which is being held in the school gym, she is chagrined to see an enormous blowup of a photograph picturing herself and Charlie as king and queen of the senior prom. The photo captures them at a moment in time when their relationship was happy and carefree, rather than sad and careworn, which is what it eventually became.

Visual metaphors of this sort abound in the movie. As a balloon floats upward toward the rafters of the gym, one of the alumni reaches for it, but it gets away. So too, many of the hopes and dreams that Peggy Sue and her classmates nurtured when they were young have eluded their grasp, driven off by the frustrations and disappointments of later life—epitomized, in her case, by her foundering marriage to Charlie. When Charlie himself makes his appearance at the reunion, he is at first barely visible in the shadowy doorway. He is but a dim figure from Peggy Sue's past, someone whom she will get to know all over again, as she relives the past and is thereby able to come to terms with the present.

With Coppola's next film, *Gardens of Stone*, the director returned to a subject he had dealt with earlier in *Apocalypse Now*: the Vietnam War. *Apocalypse Now* (1979) depicts the war itself, while its companion piece is concerned with the home-front during the same period. The first of Coppola's two Vietnam films was a mammoth production, which he shot on location in the Phillipines. The screenplay, by John Milius, Michael Herr, and Coppola, was derived from Joseph Conrad's 1899 novel *Heart of Darkness*, but the setting was updated to the period of the Vietnam War.

Captain Benjamin Willard (Martin Sheen), who is the central character and narrator of the movie, is mandated by his superior officers to penetrate into the interior of the jungle and track down Colonel Walter E. Kurtz (Marlon Brando), a renegade officer who has raised an army composed of deserters like himself and of native tribesmen, in order to fight the war on his own terms. When he locates Kurtz, Willard is to "terminate his command with extreme prejudice," which is military jargon meaning that Willard should assassinate Kurtz. Colonel Kurtz, it seems, has taken to employing brutal tactics to attain his military objectives; indeed, some of his extreme measures have sickened the members of the army intelligence staff who have succeeded in obtaining information about him.

Willard's first reaction to his mission is that liquidating someone for killing people in wartime seems like "handing out speeding tickets at the Indianapolis 500." Besides, even though Willard has been ordered to eliminate no less than six other undesirables in the recent past, this is the first time his target has been an American and an officer. He therefore decides to withhold judgment about Kurtz until he meets up with him personally.

As Willard chugs up the Mekong River in a river patrol boat in search of Kurtz, Richard Blake comments, his journey becomes a symbolic voyage "backward in time" toward the primitive roots of civilization.[10] Near the beginning of the trip Willard and the crew of his small craft witness an air attack on a North Vietnamese village carried out by Lieutenant Colonel Kilgore (Robert Duvall), which utilizes all the facilities of modern mechanized warfare, from helicopters and rockets to radar-directed machine guns. By the time that Willard's boat reaches Kurtz's compound in the heart of the dark jungle, the modern weaponry associated with the helicopter attack earlier in the movie has been replaced by the weapons of primitive man, as Kurtz's native followers attack the small vessel with arrows and spears. In entering Kurtz's outpost in the wilderness, Willard has equivalently stepped back into a lawless, prehistoric age, where barbarism holds sway.

In fact, the severed heads that lie scattered about the grounds mutely testify to the depths of pagan savagery to which Kurtz has sunk during his sojourn in the jungle. Furthermore, it is painfully clear to Willard that, despite the fact that Kurtz's native followers revere him as a god, Kurtz is incurably insane.

After he has Willard taken into custody, Kurtz spends hours haranguing Willard about his theories of war and politics, which he maintains lie behind his becoming a rebel chieftain. Kurtz does this, not only because he wants a brother officer to hear his side of the story, but also because he ultimately wants Willard to explain to Kurtz's son his father's reasons for acting as he has. Significantly, even in the depths of his madness, Kurtz has not lost sight of the preciousness of family attachments.

In Kurtz's own mind, the ruthless tactics he has employed to prosecute the war represent in essence his unshakeable conviction that the only way to conquer a cruel and inhuman enemy is to become as cruel and inhuman as he is and to crush him by his own hideous methods.

By now Willard has definitely made up his mind to carry out his orders by killing

Marlon Brando and Martin Sheen in *Apocalypse Now* **(1979). (Museum of Modern Art/Film Stills Archive)**

Kurtz; and Kurtz, who has sensed from the beginning the reason why Willard was sent to find him, makes no effort to stop him. As Willard reflects in his voice-over commentary on the sound track, Kurtz wants to die bravely, like a soldier, at the hands of another soldier and not to be ignominiously butchered as a wretched renegade. Willard accordingly enters Kurtz's murky lair and "executes" him with a scimitar. Afterwards, as Willard leaves Kurtz's quarters, Kurtz's worshipful tribesmen submissively lay their weapons on the ground before him as he passes among them. Clearly they believe that the mantle of authority has passed from their deceased leader to the man he allowed to slay him. But Willard, his mission accomplished, walks out of the compound and proceeds to the river bank, where his patrol boat awaits him.

As the boat pulls away from the shore, Willard hears the voice of Kurtz uttering the same phrase he had spoken just before he met his maker: "The horror, the horror." At the end Kurtz was apparently vouchsafed a moment of lucidity, in which he realized what a depraved brute he had become. To Willard the phrase represents his own revulsion at the vicious inclination to evil he had seen revealed in Kurtz—a tendency that Kurtz had allowed to overpower his better nature and render him more savage by far than the enemy he was so intent on exterminating.

Hence the theme of the movie is the same as that of Conrad's novel. "In *Apocalypse Now* just as in *Heart of Darkness*, the central journey is both a literal and a metaphoric one," writes Joy Gould Boyum; it is fundamentally "a voyage of discovery into the dark heart of man, and an encounter with his capacity for evil."[11] In harmony with this observation, Coppola says that he too sees Willard's journey upriver as a metaphor for the voyage of life, during the course of which each of us must choose between good and evil.

Although some critics found those scenes in which Kurtz theorizes about the motivation for his unspeakable behavior wordy and overlong, most agreed that the movie contains some of the most extraordinary combat footage ever filmed. The battle scene that particularly stands out is the one in which the officer who is aptly named Kilgore systematically wipes out a strongly fortified enemy village from the air.

Kilgore, all decked out with a stetson and gold neckerchief, looks as if he should be leading a cavalry charge rather than a helicopter attack. His fleet of helicopters is equipped with loudspeakers that blare forth Wagner's thunderous "Ride of the Valkyries" as the choppers fly over the target area. "Wagner scares the hell out of them," Kilgore tells Willard, who is observing the operation as a passenger in Kilgore's copter. As a napalm strike wreaks havoc and destruction on the village below, Kilgore exults, "I love the smell of napalm in the morning. It has the smell of victory." It is spectacular scenes like this one that have prompted some commentators on the film to rank *Apocalypse Now*, which won one of the two Grand Prizes awarded at the 1979 Cannes Film Festival, among the great war movies of all time.

There are no such stunning battle sequences in *Gardens of Stone* (1987), Coppola's other Vietnam film, since it takes place stateside. In contrast to king-sized war epic like *Apocalypse Now*, *Gardens of Stone* tells what Coppola calls a more intimate, personal story. The film focuses on Sergeant Clell Hazard (James Caan), a combat veteran who has become increasingly demoralized as he observes the army futilely waging a war in Vietnam he is convinced is unwinnable. "I care about the U.S. Army," he says to a friend; "that's my family. And I don't like it when my family is in trouble."

After four years in Vietnam, Hazard is now a member of the Old Guard, a special unit that serves as the honor guard for the burials of servicemen killed in Vietnam at Artlington National Cemetary (the gardens of stone). In practice this can involve participation in as many as fifteen funerals a day. Depressed by the continuing loss of so many young lives, Hazard sardonically tells Jackie Willow, a young recruit in the Old Guard (D. B. Sweeney), that burying is their business and business has never been better. Bright-eyed, impetuous Jackie insists that the war is not lost and that the right kind of soldier could make a difference. Hazard, on the other hand, thinks Jackie far too idealistic and tells him so repeatedly. Nonetheless, the rambunctious lad is itching to plunge into the fray, in order to do whatever he can to help with the war.

Jackie in due course is shipped overseas, where he is killed in action just a few weeks before he completes his tour of duty. During the ceremonies at graveside for Jackie, we can hear a couple of the younger members of the Old Guard muttering their favorite jingle: "Ashes to ashes and dust to dust; / Let's get this over and get back in the bus." Jackie no doubt recited this same impish little ditty when he was part of the ceremonial guard.

Hazard, who had become a surrogate father for Jackie during their time together in the Old Guard, feels as if he has indeed lost a son when Jackie is killed. The aging soldier remembers that Jackie had dreamed of winning the Combat Infantry Badge while he was in Vietnam, but did not live long enough to receive one. Hence Hazard places his own C.I.B. on Jackie's coffin before the interment, equivalent to a gift from father to son. Hazard also decides, in the wake of Jackie's death, to return to the battleground in Vietnam, in the hope that he can teach other young fighting men everything he knows about how to survive under fire, since he never got the chance to help Jackie in this way.

Coppola explains that he decided to make this muted, elegiac film about the special ceremonial unit of the army, because he has been interested in the role of ritual in army life ever since he attended a military school as a youngster. Besides, he also valued the opportunity to present an in-depth portrayal of servicemen as a sort of family whose members are bound together by a traditional code of honor and by mutual loyalty and affection. In short, his goal in making the film was to limn military men, not as conventional movie stereotypes, but as complicated human beings. He accomplished this task quite satisfactorily, as reflected in the solid characterizations of Clell Hazard and Jackie Willow and in the subtle father-son relationship that gradually develops between them.

His next subject, a biographical film about Preston Tucker, a maverick automobile designer in the 1940s, was one that had been in the back of his mind for more than a decade. Tucker was an inventive designer, but he was never able to obtain sufficient backing to mass-produce an auto based on his imaginative concepts. It is clear in viewing Coppola's "auto" biography, *Tucker: The Man and His Dream* (1988), that, as he himself says, his cinematic imagination was inspired by creating a film centering on an automaker's technical ingenuity. In essence, since Tucker's car was a mechanical miracle, he wanted his film to some extent also to be a mechanical marvel—a movie that emphasizes a variety of technical effects, from crane shots to split screens (whereby the frame is divided between two parallel scenes, shown on the screen side by side). There are, for example, some super high-angle crane shots of Tucker's dedicated crew putting together the first Tucker car, as well as some tricky split-screen shots—as when Tucker phones his wife, and we see separate shots of each of them on the screen simultaneously, as they converse about his latest inspiration. "I always like my movie's style to reflect the subject matter," Coppola explains.

It is not surprising that a movie maker named Francis Ford Coppola, who was born in Detroit, should be fascinated by someone associated with the automotive industry. (Coppola's eldest son, Gian-Carlo, who drowned in a sailing incident in 1986, shared his father's fascination: the film ends with the dedication, "For Gio, who loved cars.") Coppola has told *The New York Times* that Tucker (Jeff Bridges) developed plans for a car that was way ahead of its time in terms of engineering; yet the auto industry at large stubbornly resisted his innovative ideas. Unfortunately, Coppola commented, creative people do not always get a chance to exercise their creativity.[12]

Francis Coppola is one creative person who has continued to exercise his considerable creative talent throughout his career. He personally agrees with the tenets of the *auteur* theory, on which the present book is based, concerning the pivotal role of the director in the film making process; but he also believes that a film maker must earn the right to exercise artistic control over the movies he makes. Coppola himself has certainly earned that right.[13] The films he has directed over the years have demonstrated that, as *Time* magazine has indicated, he is one of the most gifted American directors to come across the Hollywood horizon since Stanley Kubrick. What's more, he is one of the few directors of his generation whose track record is usually enough in itself to persuade studio officials to finance a film he wants to make.

After finishing *Tucker* Coppola went on to contribute a segment to an anthology film entitled *New York Stories* (1989). In turning to his next project, he observed that he looks upon the movies he has directed in the past as providing him with the sort of experience that will help him to make better films in the future. So the only thing for a film maker to do, he concludes, is just keep going.

Part Two
Film Directors in Britain

Carol Reed accepts his Oscar for *Oliver!* (1968). (Movie Star News)

9

Carol Reed
The Disenchanted

The British film industry, as mentioned above, has maintained a symbiotic relationship with the American film industry throughout the history of the cinema. Hence the problems that confront a director working within the British studio system are largely identical with those that face his American counterpart. This is especially true since American capital has over the years become the principal source of finance for British production.

Consequently, when Carol Reed began his career in films in the mid-1930s, he had to serve the same kind of apprenticeship in the studio system as American directors who entered the film industry at that time. Reed was born in London in 1906; and, like George Cukor, he came to films from the theater and was at first assigned to be a dialogue director. In this capacity he quickly demonstrated his talent for coaching actors. Reed also felt that his background in the theater gave him a penchant for filming thrillers. "As a young man in the theater," he explained, "I became an assistant to Edgar Wallace, who wrote and produced so many melodramas. I suppose that helped me to see their effectiveness, their appealing values." Reed was shortly advanced to directing low-budget films; and once he had proved his competence and dependability at this level of production, he was promoted in the ranks of studio directors and given a greater degree of freedom in the choice and handling of the subjects he filmed.

The first film he directed, *Midshipman Easy* (1935), is a period picture based on Marryat's novel about a lad (Hughie Greene) who grows to maturity while serving on a British vessel. The young man quickly gains the respect of the older sailors on board and leads them in the capture of a Spanish merchant ship. Later he catches Don Silvio, a Spanish bandit, by masquerading as a female passenger in a coach that Don Silvio seeks to rob. The brigand escapes but is taken again in the final battle between the Spanish thieves and the ship's crew. Reed stages this skirmish with a verve that is typical of the tongue-in-cheek manner in which he directs the whole film.

Reed's early films, such as *Midshipman Easy*, are not remarkable; but then few British films before World War II were. In the silent period British film distributors depended so heavily on films from abroad, especially the United States, that in 1927 the British government established a quota system, whereby British studios regularly had to produce a specified number of domestic motion pictures if they

163

were to be permitted to continue importing movies for distribution from America and elsewhere. This led to the production each year of several "quota quickies," films that were, with rare exceptions, bargain-basement imitations of Hollywood movies, slipshod affairs turned out just to meet this need.[1] As a result, movies of artistic quality became something of a rarity among British productions and were of course the work of directors like Hitchcock and Reed.

In 1938 the Quota Act was revised with a view to discouraging the production of quota quickies. The new version stipulated that British producers must allocate sufficient funds for the making of domestic films to allow an adequate amount of time for preproduction preparation, shooting, and the final shaping of each picture. At this point Hitchcock was soon to depart for America; but English directors like Carol Reed took advantage of this increased support for British production to produce films that although still modestly made by Hollywood standards, demonstrated incontestably the artistry of which British film makers were capable.

Arthur Knight sums up the situation thus in *The Liveliest Art*: "At last the craftsmen in the British studios could take some pride in their work, and this new attitude was reflected immediately in their films. . . . For the first time there were English pictures that seemed to be looking with some insight and appreciation at the life and spirit of the country itself. They spoke of the British character, British institutions—even of social problems such as unemployment and nationalization—with unprecedented frankness and awareness."[2]

An outstanding example of this new trend in British film making was Carol Reed's *The Stars Look Down* (1940), which brought Reed serious critical attention both in England and in America. *The Stars Look Down* is an uncompromising picture of life in a Welsh mining community. A group of miners calls a strike without union support because they insist that flood waters stored up in the mine will burst forth unexpectedly, unless they are located before any further mining is done. After months of no work, the miners are forced to return to the mines without redress. The inevitable disaster occurs, and several miners perish in the flood.

The unvarnished depiction of life in a mining town that Reed gives us in *The Stars Look Down* has rarely been equaled. The opening image in the picture is of the huge machinery with which the mine is operated towering above the miners' cottages against the skyline, a shot that is repeated often in the film to remind the audience of how the mine dominates the lives of all who live within its shadow. Perhaps the strongest scene in the film is that in which the mine owner dies of a stroke just as he is on his way to save the trapped miners with the help of a map that gives the whereabouts of abandoned tunnels through which the men can escape. As he crumples to the ground in death, the map falls from his hands into a stream and floats away. From that moment the viewer knows that the trapped men are doomed.

"Reed was only thirty-three when he made this work, and he had not yet acquired the technical virtuosity of his later style," says Pauline Kael; "but this straightforward film may just possibly be his best."[3] Certainly *The Star Look Down* is among the best of Reed's films, although one hesitates to place it at the very top of the list when one considers the three motion pictures Reed made from scripts by

Graham Greene, which will be taken up shortly. At the time Reed made *The Stars Look Down*, Greene was film critic for *The Spectator*, and it is interesting to see what Reed's future collaborator thought of *The Stars Look Down*.

"Mr. Carol Reed, who began some years ago so impressively with *Midshipman Easy*," Greene wrote, "has at last had his chance and has magnificiently taken it." Greene goes on to enumerate some of the memorable scenes from the film, particularly those in which we watch the men imprisoned in the cave-in: "[T]he youth who was to have been played in a football trial on Saturday and who refuses to believe that Saturday has ever come and gone in their darkness; the old miner feeding the new young hand with cough lozenges; the man with religious mania and the boozer's muttered confession" all testify to Reed's assured direction.

Moreover, Greene mentions the authentic flavor of the film, constructed as it is of "grit and slag-heap, back-to-back cottages, and little scrubby railway stations. . . . Once before Mr. Reed tried his hand at a documentary story—*Bank Holiday* (1938). It was highly praised and was full of 'characters,' but it smelt of the studio. Here one forgets the casting altogether; he handles his players like a master, so that one remembers them only as people."[4]

Reed's next film, *Night Train to Munich* (1940), is an entertaining thriller that presages *The Third Man* and his other films with Graham Greene, just as *The Stars Look Down* foreshadows later serious works like *Odd Man Out*. Rex Harrison is Gus Bennett, a British spy tangling with Nazi agents in situations that are alternately humorous and hair-raising.

The film opens with newsreel footage of Nazi soldiers shown marching across the map of Austria, Czechoslovakia, and other countries that had already fallen under German domination by the time the film was made. Nazi agent Karl Marsen (Paul Henreid), masquerading as a Czech patriot, comes to England with orders to kidnap Herr Bomosch, an important Czech scientist working there, and bring him back to Czechoslovakia to work for the Nazis. When he succeeds in doing so, Bennett is sent to Czechoslovakia disguised as a Nazi officer to rescue the scientist and his daughter, who was abducted with him. When his ruse is discovered, all three of them make a narrow escape to Switzerland.

Rarely has a film invited comparison with Hitchcock's thrillers of the 1930s and stood up so well to the comparison. "So much is pure Hitchcock," William K. Everson points out in unpublished program notes for the film: the kindly occulist whose consulting room is a front for Nazi espionage; the rather decent villain (Marsen), who, like more than one Hitchcock villain, is a good sport about losing; and the marvelous chase sequence "that is right out of Hitchcock's top drawer." The latter scene is climaxed by Bennett jumping from one cable car to another, while the two cars pass each other over a chasm, so that he can join Herr Bomosch and his daughter, who have already gotten to safety.

Reed made two excellent films about the armed forces during the war. One was *The Way Ahead* (1944), a drama about the ordinary servicemen's view of the war, and the other was the Academy Award–winning documentary *The True Glory* (1945), about the Allied invasion of Europe. Reed and his collaborator, American filmmaker Garson Kanin, sifted through miles of footage taken by combat photographers, some of which was perhaps shot by George Stevens, at that time a member of the U.S. Signal Corps. Reed and Kanin put together a powerful document about the Allied campaign in Europe, narrated by General Eisenhower, Commander of the Allied Expeditionary Forces, and by a score of unnamed servicemen and women.

The experience Reed gained in making wartime documentaries unquestionably influenced his postwar cinematic style, enabling him to develop further in *Odd Man Out* (1947) the strong sense of realism that had first appeared in *The Stars Look Down*—a contention borne out by James DeFelice's monograph on the film.[5] The documentary approach that Reed used to tell the story of *Odd Man Out* was one to which audiences were ready to respond. Wartime movies, both documentaries and fiction films, had conditioned British moviegoers to expect a greater degree of realism in postwar films. A similar trend toward a heightened realism in the cinema was in progress in America at the same time, for the reasons given earlier.

Enterprising British producers like Michael Balcon believed that British films should be made to appeal primarily to the home market, rather than to the elusive American market that other producers like J. Arthur Rank were trying to conquer. It was the former, as things turned out, who won the day; for it was the British films that were wholly English in character and situation which were the first to win wide popularity in the United States. Among these was Reed's *Odd Man Out*.

This was the first film Reed both produced and directed, a factor that guaranteed him a greater degree of creative freedom than he had enjoyed before the war. For the first time, too, the theme that is to appear so often in his work is perceptible in *Odd Man Out*. In depicting in this and other films a hunted, lonely hero caught in the middle of a crisis usually not of his own making, Reed implies that one can achieve maturity and self-mastery only by accepting the challenges life puts in his way and by struggling with them as best he can. "What interests me," he said, "is a situation in which someone is confronted by a problem, rather than just the situation of two people trying to get together."

The character who embodies this theme in *Odd Man Out* is Johnny McQueen (James Mason), the leader of a group of revolutionaries in Belfast. An introductory preface tells us: "This story is told against a background of political unrest in a city of Northern Ireland. It is not concerned with the struggle between the law and an illegal organization, but only with the conflict in the hearts of the people when they become unexpectedly involved." This preface is important, since it makes clear that the film is primarily concerned not with a political struggle but with the human condition, specifically with the short supply of charity in the world.

After the preface Johnny and his band are shown robbing a mill in order to obtain money to finance their revolutionary activities. During the holdup Johnny shoots a policeman and is himself wounded. His confederates panic and escape without him, leaving Johnny to wander the city from noon until midnight looking for refuge. In the course of Johnny's long day's journey into night he encounters an assortment of people who admittedly do not turn him over to the police, but neither do they offer him any positive aid since they fear getting involved with him further.

His friends go in search of him, but their efforts too are ineffectual, perhaps

Odd Man Out (1947), with James Mason (center) and F. J. McCormick (right), is one of Reed's most significant films. (Museum of Modern Art/Film Stills Archive)

because their motive, whether or not they realize it, is more a concern to preserve their sense of honor by rescuing their leader than any personal care for Johnny. Even his girl Kathleen has her own self-centered concern in trying to find him before the police do, for she would rather die with him than endure a lonely life without him. No one is really capable of extending a selfless charity or compassion to Johnny for his own sake.

Despite his increasing delirium, Johnny seems to realize this. As he nears death he recites these lines form the thirteenth chapter of Saint Paul's First Epistle to the Corinthians, not only as a denunciation of a world that is bereft of true charity, but as a signal of his own spiritual conversion: "Though I speak with the tongues of men and of angels and have not charity, I am become as sounding brass; and though I have all faith, so that I could move mountains, and have not charity, I am nothing."

With *Odd Man Out* Reed proved definitively that he had full command of his directorial powers. The picture captures our interest from the outset with the robbery, photographed in a stark newsreel fashion. The tension of the scene is heightened by the insistent clamor of the burglar alarm, which can still be heard ringing in the distance while the escape car speeds away from the scene.

As the film progresses, Reed employs his camera subjectively from time to time to indicate how things look from Johnny's point of view. At times Reed tilts his camera to photograph the action from odd or distorted angles, in order to remind the viewer that Johnny is growing more frantic and delirious as his life slips away. At other times street noises and other ordinary sounds are magnified on the sound track, as if they were pounding within the head of the tormented man while he moves through the dark, sinister streets of the night city. All these details add to the impact of the film.

The Spectator hailed Odd Man Out as the first masterpiece ever to be produced by a British film studio. James Agee added, "If the world should end tomorrow, as this film rather substantially suggests that it must, and may as well, this film would furnish one of the more appropriate epitaphs: a sad, magnificent summing up of a night city." The remake of Odd Man Out by an American director as The Lost Man in 1968 only served to confirm the brilliance of Reed's film by comparison.

In 1948 Reed directed The Fallen Idol, the first of a trio of films that he made in collaboration with Graham Greene, all of which were based on Greene's fiction. In his introduction to his novella The Fallen Idol, Greene has written of the films he worked on with Reed in terms that implicitly describe the ideal relationship between an auteur director and the script writer with whom he collaborates: "Their success is due to Carol Reed, the only director I know with that particular warmth of human sympathy, the extraordinary feeling for the right face for the right part, the exactitude of cutting, and not the least important, the power of sympathizing with an author's worries and an ability to guide him."[6]

In writing the scripts for all three films on which he collaborated with Reed, Greene conferred with the director throughout the period that he was composing the screenplay. For that reason, said Greene, it is difficult in many instances to remember which of them contributed what change in the original story in each case. Greene was certain, however, that when he was adapting his novella into the screenplay for The Fallen Idol, it was Reed's idea to make the scene of the story a foreign embassy in London, with the child Felipe (Bobby Henrey) the son of an ambassador. This served not only to explain the cavernous size of the house in which Felipe lives, but also to delineate still further Felipe's feeling of being an outsider. For he is not only a child living in a largely adult world as he was in the novella, but he is also a foreigner living in an alien milieu. Hence Felipe feels doubly lonely and insecure, and is all the more apt to misunderstand what is going on around him.

Reed enables us to experience Felipe's sense of being a lonely outsider by often showing him catching glimpses of the adult world through a windowpane or through a bannister railing as he sits at the top of a staircase, remote from the adult world that he is observing. By the same token, when shooting from Felipe's point of view, Reed employs very low camera angles to show the world as a child sees it. Furthermore, the director frequently allows the viewer to hear only snatches of adult conversation on the sound track when Felipe is in a scene, to indicate how easily he misses the significance of what is being said around him.

In the opening sequence Felipe bids good-bye to his parents who are going away on a trip, leaving him in the care of Mr. and Mrs. Baines (Ralph Richardson and Sonia Dresdel), the butler and housekeeper. Felipe idolizes Baines, who manufactures adventurous stories about his past life to entertain Felipe; and Felipe, of course, believes them all. What Felipe does not understand about Baines is that he is having an affair with Julie, an embassy secretary (Michele Morgan), and that the imperious, wily Mrs. Baines is getting suspicious of her husband's behavior and beginning to badger him about it.

Events reach a crisis when Baines invites Julie to spend the day with him and Felipe, while his wife has ostensibly gone to visit her ailing aunt. That evening, after Felipe has been packed off to bed, he is abruptly awakened by Mrs. Baines, who insists that he tell her to what room Baines and the girl have retired. Frightened and confused, Felipe screams for Baines, then runs out onto the fire escape, as if sensing impending disaster. Baines comes out of the bedroom to see what is wrong and is confronted on the grand staircase by his frantic wife, while Felipe watches from the fire escape. Quite by accident the overwrought Mrs. Baines trips and falls down the long staircase to her death. From his limited vantage point, however, Felipe believes that Baines has pushed his wife to her death.

Reed has brilliantly shot and edited this whole sequence in a way that allows us to see both what actually transpired between Baines and his wife, and also how it appeared to Felipe.

At this point begins a series of spiralling ironies, in which Felipe seeks to protect his only friend by lying to the police in Baines's behalf. But Felipe's lies are so inexpert that they only serve to increase the police's suspicion of Baines. Julie begs Felipe not to tell any more lies, not even to help his friend; and Felipe resolutely goes to the police investigators to make a clean breast of the situation as he understands it—just at the moment when they are exonerating Baines.

Since Felipe believes that Baines murdered his wife, what he wants to say to the police would be enough to implicate Baines in her death once more. But none of the adults will listen to him as he insistently pulls on the police inspector's trousers. He is left standing alone and puzzled. Then, with a shrug, he runs upstairs to his nursery room where he is free of the bewildering adult world below.

But Felipe has not been bitterly disillusioned with life as is his counterpart in Greene's original novella, or as is the lad in Joseph Losey's film *The Go-Between*. In the latter picture Leo, like Felipe, becomes unwittingly immeshed in the private world of adult secrets and betrayals and is embittered for life. That these darker implications are not to be found in *The Fallen Idol* is in keeping with the relatively lighter tone of that film. Nonetheless, in *The Fallen Idol* one finds Reed's serious theme of the lonely outsider coping with a crisis not of his own devising and thereby achieving a degree of maturity. It is illustrated in a lad who is taking his first steps toward maturity by coming through a traumatic experience virtually unscathed.

In his handling of young Bobby Henrey, Reed shows his deft ability in directing young actors, thereby foreshadowing the collection of fine performances he later coaxed from the children in *Oliver!*.

After the success of *The Fallen Idol*, Alexander Korda, production chief of London Films, asked Greene to write an original story for Reed to film, to be set in postwar Vienna. Greene obliged with *The Third Man* (1949), which won the Grand Prize at the Cannes Film Festival.

The hero of *The Third Man* is Holly Martins (Joseph Cotton), an American writer of pulp Westerns, who has come to Vienna at the invitation of an old school chum, Harry Lime (Orson Welles). Upon his arrival, Martins is shocked to learn that Lime is being buried that day, having been the victim of a traffic accident. At the cemetery Martins meets Anna, Lime's mistress (Alida Valli), and Major Calloway (Trevor Howard), the British army officer in charge of investigating Lime's death.

Martins at first refuses to believe Calloway's contention that Lime was involved in the most sordid of postwar rackets: trafficking in black-market penicillin of such inferior quality that it has caused widespread sickness and death. Martins is forced to believe Calloway, however, when he discovers that Harry is still very much alive and that his "death" was part of an elaborate plot to evade the police and continue his vile racketeering. Shaken and disillusioned, Martins agrees to help the police capture Lime, and the film reaches its climax in an exciting chase through the shadowy sewers of Vienna. There is a memorable shot near the end of this sequence taken from street level, showing Lime's fingers desperately reaching through a sewer grating, in a vain attempt to escape to the street through a manhole by dislodging its cover. The pursuit finally ends with Martins obliging the gravely wounded Harry by killing him before the police can find him.

Reed attributes the phenomenal success of the picture to the fact that it was one of the first British films to be shot almost entirely on location. This enabled him to give an authentic documentary look to the film right from the opening tour of the city, in which a narrator tells the audience that Vienna is no longer the glamorous prewar city of Strauss waltzes, but a ravaged, decadent postwar city. It is just this corrupt atmosphere that Reed, with the help of Robert Krasker's Academy Award–winning cinematography, captures in the film.

Another great contribution to the movie's atmosphere was made by the haunting musical score composed by Anton Karas and played by him on the zither. Reed discovered Karas playing in a Viennese café while he was scouting locations for the film and brought him back to London to record the score. Barbara Hopkins, the sound recordist on the film, remembers that one day during a recording session Reed felt that Karas was not executing a passage with the same feeling that he had achieved when playing it the previous evening while sitting beneath Reed's kitchen table. "So Carol had his kitchen table brought to the studio. This is a man who knows what he wants," she concludes.[7]

Reed's selection of Orson Welles to play Harry Lime was another stroke of genius. Initially Welles had turned down the part, but Reed persuaded him to try playing a scene. The day that Welles arrived on location in Vienna, Reed was preparing to shoot the chase through the sewers, and Welles complained that the bad air in the sewer passages would give him pneumonia. "Finally I persuaded him to shoot the scene," Reed told me. "Then Orson conferred with the cameraman, made some suggestions; and we did the chase again. Of course he was sold on finishing the picture by then, and he gave a superlative performance."

Lime's corrupt charm is perfectly epitomized in a line Greene credits Welles with adding to his dialogue. Harry tells Holly not to think too badly of the decadence of Vienna, since out of the Italy of the Middle Ages, which was just as decadent, came

Orson Welles in *The Third Man* **(1949). (Cinema Bookshop, London)**

the Renaissance, while a respectable country like Switzerland only managed to produce the cuckoo clock. In summing up Welles's performance in *The Third Man*, Penelope Houston writes, "Harry Lime walked straight into the cinema's mythology on the strength of a line of dialogue about Switzerland and Cuckoo clocks and a shot of a hand clutching at a sewer grating."[8]

In analyzing the contributions made by Greene, Welles, Karas, and others to the film, one should not forget that ultimately it is Reed the director who must be credited with blending their work into the superb motion picture that is *The Third Man*. In his introduction to *The Third Man* Graham Greene gives an excellent example of how Reed can sense what would be just the right touch for a given scene. Greene recalled that he wanted to end *The Third Man* with Anna going away with Martins after Harry's second funeral, since he felt that the audience would not accept an unhappy ending to a thriller. Reed, however, preferred to have Anna walk right by Martins and out of the cemetery, stoically refusing to acknowledge the man who had turned Harry in to the police.

Hence the final image of the film shows the gaunt, determined Anna, staring impassively ahead as she walks toward the camera, past Martins, and out of the frame, leaving the viewer with a last, lingering shot of the bleak autumnal landscape of the cemetery, as the zither magic fades away. Greene conceded that Reed was right in the end, for the film's conclusion, done Reed's way, is perfect.

Commenting on the somber atmosphere of Reed films like *The Third Man*, Pauline Kael writes, "In Reed's postwar cities, war had changed the survivors; they were tired, ravaged opportunists who no longer felt like you or me. So the city was a nightmare city and the simple American (Joseph Cotton in *The Third Man*) or the fresh English girl (Claire Bloom in *The Man Between*) who stumbled into it was like a tourist in hell. The intrigues were part of the living rot of postwar corruption."[9]

Although *The Man Between* (1953) was not written by Graham Greene, it is a spy story that contains many of the same basic ingredients as *The Third Man*. Yet it does not approach the caliber of the earlier film. Perhaps the reason is that, as the story unfolds, the emphasis shifts from Susanne (Claire Bloom), the English girl visiting her brother, a British army doctor in West Berlin, to a middle-aged German; and the picture therefore lacks focus. Ivo, the German (James Mason), is "the man between" of the title. He is an ex-Nazi being blackmailed by Russian agents into helping them capture a West Berliner named Kastner, who has been smuggling refugees from East Berlin into the Western sector of the city.

Ivo is a man caught between the promptings of his innate human decency, which has been rekindled now that the Nazi regime of which he was a part has passed away, and the demands of the Russian agents who threaten to expose his past. One day Susanne is mistaken for a fugitive the Russians are after, and they take her to the Eastern sector. Ivo arranges to have her returned to West Berlin. He hopes to escape with her, but he is destined to remain a "man between" to the last. Susanne crosses the border into West Berlin safely, but Ivo is recognized and shot by Russian guards as he follows close behind her. The gate of the Western sector closes in front of him as he lies in the snow and dies.

Our Man in Havana (1959) is the third Reed-Greene collaboration, and, like *The Man Between*, is a spy thriller. Greene adapted the script from his own novel, which was published shortly before Castro overthrew the Batista regime in Cuba, and it deals with the last days of the Batista dictatorship.

Alec Guinness plays Jim Wormold, a diffident British vacuum cleaner salesman living in Havana who gets immeshed in a web of espionage. Reed saw the character of Wormold as a sort of plain, colorless man who usually goes unnoticed by others. "Carol and I disagreed about that," Guinness told me. "I felt that I should play Wormold as a much more clearly defined character, an untidy, defeated sort of man." Despite their differences, however, Reed and Guinness conferred throughout the filming, and Guinness evolved a performance that perfectly brings to life the Greene character.

Our Man in Havana is fairly farcical at the outset, when Wormold consistently muddles his duties as an undercover agent for the British government. But later on the mood shifts to a more serious tone, as enemy agents stalk Wormold and try to kill him. "I didn't play Wormold any differently in the latter part of the film than I did earlier on," said Guinness. "It was Carol Reed who created the more sinister atmosphere needed towards the end of the film."

Reed said that at the beginning of the film he lighted the sets for comedy, "that is, rather brightly and flatly, catching the beauty of the streets too." Then, as the picture moved toward melodrama, he used "sharp, hard lights in the night exteriors, making the streets slick and shiny, getting a brittle black-and-white feeling."[10] An example of this latter kind of lighting is in the scene in which Wormold traps and kills a counteragent who has been assigned to liquidate him. Reed lighted the scene in a murky, shadowy manner reminiscent of the night scenes in *The Third Man*. In summary, *Our Man in Havana* is an entertaining spy film; to say that it is not in a class with a masterpiece like *The Third Man* is merely to recognize that it suffers only by comparison with the standard that Reed and Greene had set for themselves by their previous achievements.

The Key (1958) is the only postwar Reed film that is set during World War II; yet its scripter, Carl Foreman, who also wrote *High Noon* for Fred Zinnemann, maintained that *The Key* is not, strictly speaking, a war movie. Foreman rather used the war "as background for a personal story in which men and women came to grips, not with death but with life, and with themselves.[11]

David Ross (William Holden), the hero, is captain of one of the ocean-going tugs of the British Salvage Service that rescue ships torpedoed or lost from their convoys. Like all of his comrades, he is a man whose existence constantly hovers between life and death because of the risky, not to say suicidal, nature of their work. Chris Ford (Trevor Howard), another tug captain, introduces David to his girl Stella (Sophia Loren) and almost immediately gives Ross a key to Stella's apartment.

Ford explains that because of the precariousness of their lives, a custom has grown up among the men of the Salvage Service, according to which whoever falls heir to Stella should pass on a duplicate key to her flat to the comrade that he wants to succeed him, should he die on a mission. "Put the key away and forget that you've got it until you need it," Chris concludes. "And don't worry; to her we're all the same man."

Inevitably, David does succeed Chris as Stella's lover after Chris is killed at sea.

But by this time, the strain of loving and losing David's three predecessors is beginning to tell on Stella. The viewer infers this in the scene in which David is using a newspaper to start a fire in Stella's hearth. As the paper begins to burn, Stella notices a picture of a tug on one of its pages. The boat seems to be going up in flames as the paper catches fire, and the overwrought Stella takes this as a premonition of David's death.

Later David returns to her after a mission on which he temporarily was thought to have died in action. Even though he is now safe, Stella vows that she will never again go through such an ordeal. She decides to take the next train for London and a new life. As the film was originally shot, David rushes to the depot to make Stella change her mind but arrives too late to stop her departure. He forlornly turns around and walks away, lost from view in a cloud of smoke and steam as he murmurs, "I'll find her when I get back to London. I'll find her."

Reed liked this ending, which recalls the conclusion of *The Third Man*. But the American distributors of the film prevailed on him to alter the film's last scene, so that Ross catches the train and is reunited with Stella on board. Reed has since regretted that decision. "A man and a woman don't always get together in life," he said. "I don't like to tie up things too neatly. Life isn't like that." Unquestionably Reed's original ending for the film is much more in keeping with the thrust of the whole film as outlined here, indicating once more that the industry should have deferred to the artist and not the other way around.

In 1963 Reed made another in his series of thrillers, *The Running Man*, with Laurence Harvey, Lee Remick, and Alan Bates. He followed this in 1965 with *The Agony and the Ecstasy*, with Charlton Heston as Michelangelo and Rex Harrison, who had not appeared in a film for Reed since *Night Train to Munich*, giving a splendid performance as Pope Julius II, the artist's volatile patron.

"That picture didn't turn out right," Reed conceded; it was made, he explained, at a time when Hollywood was excited about movie epics that were long enough to have an intermission like a play. Reed would have made the film differently, had he been given the choice. "I would like to have made a shorter, tighter film, rather than a three-hour extravaganza with an intermission." In his view there were simply too many scenes of Michelangelo painting, and too many scenes of him quarreling with the pope over their artistic differences about his religious paintings; moreover, the scenes in question often went on too long. "It's a funny thing," he observed; "a scene can be good at three minutes; and if it's overwitten into four, the extra minute weakens it. On the other hand, a ten-minute scene may not be too long if there is ten minutes of material there to develop."

Reed also noted that he soft-pedaled the notion that Michelangelo might have been homosexual, because there is nothing conclusive about this in any of the documentation about him. "It seems quite certain that he wasn't interested in women," said Reed; "but that may have been just because he was so wrapped up in his work. I didn't think that it was right to write into the screenplay something that the historians themselves weren't sure about."

At all events, none of the films that Reed made in this period was outstanding. But he proved with *Oliver!* (1968) that he was back in top form, winning the

Academy Award as best director, while the film was named best picture of the year. *Oliver!* was not based directly on Dickens's novel, as was David Lean's 1951 *Oliver Twist*, but on Lionel Bart's musical play. Reed brought it to life on the screen as one of the last big budget musicals, just before rising production costs made musicals designed on this scale prohibitively expensive.

In any screen musical there arises the perennial problem of getting the film audience to accept the theatrical convention of characters bursting into song to express their feelings amid realistic settings. Reed solved this problem by having production designer John Box create sets that were somewhat stylized representations of nineteenth-century London. He also evoked stylized performances from his actors, particularly from Ron Moody as the villain Fagin, in order to make movie realism meet musical romanticism half way. Fagin, however, is not quite the despicable villain that Dickens portrayed, but an eccentric impresario who trains poor boys like Oliver (Mark Lester) "to pick a pocket or two," in order to teach them to survive in the tough London slums.

Consequently Oliver emerges, like Felipe in *The Fallen Idol*, as a "boy between," a lad wedged somewhere between the world of childhood to which he really belongs and the adult world into which he has been prematurely thrust by circumstances. In her review of *Oliver!*, Pauline Kael paid Reed a tribute that sums up his work in the cinema: "I applaud the commercial heroism of a director who can steer a huge production and keep his sanity and perspective and decent human feelings as beautifully intact as they are in *Oliver!*.[12]

Reed has succeeded in *Oliver!* in integrating the songs and dances with the plot so that all three combine to move the story forward. For example, Fagin sings a song to explain his philosophy of life to Oliver ("You've Got to Pick a Pocket or Two") and then has some of the boys go through a demonstration of the art of pocket picking that amounts to a miniballet.

Reed was convinced that the only way to insure the overall artistic unity of a film is to oversee the production from the earliest stages of planning right up to the last stages of postproduction. "Not enough directors are willing to do this," he said. "After shooting is over they're thinking of their next picture and are willing to turn the current one over to the studio to cut. To make a good film you have to sit down at the Movieola day after day, running the footage over and over." After a while, "you begin to see the picture taking shape, establishing a rhythm of its own. That's when you begin to feel the picture's natural pace and you develop it."[13]

The Public Eye (1972; British title: *Follow Me*) brought Reed back to the contemporary scene with story of Charles Sidley, a staid British accountant (Michael Jayston), who hires a detective (Topol) to shadow his wife Belinda (Mia Farrow), whom he suspects of taking a lover. In actual fact the bored young wife spends most of her time touring London and going to horror movies. In time the detective becomes her constant and amusing companion in these diversions, although she has no idea why he is tagging along after her. When she finds out, she leaves her husband; but the detective patches things up between them by suggesting that they both tour the city in the same fashion that Belinda and he had done.

A flimsy plot, to be sure, but one which Reed invests with charm, especially in his

Mark Lester, Jack Wild, and Ron Moody in *Oliver!* (1968). (Museum of Modern Art/Film Stills Archive)

handsome shots of London in summertime. One day in late summer I watched Reed shooting a scene for the film on location in the Mayfair section of London. Reed, a tall, mild-mannered man, seemed to be everywhere at once: chatting with the proprietress of the hat shop who had given over her establishment for the day's shooting; whispering directions to Mia Farrow, who was to enter the shop from a cab at the curb; and advising Topol, who was having trouble starting the motor scooter on which he was to enter the scene. Here was a man to whom no detail of the production was too minor for his attention, a craftsman who polished every aspect of a film on which he worked.

A genuinely self-effacing man, Reed was never impressed by the awards and honors that he garnered throughout his career (he was knighted in 1952). Summarizing his own approach to film making, he once said, "I give the public what *I* like," and hope they will like it too.[14] More often than not, they did.

10
David Lean
The Undefeated

Even though David Lean adapted to the screen several literary works by worthy authors ranging from Charles Dickens to E. M. Forster, there is little question that, despite their distinguished literary antecedents, he is really the creative genius behind the films that bear his name. In discussing the degree of personal involvement in his motion pictures, Lean pointed out that his work on a film began at the script stage and continued throughout the film making process, as one would expect with an *auteur* director.

"In the early stages I suppose the director is, as it were, a shaper of the film. And then, of course, as the shooting gets nearer, he takes more and more responsibility," he said. "One tends to put one's own point of view over through the actors. And so, a kind of personal taste or touch will come out. Above all, the director chooses what the audience sees, and when. He decides whether you shall see it in a close-up or long shot. . . . So that in itself has quite an effect, of course."[1] Once the film was finished, Lean said, he was particularly interested in supervising the editing. Since he had been an editor, he found it hard to keep his hands off the celluloid. Furthermore, he always tried to shoot with a plan for editing the film in mind, in order to be sure to get the shots he knew would be needed.

The successful films Lean made more than justify the artistic independence that producers extended to him. "This question of freedom, it's a question of one's record, I suppose; and I suppose that I've had a fairly good record," he noted. "The financing of movies is a big gamble, and, considering the high stakes involved, I feel that I have been treated well. On the whole my own final cut of a picture has been allowed to stand. This may be partly due to the fact that I was an editor for many years and am generally more ruthless than the producer."[2]

David Lean was born in Croydon, England, in 1908 and got his first job in a film studio as a teen-ager serving tea to the cast and crew during breaks in shooting. At the age of twenty he became an assistant cameraman. He eventually became an assistant director and then an assistant editor. After a term spent in editing *British Movietone News*, he graduated to editing feature films. Among them are the screen adaptations of two plays of George Bernard Shaw, *Pygmalion* (1938), the musical version of which George Cukor filmed as *My Fair Lady*, and *Major Barbara* (1941).

"I became a good cutter," Lean recalled, "and I was offered the chance to direct low-budget films. But I said no because if I made a film of this sort and it flopped,

Peter O'Toole and David Lean on location for *Lawrence of Arabia* **(1962), for which Lean won an Academy Award. (Cinema Bookshop, London)**

people would say that I had done a poor job, not that I hadn't had enough time or money to make it right." Lean's first real break came when Noel Coward offered him the chance to codirect *In Which We Serve* (1942), for which Coward had written an original script.

Coward based *In Which We Serve* on the exploits of his friend Lord Louis Mountbatten, captain of the destroyer H.M.S. *Kelly*, which was torpedoed by the Germans in the battle of Crete during World War II. The film's preface says, "This is the story of a ship"; but it is also the story of her crew, whose mutual loyalty is grounded in their devotion to their ship, the *Torrin*, just as the group unity of the flight crew in Howard Hawks's *Air Force* is focused around their bomber, the *Mary Ann*.

The picture begins with the sinking of the *Torrin* by the Germans in the Mediterranean and then focuses on a group of her survivors as they cling to a life raft floating in the sea. Each of them recalls in a series of flashbacks how his life has been inseparably involved with the fortunes of his ship ever since he joined her crew. *In Which We Serve* ends with the rescue of the survivors of the *Torrin* and their eventual dispersal for new assignments. The film concludes with the following spoken narration: "Here ends the story of a ship. But there will be other ships, for we are an island race. There will always be other ships, and other men to sail in them. They give to us and to all their countrymen eternal pride."

Lean and Coward brought to bear the realistic techniques being used in wartime documentaries to give their film an urgent sense of authenticity, to which Lean's experience as a newsreel editor contributed a great deal. Coward, who played the ship's captain, was so pleased with Lean's work on the film that he invited Lean to film any of his plays that he chose. Accordingly Lean formed his own production unit and did screen treatments of a trio of Coward plays: *This Happy Breed*, *Blithe Spirit*, and *Brief Encounter*. The choice of film subjects that Lean made from Coward's work reflected the changing tastes of the mass audience during and after the war.

The budding realism that had been initiated in British cinema in the late 1930s by films like Carol Reed's *The Stars Look Down* continued to grow in British films during the war years because of morale-building movies like *In Which We Serve* and *This Happy Breed* (1944), which is about the people on the home front.

Nevertheless escapism dominated most of the output of British studios during the war. Penelope Houston writes: "Escapism in the British cinema during the war and after involved endless permutations of the same star équipe, as James Mason and Stewart Granger, Margaret Lockwood and Phyllis Calvert, flung themselves into Regency disguise, took to the roads as highwaymen, poisoned off old retainers (with, if memory can be trusted, doses from large bottles obligingly labelled 'poison'), and cheated each other out of inheritances. . . . One way or another, this was a cinema for a society weary of restrictions and ration-books; and it seems more than mere coincidence that it barely survived the end of rationing." (In fact, after a steady diet of historical epics of this sort, one small-town exhibitor is said to have written to his distributor at the time, "Don't send me no more pictures about people who write with feathers!")

Lightminded farces, as well as historical spectacles, were also part of this trend in escapist entertainment; and to the former genre Lean contributed *Blithe Spirit* (1945), in which Rex Harrison plays a harried husband named Charles, whose first wife Elvira comes back to haunt him after he marries his second wife Ruth. Margaret Rutherford contributes to the mad mischief as Madame Arcati, the wacky medium who rides a bicycle as if it were a broomstick and whom Charles enlists to help him get rid of the spirit of his departed spouse.

Unfortunately, Elvira is not to be so easily disposed of. She sabotages Charles's car, in order that he will die in an auto accident and join her in the great beyond. But Ruth takes the car out for a spin before he does; and hence it is she, and not Charles, who joins Elvira in the hereafter. As a result of this neat plot twist, Charles now has, not one, but two deceased wives to haunt him.

Only when Lean borrows gimmicks from other films about ghosts does this movie become unconvincing, opines Michael Anderegg in his book on the director. Thus the "invisible" Elvira driving a car, says Anderegg, is "too hoary a cliché to be very funny."[3] To set the record straight, Anderegg's memory has played him false, since the scene as described is not in the film. All in all, in *Blithe Spirit* Lean has served up a delightful comic fantasy.

Then, when realism gained the ascendancy in postwar British cinema, Lean turned to Coward's bittersweet one-act drama of middle-aged romance, *Still Life*, which became Lean's first important international success, *Brief Encounter* (1945). Laura Jesson (Celia Johnson), a housewife who goes to town once a week for shopping and a matinée at the pictures, meets Dr. Alec Harvey (Trevor Howard) on one of her excursions; and their casual relationship slowly develops into romance. Both of them, however, mutually agree to part in order not to jeopardize the happiness of their respective families. The plot of *Brief Encounter* is reminiscent of the kind of romantic tale that fills the pages of the "true confessions" type of magazine; but Lean treated his material with a degree of taste that this type of story rarely receives. The scene in which Laura and Alec see each other for the last time is an index of the skill with which Lean keeps the tender moments of the film from slipping into sentimentality.

Alec and Laura sit in the grubby tearoom of the railway station waiting for Alec's train, which will arrive before Laura's. Suddenly their quiet intimacy is interrupted by Myrtle Bagot, a gossipy friend of Laura's, who joins them and begins chattering in her usual inane fashion. Alec and Laura can say nothing to each other, realizing that this unfortunate happenstance has robbed them of the opportunity of even saying good-bye. Over Myrtle's prattle Alec's train can be heard pulling into the depot. Alec slowly rises, and we see in close-up his hand gently come to rest on Laura's shoulder before he goes out into the night. Laura is left staring blankly at Myrtle, who does not even notice that no one is listening to her.

Suddenly, at the sound of an oncoming train speeding toward the station, Laura rushes out onto the platform. As the lights from the windows of the passing train flash across her face, we know that she has conquered her impulse to commit suicide, in favor of her resolution to return to her husband and two children. This is a moment of triumph for Laura, whose sense of devotion to her family has over-

Brief Encounter **(1945) has Celia Johnson and Trevor Howard playing the leads in Lean's classic love story. (Museum of Modern Art/Film Stills Archive)**

come her despair at losing Alec. Implicit in this scene is the theme that would become prominent in Lean's work. 'I am drawn to the person who refuses to face defeat,'' he said, "even when they realize that their most cherished expectations may go unfulfilled." In retrospect one sees that this theme was already beginning to take shape in the story of the survivors of the *Torrin* in *In Which We Serve* and in the family facing wartime privations in *This Happy Breed*.

Great Expectations (1946) was the first of Lean's two adaptations of Dickens. Everywhere in the film there is evidence that the experience Lean had gained in his years as an editor had taught him how to build a scene with perfect timing. The opening sequence of *Great Expectations* is justly famous in this regard. The boy Pip, who has come to the cemetery to put flowers on his mother's grave, is frightened by its eerie atmosphere, which is heightened by the ominous sound of the wind moaning through creaking tree limbs. As Pip turns away from the grave to depart, Lean's camera moves slightly ahead of him to reveal a ferocious figure moving into the frame; just at that moment Lean cuts to a close-up of the brutish convict Magwitch, who grabs Pip and claps his hand over the boy's mouth. Lean allows the audience to see Magwitch a split second before Pip does, thus creating a sense of shock in the viewer that is immediately reinforced by Pip's own terrified reaction.

What he was trying to do in the scenes of Pip's childhood, Lean explained, was to make everything in the film larger than life, as it is in a boy's imagination. "The scenes of the boy Pip lying terrified in his bedroom after a night of fear, then creeping downstairs at dawn" and stealing food at the behest of the convict hiding out on the moors, "was something Dickens wrote as if he were right inside the boy himself. We tried in the film to make the audience share Pip's fears."[4]

In *Oliver Twist* (1948), Lean told the whole story from the point of view of a small boy, as he had done in the early sequences of *Great Expectations*. "The whole film was outsized," Lean remembered, "from the stylized sets built in forced perspective" to the stylized performances of the villains of the piece, Bill Sykes and Fagin. The role of Fagin, the old Jew who takes orphan boys under his wing to teach them to be successful pickpockets, was played by Alec Guinness. The actor copied the Cruishank illustrations from the first edition of *Oliver Twist* in creating his make-up for the part. "We made Fagin an outsize, and we hoped, an amusing Jewish villain," Lean said.[5]

Nevertheless, because of the touchy temper of the times, in which the memory of the Nazi annihilation of the Jews was so recent, Guinness's portrayal of Fagin was criticized as anti-Semitic, and the release of the film was delayed for a time in America and elsewhere. In his own production notes for the film, Lean had written that he wanted Fagin to start off in Oliver's eyes "as an amusing old gentleman; gradually this guise falls away and we see him in all his villainy."[6] Guinness accomplished this change perfectly. He projects Fagin as a grotesque individual who is nevertheless not entirely devoid of human qualities, even of a sense of humor. Indeed, the conception of Fagin in Carol Reed's *Oliver!* (1968), the musical version of *Oliver Twist*, owes more than a little to Guinness's portrayal of the old Jew.

For the film's initial release in America however, seven minutes were cut from Fagin's scenes. Most of the footage that was removed involved his comedy scenes early in the picture. "This left Fagin as a straight Jewish villain," Lean pointed out. "In my opinion this version was anti-Semitic."[7]

In 1950 Lean made a curious film called *Madeleine*, a documentary-type murder mystery that, like the actual case on which it was based, is left unsolved at the end. The audience somehow feels cheated when no final explanation of the facts is offered in the film. Lean, however, is in perfect accordance with the known facts in leaving the viewer with a question mark rather than a solution to the case of Madeleine Smith, a young lady of a genteel family of the last century accused of murdering her lover.

"In this great city of Glasgow," says a narrator voice-over on the sound track as the camera moves along the streets of the city, "there is a square which has nothing remarkable about its appearance; but there is one house that is exceptional: number seven. This house, which still remains, was the home of Madeleine Smith; perhaps her spirit still remains there, to listen for the tap of Emile L'Angelier's cane at her window." With this spoken introduction, the setting shifts from present day Glasgow to the day when Madeleine's father bought the house for his family.

The Smith family lives a very proper but stodgy existence, which bores Madeleine (Ann Todd). One night, some time later, while she is playing and singing listlessly for her family, the shadow of a man cavalierly twirling a cane appears on the sidewalk before the house. Madeleine knows that it is time for her rendez-vous with her lover Emile (Ivan Desny) and begs off continuing her concert. She rushes through the corridors of the mansion toward her tryst with her lover accompanied by a lush waltz on the sound track, symbolizing the romance that Emile has brought into her dull life.

Lean uses several visual images to indicated that the love of the wealthy Madeleine and the impecunious Emile is outside the conventions of the society in which she moves and therefore must be kept a secret. In one scene she and Emile are walking in the woods and hear the sound of bagpipes accompanying a dance in a nearby dance hall. Madeleine begins dancing a reel to the music issuing from a party of happy dancers that she and Emile can never join.

When Emile insists that Madeleine break her engagement to a man of her own class and marry him, she refuses, finally realizing that there is little but lust keeping them together. Emile counters that he will blackmail her into marrying him; instead he dies a short time later of arsenic poisoning. The ensuing trail, in which Madeleine is accused of having murdered Emile, should be the high point of a film that has built steadily in suspense from the beginning. Instead, the viewer's interest wanes as he listens to the lawyers for the prosecution and for the defense match wits in rather intricate arguments, punctuated by snippets of testimony from the witnesses for both sides.

The final verdict is one that could be given only in Scotland: Madeleine's guilt, says the jury, was "not proven." That verdict, the narrator explains, "means that Madeleine Smith left the court neither guilty nor not guilty, because the charge was 'not proven.'" He continues, "Madeleine Smith, you have heard the indictment: were you guilty or not guilty?" Madeleine looks into the camera as she drives off from the courthouse in a carriage, and a wry smile crosses her face. With that, the film ends. Lean's steadfast objectivity, which has led him to give no hint whether Madeleine's guilty or innocence is the more probable, succeeds in leaving the audience with the feeling of frustration that comes from witnessing a stalemate.

The Sound Barrier, Lean's next major film, appeared in 1952 after he had thoroughly researched the test flying of jet planes. Ralph Richardson won a New York Film Critics' Award as John Ridgefield, the owner of the Ridgefield aircraft factory, who is seeking to make a significant breakthrough in aviation by developing a plane that will fly faster than the speed of sound.

Ridgefield has an abiding sense of concern for his pilots who daily risk their lives in trying to achieve this goal, which will help push back still further the frontier of man's knowledge of space. A personal crisis develops when Tony Garthwaite, Ridgefield's son-in-law, is killed in the course of test flight. Ridgefield not only has to face his daughter Susan (Ann Todd) afterward; but he must re-examine in this moment of defeat whether or not he has a right to fulfill his great expectations of breaking the sound barrier if the price must be paid in human lives. After much soul-searching, Ridgefield decides that the experiments must continue.

"I am drawn to the person who refuses to face defeat," Lean said. And so his sympathies—and ours—are with Ridgefield as he sits tense and anxious in his office listening to the voice of Philip Peel, Tony's successor as chief test pilot, over a loudspeaker, while Philip describes what is happening to him and his plane as he tries to succeed where Tony has failed. Lean suggests how Ridgefield is living through the test pilot's experience with him by photographing Ridgefield for a moment at a tilted angle, as if the executive were in the cockpit with Peel, hurtling through space, plunging into a dive, and then levelling off again.

After the ordeal is over and Peel has accomplished his mission, Ridgefield philosophizes to his daughter Susan that man ultimately has the advantage in his fight to conquer the universe. This is because he has the weapons of courage and imagination with which to carry on the struggle—virtues with which her late husband was certainly imbued.

In *Summertime* (1955) Lean turned his hand to subject matter that was less cosmic in nature, but no less worthy of his talents for that. *Summertime* present Katharine Hepburn in one of her most engaging performances. She plays Jane Hudson, a spinster taking her first European vacation, who grows lonely in Venice after the excitement and novelty of sightseeing have worn off. Like a dreamy schoolgirl, she becomes enchanted with Renato De Rossi, a handsome Italian (Rossano Brazzi), who, it develops, is a married man separated from his wife. When Jane learns this, the hapless tourist cuts her vacation short and boards the boat train for home, disappointed, but somewhat the wiser, no doubt, for the experience.

Lean, who won the New York Film Critics' award as best director of the year for this film, brilliantly captures the glories of Venice in colorful images that pervade the picture. *Summertime* represents the blending of the talents of a resourceful director and a sensitive actress in the filming of a charming bittersweet comedy.

Between 1957 and 1966 Lean made a trilogy of movies that examine three men, each of whom seeks to make his personal vision a reality: *Bridge on the River Kwai*, *Lawrence of Arabia*, and *Dr. Zhivago*. Lean made all three of these films for American producers, for these ambitious productions could not have been financed by the British film industry. Yet they remain inherently British films since they not only were made by a British director who was given a free hand, but were peopled largely with British actors, and staffed behind the cameras primarily by British technicians as well.

The Bridge on the River Kwai (1957) climaxed the professional association of Lean and Alec Guinness, which began with *Great Expectations*, when both received Academy Awards for their work on *Kwai*. The film was also voted the best picture of the year by the Motion Picture Academy. Yet Guinness at first turned down the screenplay of what was to become his best-known role because, he told me, "It was rubbish: filled with elephant charges and that sort of thing. After the script was revised I turned it down a second time because I found Colonel Nicholson a blinkered character. I wondered how we could get audiences to take him seriously." Guinness finally accepted the part, however, and went with Lean on location to Ceylon to make the picture.

Kwai deals with a British battalion captured by the Japanese in 1943. Colonel Nicholson first endures torture rather than allow his officers to do hard labor, which

Alec Guinness in *The Bridge on the River Kwai* (1957), for which both David Lean and Guinness won Oscars. (Cinema Bookshop, London)

is contrary to the Geneva Convention. Nevertheless, he later does something of an about-face, by having all of his men, officers included, contribute to the building of a bridge to accommodate the Burma-Siam railway. Nicholson becomes so obsessed with the idea of making the bridge a tribute to British know-how and resourcefulness that he even tries to prevent a group of Allied commandos from blowing it up. But Nicholson and the bridge are finally destroyed together—ultimately, we infer, with Nicholson's complicity.

"Madness, madness," shouts a British army doctor, as he sees the commemorative plaque that Nicholson had placed on the bridge floating away with the rest of the debris after the explosion. But perhaps Nicholson was not entirely mad in his unswerving determination to erect the bridge. As the producer of the film Sam Speigel put it, "Man came into this world to build, and not to destroy. Yet he's thrown into the necessity of destroying, and his one everlasting instinct is to try to save himself from having to destroy."[8]

Spiegel's remark is totally consistent with Lean's approach to the film, for he presents Nicholson throughout as a character who deserves our compassion, even though he is eccentric to the point of neurosis. Lean has said jokingly that *Kwai* was about a stupid nut, while *Lawrence of Arabia* was about a brilliant nut; and that is why he was drawn to do *Lawrence* next.

Because making *Lawrence of Arabia* (1962), Lean strove to probe deeply into the enigmatic personality of T. E. Lawrence, on whose life the film was based. Indeed, Lean always studied the personalities of the principal characters of a film that he was about to make, even if the story was wholly fictional. "I know the characters backwards when we start to shoot," he said about his preparations to direct a film. "As Noel Coward used to say, 'You ought to know what they would eat for breakfast, though you never have a scene in which they eat breakfast.'"

Lawrence, which also won best director and best picture Oscars, had a literate script by Robert Bolt, who was to write Lean's next two films, *Dr. Zhivago* and *Ryan's Daughter*, as well as *A Man for All Seasons* for Fred Zinnemann. Bolt specialized in the kind of script that focuses on a personal narrative played out against the background of epic historial events—just the kind of material in which *Kwai* proved that Lean excelled.

In *Lawrence of Arabia* Lean and Bolt chronicled the life of Thomas Edward Lawrence (Peter O'Toole), a British intelligence officer stationed in Cairo during World War I. Lawrence convinces his superiors to let him seek out the Bedouin chief, Price Feisal (Alec Guinness), in the desert and help him to unite the Arab tribes against their common enemy, the Turks, with whom the British are also at war. Lawrence becomes the charismatic leader of the Arab hordes. He first leads them to victory against the Turks; then he champions Arab nationalism in order to gain political independence for them from the British, after he discovers that his own countrymen are using the Arabs merely as pawns in their political maneuvers in the Middle East.

But Lawrence unfortunately turns out to be a man defeated by his own capacity for greatness. As the Arabs begin to treat him like a god, he becomes vain, egocentric, and erratic. The most brilliant scene in the film shows us how Lawrence has become mesmerized by the adulation of his Arab warriors. After he and his men have destroyed a Turkish train, Lawrence jumps atop one of the cars to accept the cheers of his men. As he stands there wearing the dazzling white robes of a Bedouin chief, he is suddenly stunned by a bullet that just misses wounding him critically. He looks down to see that a dying Turk is firing at him from the ground. An expression of amazement crosses Lawrence's face; for he has been jolted into realizing that he is, after all, still a mortal man and not the god that his warriors seem to believe him to be.

This realization that his days of glory may be numbered subconsciously leads Lawrence to ever more barbarous attacks on the Turks, even to the senseless slaughter of a whole caravan of Turkish soldiers, against whom he leads his men with the savage cry, "No prisoners." Eventually Lawrence realizes how ruthless he has become; in addition, he sees that his attempts to form a Pan-Arabia are doomed to frustration by the factiousness of the Arab tribes and by the continued meddling of the British in Arab affairs.

He therefore decides to return to his former rank in the British army and go back to England. As he is driven to the airport, a truckload of British soldiers passes him on the road; and none of them recognizes him, implying that Lawrence is already becoming a forgotten man. Lean underscores this point further by cutting to a shot of Lawrence's face as seen through the dusty windshield of the car. His tarnished image has already begun to fade, for his moment of glory has passed.

To make *Lawrence*, Lean went on location to Jordan and photographed the desert in striking images that vividly communicate to the viewer the experience of living in the relentless heat of the desert. Lean's ability to immerse his audience in the environment of the story he is telling is epitomized in the breathtaking shot of the blazing sun slowly rising on the horizon over the rim of the infinite desert, which stretches into the measureless reaches of space, dwarfing man and his petty pretensions by comparison.

Lawrence's tragedy, like that of Colonel Nicholson, is in his being robbed of the dignity that might have accompanied an honorable defeat by the fatal flaws in his character which were exposed by the crises he faced. In both cases, the would-be hero was stubbornly determined to surmount staggering odds but was revealed in the process to be a self-deluded man who was as dedicated to his own self-esteem as to the principles he was championing.[9]

Lean never ceased to be concerned with the individual and his ability, or lack of it, to measure up to the demands that life can make on him; and this is borne out in the third film of the trilogy. "The Russian Revolution itself was a towering historical event," Lean said, "but *Dr. Zhivago* (1965) is not the story of the Revolution. The drama, the horror, and the turbulence of the Revolution simply provide the canvas against which is told a moving and highly personal love story." In *Zhivago* Lean zeroes in on a group of individual human beings, heroic in their efforts to survive the onslaughts of historical events that are shaping their lives but over which, ironically, they have no control. The Revolution itself remains in the background of the story, but it is always there.

Lean decided to film *Dr. Zhivago* after reading Boris Pasternak's novel to pass the time on a sea journey. By the time he had finished it, he declared to himself, "I don't see how it is to be done, but we must do it."[10] Lean shot thirty-one hours of film in ten months and then spent an additional ten weeks editing down this footage to the final running time of just over three hours. Lean oversaw every aspect of the production of a film made on the grand scale of *Zhivago* just as personally as he did in the days when he was making "smaller" films. That is why his later epics are just as unmistakably David Lean films as his earlier motion pictures.

Since Dr. Zhivago himself is an observer more often than he is an actor in the novel, it is his mistress Lara who impressed Lean as its most interesting character. Nevertheless Yuri Zhivago (Omar Sharif) is still at the center of the film; for he is the link between all of the various characters, each of whom in his own way is trying to survive the critical period of the Revolution. As Richard Schickel wrote, "The action of the film may be described very simply as the disillusionment—but not the souring—of Yuri Zhivago. One by one his hopes of preserving his identity as doctor, as poet, as family man, as unique individual are casually and wantonly destroyed by a Revolution with which he mildly sympathizes, but in which he does not want to involve himself. Finally, and most cruelly, the one thing the Revolution has given him—the opportunity to possess physically his great love, the magnificent Lara (Julie Christie)—is taken from him too."[11]

Zhivago survives even this loss, but eventually he dies of a heart attack in the street. Yevgraf, Zhivago's half-brother (Alec Guinness), who narrates the film, make the final reflection on Zhivago's life to a young girl who may be the love-child of Zhivago and Lara: 'We've come very far very fast. But do you know what it cost?" She is then left to ponder, as is the audience, the tragic implications of the story that she has been told.

Although Lean for the most part keeps the Revolution in the background of the film, when he chooses to bring it to the foreground, he does so in the same way that Russian director Sergei Eisenstein handled the abortive Revolution of 1905 in his classic silent film, *Potemkin* (1925); that is, by choosing incidents that are relatively insignificant in themselves, but that are symbolic indications of the thrust of the entire revolutionary effort. For example, in order to dramatize the tyranny that led to the 1917 Revolution, Lean stages a scene in which a detachment of Cossacks massacres a group of peaceful demonstrators. Lean suggests the slaughter in a rapid succession of images blended into a superb wedding of sight and sound: the slashing of sabers, the stunned expressions of terrified peasants, the drum of the marching band rolling into the mud, blood speckling the snow.

The whole film is, like *Lawrence of Arabia*, a masterpiece of understatement. Often feelings are only hinted at and words are left unarticulated, in order to let viewers gradually discover for themselves the full implications of the story as it unfolds. Characteristically, Lean has succeeded in compressing much of the meaning of the novel into cinematic imagery. In one sequence, as Russian soldiers sporting new boots march across the screen on their way to fight in World War I, Yevgraf comments on the sound track that the boots will eventually wear out. Later, at the close of the scene in which a group of war-weary troops have killed the officers who tried to stop their ignominious retreat, one soldier pauses to pull off the boots of a dead officer to replace his own. The soldiers' boots, Yevgraf observes, have finally worn out—like the wearers' enthusiasm for their cause.

Another unforgettable image in the film is that of Lara photographed through a frosted windowpane; as a candle flame gradually melts the frost, we see more and more clearly the silent anguish in her soul mirrored on her face. She is Lara as Pasternak saw her, a woman of great devotion and spiritual beauty—martyred, stubborn, extravagant, adored.

This description would also fit perfectly Rosie Ryan, the heroine of Lean's next film, *Ryan's Daughter* (1970), which takes place during the Irish Revolution of 1916. Although *Dr. Zhivago* earned an enormous amount of money, MGM, the company for which Lean made it, had fallen into a financial crisis by the time he began shooting *Ryan's Daughter* in February 1969. In the year and a half that Lean took to complete the film, the studio administration had changed three times; yet Lean went ahead making his film his own way.

That *Ryan's Daughter* falls below the exacting standard set by Lean in his previous epic films is therefore not due to studio interference, but to the fact that Robert Bolt's original screenplay failed to create a dramatic line strong enough to support the weight of a film nearly three hours in length. Whereas the Russian Revolution acts as a constant presence in *Dr. Zhivago*, the Irish Revolt hardly ever intrudes on the story of Rosie Ryan, beyond providing the reason why the towns-people are so horrified to learn that Rosie (Sarah Miles) is cheating on her middle-aged husband (Robert Mitchum) with an officer in the British army of occupation (Christopher Jones).

Rosie Ryan is a Lean heroine of the same stamp as most of his heroes. When her affair is discovered, her marriage is ruined, and she is forced to leave town. Yet she rises above all her misfortunes and resolutely looks to the future, in the hope of starting a new life elsewhere. Once again it is clear that Lean has been drawn to a person who refuses to face defeat.

After the disappointing public response to *Ryan's Daughter*, Lean was involved with various projects that did not reach fruition. During a time when economic pressures in the movie industry were making it less and less feasible to produce the sort of large-scale epic films he had become accustomed to making, Lean found it difficult to come up with a viable project; nor was he in a hurry to do so. He had often said, "I would rather make one good picture in three years than four others in the same time."[12] As a matter of fact, from *River Kwai* onward, there had usually been a span of roughly five years from one Lean picture to the next. This time, however, it was to be a decade before he launched another production.

Finally, in 1981, he turned to E. M. Forster's 1924 novel, *A Passage to India*, a subject he had first considered filming in 1960, after seeing a stage adaptation of the book. Plans went ahead for the production, which was shot primarily on location in India; and the finished product proved to be an impressive Lean offering well worth waiting for, a film that was welcomed by audiences everywhere.

Mrs. Moore, an elderly British matron (Peggy Ashcroft), accompanies Adela Quested (Judy Davis), the young woman who plans to marry Mrs. Moore's son Ronny, on a trip to India, where Ronny serves as a British magistrate in Chandra-pore. During their sojourn in India the pair become acquainted with Cyril Fielding, the principal of the local government school (James Fox), who in turn introduces them to a couple of his Indian friends, the venerable Professor Godbole (Alec Guinness) and young Dr. Aziz (Victor Banerjee). The impetuous Aziz is so grate-ful because the two English women do not treat him with the condescension he has learned to expect from the British that he invites them to make an excursion with him to the famed Marabar Caves.

After they arrive at the cave site, Mrs. Moore, who is overcome by the heat and fatigue, has a dizzy spell, leaving Adela and Aziz to proceed on the tour alone. The situation turns tragic when Adela hysterically accuses the young doctor of attempt-ing to assault her in the dark recesses of one of the caves. The sensational trial of Aziz inevitably sets Indian against Englishman; so that, regardless of the verdict, it is painfully clear that Anglo-Indian relations have been severely damaged for some time to come. That is implicitly what Mrs. Moore means when she stoically refuses to appear in court as a witness, explaining that "nothing I say or do will make the slightest difference."

Lean's film, which he scripted and edited as well as directed, closely adheres to the novel in implying Aziz's innocence, leaving the filmgoer to infer that Adela's fancied rape was most likely the product of her own sexual fantasies, subconscious-

Judy Davis and Victor Banerjee in *A Passage to India* **(1984). (Museum of Modern Art/Film Stills Archive)**

ly stoked by her suppressed attraction to the handsome Indian. In any event, when Adela herself testifies at the trial, she has the gumption to admit her confusion about what happened and to withdraw her charges against Aziz. In the epilogue that rounds off Lean's compelling film, Aziz and Fielding, who championed Aziz's innocence all along, confirm their comradeship; and their mutual gesture suggests that understanding between different races and nations must begin with communication between individuals.

When one considers the positive public response to many of Lean's movies, it is evident that few directors have commanded such a large portion of the mass audience. Commenting on the popularity of his films, Lean, who was knighted in 1984, once remarked that, if his movies have pleased a lot of people, presumably it meant that he was something of a common denominator. Like the average filmgoer, he explained, "I like to be excited when I go to the movies. I like to be touched. And I like a good yarn, I suppose." Elsewhere he added, "I'm a picture chap. I like pictures, and when I go to the movies I go to see pictures. I think dialogue is nearly always secondary in a movie. It's awfully hard, when you look back over the really great movies that you see in your life, to remember a line of dialogue. You will not forget the pictures."[13]

Joseph Losey (center) directs Dirk Bogarde (left) in *Modesty Blaise* (1966). (Cinema Book-shop, London)

11
Joseph Losey
Decline and Fall

Probably no film maker in this book had to face greater obstacles in achieving artistic control of his films than Joseph Losey. Yet he went on working until he won it, for he firmly believed that a director's films should be distinguished by a strong personal style if they are to be taken seriously. "A film must bear a director's stamp, or it's nothing," said Losey, thereby implicitly endorsing the *auteur* theory. He therefore fought from the beginning of his career for the right to make films that bear his stamp, first in Hollywood and later in England, where he took up residence as a permanent member of the British film making community.

Losey was born in La Crosse, Wisconsin, in 1909. After attending Dartmouth and Harvard, he tried a variety of jobs. He reviewed plays for *Theater Arts* and became a roving reporter for *Variety*. He was stage manager for the first shows at Radio City Music Hall in New York and later for several Broadway plays, until he became a stage director himself. His first big break as a director in the professional theater was *The Living Newspaper* (1936), a project of the Federal Theater that provided work for some of the thousands of unemployed actors, writers, and technicians during the Depression. He directed several more plays in the legitimate theatre and then, like George Cukor and Carol Reed, two other film directors who got their start in the theater, was offered a contract to direct motion pictures.

Losey went to Hollywood briefly in 1938 and went on to make educational shorts in New York before joining the Signal Corps in 1943, as did other Hollywood directors like George Stevens. When he returned to Hollywood after the war, he made another short, *A Gun in Hand* (1945), which was part of the *Crime Does Not Pay* series on which Fred Zinnemann had spent part of his apprenticeship in the MGM shorts department.

The officials at MGM gave no indication that they intended to elevate Losey to feature production in the foreseeable future, and so he was delighted to accept an offer from Dore Schary, the production chief at RKO. Schary had instituted a policy of encouraging independent film makers to direct films for his studio. Losey's first motion picture for RKO was *The Boy with Green Hair* (1948), but long before it was finished Howard Hughes had taken over the studio. Schary and his policies were out, and Losey's long-standing struggle with the studio system was under way. Every day he received memos from Hughes scribbled in pencil about changes in the script and footage that had to be reshot. Losey carried on as best he could under these unfavourable conditions.

The Boy with Green Hair is an allegory that uses the lad's green hair as a symbol of the need for peace and international understanding in the world. This film is not typical of Losey's subsequent work, which is firmly rooted in realism rather than in fantasy and which seeks to explore problems rather than to solve them. Losey prefers to make films that "disturb and stay with the viewer after he has seen them," rather than pictures that offer easy answers to life's difficulties.

His first feature, although untypical of his later films, nevertheless sounded a thematic chord that would reverberate through his subsequent films. "I think, basically, if I have one theme," he said, "it is the question of hypocrisy: the people who condemn others without looking at themselves."[1] In *Boy with Green Hair* this theme is concretized when the townspeople ostracize the boy (Dean Stockwell) because his green hair makes him different. "After more than thirty years of film making," Losey commented, *"The Boy with Green Hair* seems somewhat sentimental to me now; it did not, of course, when I made it."

Certainly no other Losey film could be called in any way sentimental, since he specialized in making films that offer the viewer an uncompromising look at life. Often the problems Losey treats in his movies have a social dimension. This is true, he feels, not only of his films that deal with subjects such as racial injustice (*The Lawless*) or war (*King and Country*), but also of those who deal with educated people such as *The Servant* or *Accident*. "If you make a film about coal miners, it is immediately considered to have social significance, whether it does or not," he pointed out; "whereas the social significance of other films is often overlooked."

Losey's second film, *The Lawless* (1949), is a stark story of another kind of hypocrisy: racial prejudice. It concerns a Mexican youth accused of raping an American girl in a small American border town and was made for the independent producers Pine and Thomas.

After *The Boy with Green Hair* Losey was more confirmed than ever in his resolve to work in Hollywood with the kind of freedom that he had been promised at RKO, but that had not been forthcoming after Hughes's takeover of the studio. Hence he turned to independents like Pine and Thomas for work. "I did independent films which had major backing and major distribution," he said, but that were not controlled by the big studios. "We had marvelous crews, and we prided ourselves in working very fast and very efficiently."[2] At this period in his career Losey did not have the latitude to choose the subjects that he wanted to film; yet he never took on a project that he thought had nothing to offer him.

Because of the trend toward realism in postwar cinema, already noted, Losey was able to shoot *The Lawless* almost entirely on location, with the townspeople appearing as extras and in bit parts. Shooting on location not only enabled Losey to give the film a feeling of authenticity, but also helped him to stay within his tight budget for the picture, which was $150,000.

He next made a grim crime film, the *The Prowler* (1951), for producer S. P. Eagle—really Sam Spiegel, who later produced some of David Lean's films. Spiegel budgeted the film at $700,000, still a slim sum by Hollywood standards, but a king's ransom compared to the budget of some of Losey's other early films. "I owe Spiegel a great deal," said Losey, "because I know nobody else in Hollywood at that time who could or would have given me that kind of freedom or implementation."

The hesitation of other producers to hire Losey was not just because he had only two feature films to his credit, but because suspicion that he might be a Communist had already begun to be asserted. While he was still at RKO, Losey had been offered an impossibly ridiculous script entitled *I Married a Communist* to direct, and he promptly turned it down. It was only afterwards that he learned that this script was a touchstone for establishing whether or not a director had Communist leanings. If a director refused to make *I Married a Communist*, he immediately became politically suspect. Losey was the first of thirteen directors to be so tested. The film was finally made by Robert Stevenson and can still be seen on the Late, Late Show under the title *The Woman on Pier 13*.

These were the tense Cold-War years that spawned Senator Joseph McCarthy's witch-hunt for Communists and the House Unamerican Activities Committee hearings, which eventually would force Losey to migrate to England, just as Charlie Chaplin was forced to move to Switzerland. Meanwhile, although the clouds were still gathering around Losey's Hollywood career, he was still able to make two more films there. Then he went off to Europe to shoot an Italian-French-American Coproduction, *Stranger on the Prowl* (1952), starring Paul Muni. During shooting, Losey was notified that he was under investigation by the House Unamerican Activities Committee, which meant that he was blacklisted from further work in Hollywood. Losey completed the picture he was working on; but his name was taken off the credits and replaced by "Andrea Forzano," the son of one of the film's coproducers. The picture had only a brief release and then sank without a trace.

When Losey sought to track down why he had been blacklisted, he found that, besides his refusal to direct *I Married a Communist*, he was also suspect because he had supported Adrian Scott, the producer of the *The Boy with Green Hair*, when Scott had been blacklisted before him, and because of his association with blacklisted writer Bertolt Brecht, whose play *Galileo* Losey had directed on Broadway in 1947.

Losey went to England in 1952, where he took whatever work he could find. At times he lived on the occasional £75 (about $225 in Losey's estimate)—the sum that he could earn by writing documentary scripts for the British Transport Commission. He was hired to direct two low-budget features, neither of which carried his name. *The Sleeping Tiger* (1954) was credited to "Victor Hanbury," the film's producer, and *The Intimate Stranger* (1955) to "Joseph Walton," which happened to be Losey's first and middle name. "*Time Without Pity* (1956) was the first film anybody in Europe had the courage to put my name on," he says.

Losey also augmented his slender income by making television commercials. "I had no objection to doing TV commercials," he said. "It was a way of avoiding doing films which I didn't want to make." Because he brought his cinematic skill to bear in making these commercials, the British Film Institute included several of them in its 1967 retrospective of his work.

The first films that Losey made in Britain were, like most of his American films, done on a meager budget; and Losey taxed his ingenuity to give each film a professional look that belied the circumstances under which it was made. "We thought the script was frightful," said Dirk Bogarde, the star of *The Sleeping Tiger*. "Joe had to embellish this rubbish, as he always had to do; and in consequence it was much more exciting to do."[3] *The Sleeping Tiger* was the first of five films Bogarde made with Losey; and the latter said of their professional relationship, "It is very rare to find an actor who is willing to risk appearing in films that depart from established formulas as mine do."

In making *The Sleeping Tiger* Losey sought to depart from the established clichés of domestic melodrama, with which the script was permeated. For one thing, he tried to examine a little more deeply than the script might have warranted the emotional problems of Glenda Esmond (Alexis Smith), the wife of psychiatrist Clive Esmond (Alexander Knox). Glenda has become infatuated with Frank Clements (Dirk Bogarde), a young thief who had tried to rob Dr. Esmond. Instead of turning him over to the police, Esmond has made him a guest in his house and is trying to cure him of his evil inclinations by therapy.

When Esmond finally despairs of helping Frank, he decides to give himself up to the police for harboring a criminal. Glenda, however, cannot accept the loss of both lover and husband that this will entail. "You're not going to give me notice," she screams at Esmond, "like a servant or waitress." The film ends when Glenda, in a fit of hysteria, drives her car through a billboard and is killed. Pictured on the poster is a tiger, which is part of an ad for Esso gasoline. The tiger recalls Esmond's earlier statement that "all of us are capable of anything, given the right provocation. In the dark forest of every personality is a sleeping tiger." Of course Esmond had made the remark with reference to Frank's life of crime and had no idea at the time that it would soon be applicable to his wife.

Of *The Sleeping Tiger* and his other early British films, Losey said, "I was still a foreigner in England —I'm a foreigner wherever I am and always will be —and my eye was foreign, seeing strange things which now would be quite ordinary to me."[4] As a foreigner Losey was fascinated by the class system in England, and the films he made there have often explored how chaos and tragedy can result from the rigid maintenance of class barriers. Losey's interest in the class consciousness inherent in British society is closely related to his more basic theme of hypocrisy.

In discussing his later film *Accident* with me, Losey formulated this concept more fully in terms that transcend that particular film and give us an insight into the personal vision that underlies his pictures. "*Accident*," he said, "is about a kind of moral bankruptcy, which is almost amoral, in contemporary society, among people who have every resource of our so-called civilization, and who are worse off than their grandfathers were in terms of coping with life. It is about conspiracy and betrayal between human beings, despite their declared loyalties. It is about people's failure to recognize themselves, what they are really like."

Although Losey was thinking specifically of *Accident* when he articulated this triple theme—moral bankruptcy, human betrayal, and failure in self-knowledge— it underlies in varying degrees most of the films that he has made. In *The Sleeping Tiger*, for example, Glenda fails to realize how deep in her sexual frustration because of her husband's emotional neglect of her, until she becomes attracted to a younger man. When she does, she is more than willing to betray her husband to punish him for his past failure to give her fulfillment, by seeking to find it with Frank. In addition, the case of Glenda Esmond illustrates how Losey often shows the erosion of moral values in modern society infecting first of all the most privileged members of society, who have obviously forgotten the meaning of noblesse oblige, and then spreading to the other levels of society.

As James Leahy says very perceptively, "Inherited wealth, position or influence may insulate the individual from the struggle for survival, but such an inheritance can easily be dissipated; and the individual who suddenly loses his protection, and who is left to defend himself by his own efforts and personality, is faced with a struggle which is usually too much for him."[5] This is true of the debt-ridden aristocrat Paul Deverill in *The Gypsy and the Gentleman* (1957), just as it was true of Glenda Esmond. Luxury has not prepared Paul (Keith Mitchell) for life in a world where only the fittest survive and are capable of enterprise. Paul throws aside convention to marry Belle, a gypsy (Melina Mercouri). But his action is not a democratic gesture, merely a succumbing to his sexual passion.

Belle secretly despises Paul and contrives to have her unsuspecting husband employ her lover as a hired hand on the estate, so that she can go on being his mistress. Paul becomes more and more depraved under the spell of his gypsy wife; and when he realizes how far he has sunk, he drowns both Belle and himself, thus dragging her down with him to the bottom of the river, just as she has dragged him down to her level. But Belle did not so much corrupt Paul as expose the weaknesses in his character, in the same way that Tony's servant manipulates him in *The Servant*.

It was Losey's next film, *Blind Date* (1959), that first gained him widespread critical attention. Once more he had been given a melodramatic story to tell, which he struggled to invest with some human values and psychological depth. Although the plot is basically that of a murder mystery, it also involves the love of Jan, an impecunious painter (Hardy Kruger), for the wealthy Lady Fenton (Micheline Presle). Accordingly Losey decided to tell his story in the context of the British class system.

He chose to make the artist a coal miner, "somebody who was self-made and still painted from the memory of his earlier experiences," Losey explained.[6] He likewise decided to give Inspector Morgan (Stanley Baker) a working-class background that would prompt him to sympathize with Jan when the latter is unjustly accused of the murder of a high-class call girl. When the evidence begins to imply that Lady Fenton's husband, Sir Howard Fenton, a high ranking government official, is implicated in the girl's death, the Assistant Commissioner of Police, Sir Brian Lewis, who obviously wants to protect a member of his own class, insists that such a possibility is inconceivable. "It's a question of background,"says Sir Brian.

Morgan is tempted to believe him, but he relentlessly pursues his investigation until he uncovers the real facts. Lady Fenton killed the call girl, who was her husband's mistress, and then sought to frame Jan for the murder. When he realizes how his ingrained respect for the upper classes had clouded his vision in working on the case, Morgan tells Lady Fenton that he now understands that she had counted on the fact that he would not be able to bring himself to believe that a member of her class would be capable of such behavior.

Ironies of this kind occur in the film from the very beginning. The movie opens with shots of the Houses of Parliament, Westminster Abbey, and the Palace of

Saint James—all symbols of traditional British values. Then the picture goes on to show Jan, a young innocent ensnared in a sordid scandal involving a high government official who is committed to preserving those values, and the official's wife. Jan's working-class background in the coal mines was a clean existence, for he had never been soiled by coal dust in the way that he has been stained by his attachment to Lady Fenton. Significantly, Morgan, one of his own class, rescues Jan just in time from the near disaster that his relationship has caused him.

The world of *The Criminal* (1960) also pictures a tightly knit class structure. But it is that of the underworld, in which a man's status in the crime network is carried with him into prison, where it dictates both the influence he exerts over his fellow prisoners and also the bargaining power he has with prison officials. Criminals have their own code, said Losey; "and their codes of loyalty and behavior are absolute. If you violate them, the penalties are much greater than in the outside world."

Johnny Bannion (Stanley Baker) is influential in this underworld setup whether he is in or out of prison. Nevertheless, Johnny is radically a loner by nature, who values his personal individuality highly. He therefore is gradually becoming obsolete in the world of organized crime, which is becoming more of an intricately constructed big-business operation all the time. "Your sort doesn't fit into an organization," Mike Carter, an old cohort of Johnny's (Sam Wanamaker), warns him when Johnny gets out of prison. Carter secretly hopes to displace Johnny as leader of the gang and is counting on Johnny's stubborn personality to help him dislodge Johnny from his position in the mob.

The gang stages a racetrack robbery, and in the ensuing fight among members of the group over the loot, Johnny is killed. His death proves that, just as Carter predicted, there is no longer a place for the Johnny Bannions in the big business of crime.

Losey's continuing insistence on making a picture as he conceives it should be made was illustrated during the shooting of *The Criminal*. He refused to film the race track robbery in detail, à la Stanley Kubrick's *The Killing*, as the film's distributors wanted him to. "It seemed to me the important thing was to see the exterior aspect," Losey explained, "to see how they got in, and then see them come out and escape. The fact that inside somebody points a gun at somebody else and someone puts lots of money into satchels is not to me interesting." Losey added that his attitude had sometimes caused motion picture distributors to complain, "He made his film, he didn't make *ours*." To this Losey responded, quite characteristically, "Well, I make my film; and I don't know what their film is."[7]

This director's determination to make a film the way he envisions it was fully vindicated when he directed *Eve* (1962). The movie starred Jeanne Moreau in her definitive performance as a femme fatale. After the unfavourable reception of the picture at its Paris premiere, the French producers panicked and cut the film severely without Losey's knowledge or consent. They furthermore altered some of the dialogue, redistributed the music on the sound track, and redubbed some of the actors' voices. Originally Losey had Anna Proclemer dub the lines of the Italian actress Virna Lisi, but the producers redubbed Lisi's dialogue with the voice of another actress.

When the resulting film was released internationally in this mutilated version, it was harshly criticized for precisely the things for which Losey was not responsible. For example, one critic referred to the "all-American" coed-type voice that had been attached to Virna Lisi in the film. "In my version," Losey pointed out, "Anna Proclemer's dubbing of her was a great performance, and along with Virna Lisi's very great beauty and expressiveness, I would have thought it a considerable performance."[8] The British Film Institute's National Film Archive in London owns the only known print of *Eve* that has the original Losey sound track. Its existence testifies that the butchery of Losey's film by its producers ranks as one of the worst examples of interference with the work of a film artist on record.

After the disaster that attended Losey's work on *Eve*, he made the first of three films in collaboration with playwright Harold Pinter, *The Servant*, which was followed by *Accident* and *The Go-Between*. The creative association of Losey and Pinter has proved as fruitful as that of Carol Reed and Graham Greene. Losey had wanted to film Robin Maugham's novella *The Servant* with Dirk Bogarde after they had finished *The Sleeping Tiger* in 1954, but Bogarde had other commitments; and so the idea was shelved. Then a producer hired Pinter to do a screenplay of the book, and Losey and Bogarde renewed their interest in the project.

Losey shot *The Servant* (1963) in seven weeks, despite an attack of pneumonia. The resulting movie is a chilling parable of Innocence corrupted by Evil. Its distributors, however, were wary of its commercial potential and delayed its release until after it had triumphed at both the New York and Venice Film Festivals. Losey's concern for the moral bankruptcy of contemporary society, particulary among those of background and education, is nowhere more strongly stated than in *The Servant*.

Tony, a young aristocrat (James Fox), lacks any moral convictions or realistic personal goals. As a result he is easily dominated by others who possess more forceful personalities than he does. Tony is by turns dominated by his finacée Susan (Wendy Craig); then by his infatuation for Vera (Sarah Miles), his maid; and finally and most completely by his servant Barrett (Dirk Bogarde), who methodically reduces the weak-willed Tony through drugs and alcohol to a total wreck. Because Barrett resents being the servant of someone whom he considers in many ways his inferior, he not only plots to take over the household, but derives perverse pleasure from degrading Tony as a human being as well.

There is a definite visual pattern in the film that emphasizes the changing relationship of Tony and Barrett. The first time Barrett and Tony meet, Barrett sits during the interview while Tony stands over him, asking him questions. Tony is in the foreground and Barrett in the background. As the film progresses and Tony gradually submits to Barrett's stronger personality, Tony loses ground—literally and figuratively. Barrett comes more to the fore, and Tony sinks into the background and into insignificance. Barrett is now placed in positions where he stands above Tony. The key scene on the staircase ties all of this symbolism together. Barrett strengthens his hold on Tony by threatening to leave. Tony stands above Barrett on the stairs to block Barrett from going to his room to pack. But Barrett pushes past him as they talk; and the scene ends with Tony kneeling below Barrett

Wendy Craig, Dirk Bogarde, and James Fox in *The Servant* (1963). (Cinemabilia)

on the stairs, begging him to stay. Barrett by this point is very much in command of the situation.

Finally, at the end of the film, when Barrett's triumph over Tony is complete, he locks the front door, sliding the bolts like a jailer. Then, as Barrett ascends the stairs on his way to sleep with Vera in the master bedroom, he passes Tony, groveling on the stairs in a drunken stupor. Losey photographs Tony, imprisoned as he is by his addiction to alcohol and drugs as well as by his emotional dependence on Barrett, through the bars of the bannister railing.

There is no last-minute rescue of Tony to soften the impact of the film; and to those who therefore think a picture like *The Servant* to be pessimistic, Losey replied, "I don't regard my work as being particularly pessimistic because I think pessimism is an attitude that sees no hope in human beings or life in general, that has no compassion therefore; and to have compassion, I strongly believe you have to examine the worst, the msot tragic, the most crucifying aspects of life as well as the beautiful ones, and also the things that corrupt life, distort it, destroy it."[9]

Losey's second film with Pinter, *Accident* (1967), also ends with the main character being shut in with the life that has become the pattern of his existence. But in this film the hero's action represents a decisive renewal of commitment to his family, rather than a final descent into degradation.

Accident begins with an auto crash involving two aristocratic Oxford students, William (Michael York) and Anna (Jacqueline Sassard). William is killed in the accident; but Anna, his financée, escapes. A series of flashbacks trace how two middle-aged Oxford dons, Stephen (Dirk Bogarde) and Charley (Stanley Baker), rivaled William for Anna's affections, and how the accident has changed all of their lives. "I guess it's really about how civilized and courteous people can often be as vicious underneath as the lower classes," Losey explained. "In some way, everyone affects everyone else in life. Sometimes we have the most powerful effect on others when we least suspect it."[10]

The tempo of *Accident* is rather slow, and Losey said that he paced the film this way for a purpose: "I agree with the critic who said the *Accident* has the tempo of breathing. I took a certain risk in doing the film this way. Unless you accept the pace of the film from the start, the picture will not work for you. You have to look and listen all the time while you are watching the film, which is a great effort for the majority of people who no longer read books. But I think it is time that people took the time to look and listen to films."

Since the dialogue of *Accident* is sparse, as is usually the case with a Pinter script, the viewer must be alert to what the visuals are telling him. As Tom Milne wrote of *Accident*, "it is in the gaps that the real story is told."[11] The rivalry for Anna between Stephen and Charley on the one hand, and William on the other, never breaks into open warfare. Yet throughout an apparently calm luncheon party at Stephen's home on a sunny Sunday afternoon, a cold war is waged; and several skirmishes are won and lost. William, with his blond hair and white tennis outfit, looks like an Adonis on the court, an unwelcome reminder to the two older men of their years.

As the day wears on Stephen subtly encourages William to match him and Charley drink for drink. When finally William collapses in a stupor, Stephen says jeeringly, "You're drunk, *boy!*" It is one of the few times in the film when Stephen, or anyone else for that matter, raises his voice. The rivalry continues when Stephen visits William's estate and joins in a game with William's aristocratic friends. "Only the old men watch," William says tauntingly, "and the ladies." That age has been the real source of the rivalry is made clear by the fact that Stephen does not object later when he comes home one night to find Charley and Anna using his house for a rendezvous, while Stephen's family is away.

Nevertheless Charley has betrayed him, and there are a number of such betrayals in *Accident*. Anna later becomes engaged to William and asks Stephen to tell Charley, her erstwhile lover. When Anna is in a state of semi-shock after the accident, Stephen brings her to his home and virtually overpowers her, on the same night his wife is having his third child in the hospital.

It is the accident that kills William which jolts Stephen, Charley, and Anna into facing themselves as they have failed to do before. Afterward Anna leaves the university, Charely is crushed that his interest in her is not enough to keep her there, and Stephen settles down with his family to accept the approach of middle age. At the final fade-out Stephen plays with his children on the lawn, then takes them into the house. The camera draws back from the house, and we hear the echo of the crash with which the film opened. Losey in the last scene has tied together the theme and plot of the film with this last, lingering image.

"Stephen goes into the house," he explained, "taking along his children, and shuts the door. He is shut in with the life he has elected to lead. But he is a qualitatively different person than he was in the beginning of the story. The accident which killed William has changed the lives of everyone involved." Hence the echo of the crash at the end of the film reminds us of the accident that has finally brought Stephen to his senses and forced him to straighten out his life.

Richard Roud has written that both Losey and Pinter are fascinated by depicting a privileged world, "from the smart Chelsea house of *The Servant* to the spires of Oxford in *Accident*, and now, in *The Go-Between*, the splendors of upper-class life at the turn of the century."[12] *The Go-Between* (1971), which won the Grand Prize at the Cannes Film Festival, is very likely Losey's masterpiece.

Losey and Pinter wanted to film L. P. Hartley's novel after they finished *The Servant*, but problems in obtaining the rights forced them to postpone the project, as they originally had had to put off filming *The Servant* for some years. Production finally got under way in the summer of 1970. Losey moved his cast and crew into a rambling old country estate near Norwich for an eight-week shoot.

The title character is twelve-year-old Leo Colsten (Dominic Guard), a boy from a working-class background who is invited to spend the summer with the wealthy Maudsley family. Leo feels very much an outsider until Marian Maudsley (Julie Christie) asks him to carry notes back and forth between her and Ted Burgess (Alan Bates), a tenant farmer on the estate. These errands make Leo feel needed and therefore wanted.

Alan Bates described the plot this way: "It's primarily about Leo's adolescent state, his maturing—he is suddenly involved in this love affair between an upper-middle-class girl and the local tenant farmer. The boy virtually becomes their go-between without knowing what he's doing. It's a socially dangerous affair for them to be having, one that results in tragedy, and it has an effect on the boy that lasts throughout his life."[13]

When Leo begins to suspect that there is something wrong about his serving as messenger for Marian and Ted, he tells Marian that he does not want to carry any more notes. She explodes at him in a way that makes him realize she has only been using him all along and has never really liked him. Leo is further disillusioned when Lady Maudsley (Margaret Leighton), who suspects what is going on between Marian and Ted, forces Leo to lead her to their place of assignation. Leo, torn between his unwillingness to break his promise of secrecy to Marian and Ted on the one hand, and his conviction that he owes obedience to Lady Maudsley on the other, takes her to the barn where Marian and Ted meet.

It is a shattering moment when they burst into the bar and discover Marian and Ted making love. The camera stays on Lady Maudsley as she turns Leo's head away from the sight and buries it in her breast. But it is too late to protect Leo's innocence any longer. Significantly enough, it is on Leo's thirteenth birthday that he has been thus traumatically initiated into the adult world.

In the course of the film there are fragmented flashes forward to an old man in the present visiting the Maudsley estate. The viewer gradually realizes that this elderly gentleman is Leo in old age (Michael Redgrave), come to revisit the scene of that summer of so long ago. "You ought to be married," the aged Marian tells

Dominic Guard and Margaret Leighton in *The Go-Between* (1971). (Author's collection)

him; "you are dried up inside." Leo, we infer, never recovered from his disillusionment at learning how he had been manipulated by those whom he loved and respected and has become a cynical old man.

As in Pinter's other scripts for Losey, much more is implied in the dialogue than is ever articulated by the characters. For instance, Hugh Trimingham, who is engaged to Marian and suspects early on that she is seeing Ted, chivalrously remarks that "nothing is ever a lady's fault" and coolly suggests that Ted join the army. In actuality Ted shoots himself with his hunting rifle, Hugh marries Marian, and the superficial veneer of genteel respectability descends once more on Maudsley Manor.

Losey handles every aspect of the film brilliantly. The lush color photography of Leo's summer at the Maudsley estate reflects how the lad is dazzled by the wealthy surroundings that the Maudsleys take for granted and offers a sharp contrast to the pallid hues of the scenes in which the elderly Leo returns to revisit the estate. "The past is a foreign country," he muses; "they do things differently there." Leo was a foreigner in the land of his social betters; and the way he was exploited—first by Marian in making him help her carry on her affair and then by her mother in making him help her spy it out—has left him with the abiding feeling that he is an outsider who can trust no one.

The opulent look of the film belies the stringent budget that Losey was working with. "I think the degree of freedom in film making is in inverse proportion to the amount of money expended," he said. "That's why I try to stay within a relatively low budget. In the case of *The Go-Between* I was originally promised a budget of $2.4 million; and this was cut back to $1.2 million, which means that I eventually made the film for half of what I had originally counted on. There are two ways to cut a budget: speeding up the schedule, which involves trimming all down the line, and working on a percentage basis. I used both methods in this instance. I cut a month off the shooting schedule and worked for no salary, in favor of working on a percentage of the film's eventual profits. The producer, the writer, and some of the actors agreed to do this, too."

When people in the industry suggested that Losey's experience in making *The Go-Between* on half of the original budget proves that picture making costs more than it has to, he replied, "Why should writers, actors, and directors take all of the risks in making a film, and not the studio? Had *The Go-Between* not been a success, it would have meant that those of us working on a percentage basis would have taken the financial loss, when some of us had been involved in the project for close to eight years. These are some of the realities that face the artist working in an industry." One executive at the studio where *The Go-Between* was made, however, proved very cooperative: Bryan Forbes. "We owe Bryan Forbes a great deal," Losey pointed out. "While he was in charge of the studio he fought to get the film made. The kind of interference that other film executives try to exercise, however, often causes a film to lose rather than to make money. If some of the front office people had had their way, *The Go-Between* would have been shelved. If distributors would only be willing to sell the product that the director delivers to them, they would make more successful films in the long run."

Losey had an even tighter budget and shorter shooting schedule when he made *King and Country* (1964) than he did for *The Go-Between*. "The film was set up, shot, edited, and finished in three months," he said. "When one works on a film so intensively for a short period, you wonder what you will have when you are finished. That is why I was pleased with the way *King and Country* turned out."

Like Kubrick's *Paths of Glory*, Losey's film is not just an antiwar movie, but a study of the way the class divisions of the European social system have operated during wartime between officers and enlisted men. *King and Country* centers on Hamp (Tom Courtenay), a young soldier who is court-martialed and executed during World War I for desertion. The tribunal senses that the lad was driven to desertion, not by disloyalty, but by emotional fatigue and horror at the carnage of war. "I just started walking away from the guns," he explained at his trial. "I thought I was walking home." But the youth is nonetheless sacrificed to the impersonal military code that recognizes no exceptions.

The film opens with the camera examining the War Memorial at London's Hyde Park Corner, which is dedicated to those who gave their lives for king and country in World War I. It pauses on a single phase of the memorial's inscription: ". . . the royal fellowship of death." Above these words is a rather stylized figure of a dead soldier lying in state. By implication the memorial is for Hamp too, even though he was shot down not by the enemy but by a firing squad as a victim of the inflexible military code.

The close-up of the idealized statue of a dead soldier is followed by a series of grimly realistic still photos from the Imperial War Museum of actual corpses lying on the muddy battle fields of World War I. The last of these photos dissolves into a shot of the doomed Private Hamp lying on his bunk awaiting trial.

In *King and Country* Losey makes his indictment of the injustices of war through powerful imagery rather than through spoken dialogue, and thus he avoids the polemical approach to which this type of story lends itself. There is, for example, the mock trial of a rat by a group of tired and tense soldiers that is intercut with Hamp's trial and thus serves as a comment on it.

The tribunal that condemns Hamp is apparently confident that it is upholding the traditional military code of honor. The false sense of values on which they base their decision is made clear by the prosecuting attorney, who snaps at the well-meaning but ineffectual defense lawyer (Dirk Bogarde), "A proper court is concerned with law; it's a bit amateur to plead for justice." Yet how different the tribunal's action seems to us when viewed through Losey's critical camera.

Modesty Blaise (1966), although it is done with a lighter touch than most of Losey's work, nevertheless takes us into the same dark corners of human existence that he has explored in his other films. Modesty (Monica Vitti) and Willie Garven (Terence Stamp) are pitted against Gabriel (Dirk Bogarde), an evil genius bent on capturing a shipment of diamonds. The perverse Gabriel, amid the gimmicks and gadgets of his mountain retreat, reminds one of Losey's remark about people who have "every resource of our so-called civilization" at their disposal and use them for their own selfish purposes. Hence even this film, although it is shot in blazing color, has a tinge of black comedy.

Losey's usual concern for human betrayal as an index of the loss of values in the modern age serves as a source of satire in *Modesty Blaise*, in which there are so many spies and counterspies, agents and double agents, that one is not always sure who is betraying whom, or why. The word *trust* comes up frequently in the dialogue, always in an ironic context. To a government official who asks if Modesty can be trusted to help protect the diamond shipment, Sir Gerald Tarrant (Harry Andrews) responds, "We don't trust her, we merely use her."

When the material calls for it, Losey can be a magician who conjures up a story rather than tells it. This is how he handled the bizarre plot of *Modesty Blaise* and even the much more serious, although equally bizarre story of *Secret Ceremony* (1969). In the latter movie Mia Farrow plays Cenci, a rich and neurotic girl whose mother has died. She coaxes Leonora, a fading prostitute (Elizabeth Taylor), to share her large and looming mansion with her as her make-believe mother. Since Leonora has lost a daughter of her own, she consents to the masquerade. But matters become more complicated with the appearance of Cenci's estranged stepfather (Robert Mitchum), whom Cenci implies had seduced her sometime in the past. A savage psychological battle ensues between the make-believe mother and the stepfather for possession of the girl's affections, leading to multiple tragedy.

Cenci, having rejected her frustrating illusions and found nothing in reality to compensate for them, takes a fatal overdoes of drugs. The scene in which she refuses a reconciliation with Leonora, who has no idea that Cenci is dying, is the most gripping in the picture. As the door closes behind Leonora, the camera swings

Richard Burton and Alain Delon in *The Assassination of Trotsky* **(1972). (Cinemabilia)**

slightly upward to reveal Cenci, now mutely trying to cry out to Leonora from the balcony above to save her from the oblivion that is overtaking her. But Leonora, unaware that Cenci needs her help, leaves her to die.

Losey's color camera explores the elegantly overdecorated house with a precision and care that almost imparts to it a life of its own, like Tony's mansion in *The Servant* or Maudsley Manor in *The Go-Between*. His restrained direction has fashioned from his unpromising material a brooding study of the corruption of Innocence and the abiding presence of Evil, which is also reminiscent of *The Servant*.[14]

In *The Assassination of Trotsky* (1972) Losey turned for the first time to actual historical events as the source for a film. Alain Delon plays Frank Jacson, who murdered Leon Trotsky (Richard Burton) in his Mexican retreat. The film covers the period from the first attempt on Trotsky's life by a group of Stalinists up to Trotsky's death a couple of months later. "Some people have complained that the film doesn't give sufficient information about the background of Trotsky's life," Losey commented. "The title, I thought, would have made the intention of the picture clear; that is, to treat only the last months of Trotsky's life. Nevertheless, I had intended to include newsreel material in the film about Trotsky's past; but not much exists, and what does is scratched and faded. I even spent a lot of time and money trying to get some of this newsreel material into the film, but finally had to give up." In the film as it stands Losey has recreated with scrupulous care the last months of the doomed revolutionary. Losey, of course, was an exile himself and hence was attracted to the story of Trotsky.

Losey zeroed in on the life of another historical figure in *Galileo* (1975), which he made in England for the American Film Theater series of filmed plays. "I had done *Galileo* on the stage with Charles Laughton in the title role, and wanted to film it then, but the project fell through," Losey recalled. "The AFT gave me a one million dollar budget, so I had to find ways of simplifying the production," since a historical film could have realistically cost much more. "But this was good discipline for me, and was not at all detrimental to the film"—just as working on a slim budget had definitely not hurt another of his costume dramas, *The Go-Between*.

Galileo relates the life of the seventeenth-century Italian astronomer Galileo Galilei (Topol), who came under fire from the Vatican over his scientific theories, which at the time were thought to be in conflict with Church doctrine. Long after Galileo's death his theories were ultimately acknowledged to be in harmony with the tenets of Christian theology; but Losey was interested not so much in portraying a controversy involving science and religion as in delineating the age-old struggle between the individual and authority. *Galileo* is really about "individual responsibility," Losey commented. Perhaps with his own experience with the House Unamercian Activities in mind, he added that, in keeping with its literary source, the film implies that 'the human race isn't going to survive if people consistently . . . allow themselves to be intimidated. That's the magnificence of that play."

Because the movie's action seldom strays beyond a few basic sets, the film was dismissed by some as a mere photographed stage play. Yet Losey adroitly brings the play to life on the screen by keeping his camera on the go, as it roves from one character to another, capturing every significant gesture and remark, while Galileo engages in lively debate with the churchmen over his scientific research. In committing to celluloid a play he had wanted to film for more than a quarter of a century, Losey accomplished the fulfillment of a long-cherished wish and created a worthy cinematic transcription of a great modern drama in the bargain.

Later in the 1970s Losey went to France to make a trio of French-language films: *Mr. Klein* (1976), *Southern Routes* (1978), and *The Trout* (1982). He joked at the time that, no matter where he went to make a movie, he was still considered a foreign director. If the British regarded him as an American, the French, he said, thought of him as British. For a while it appeared that, after three decades, the expatriate director would make one more picture in his native country; but it was not to be. Losey advised me in a letter from Paris at the time that, to his keen disappointment, the production of a film he was to have made in America had been postponed indefinitely.[15] He eventually returned to England to film *Steaming* (1985), adapted by his wife Patricia from the play by Nell Dunn. The movie, which depicts the interaction of a group of women in a London steam bath, has an all-female cast, like Cukor's *The Women*. Losey described *Steaming* as "a film about a shelter or refuge, an enclave for a group of women 'regulars' in a Turkish bath," who derive mutual support and understanding from sharing with each other their thoughts on life, love and other common concerns. Losey, whose early experience as a director in the professional theater had taught him how to bring out the best in his actors, obtained ensemble acting of a high order from his top-flight cast, headed by Vanessa Redgrave and Sarah Miles.

Steaming was to be Losey's last film, and, characteristically, he finished shooting the picture on schedule, despite his declining health. "It was so important to Joe to finish his work on *Steaming*," Patricia Losey has said. "It's so important to all of us who were involved that he did."

Writing of Losey's career, Rex Reed has observed, "Seldom has there been a case of native talent treated so badly by the industry that bred him."[16] "Working like this over the years," Losey reflected, "sacrificing the big, juicy jobs for the things I believe in, and doing it with no money and little encouragement, it's been exhausting." Yet, when one ponders the impressive group of films that Losey was able to make with all of the obstacles in his path, one wonders if he would have had it any other way.

12
Bryan Forbes
The Kitchen Sink-Drome

"What the British film has always lacked has been—except in rare hole-in-the-corner movements—its own inspiration," William Whitebait wrote in 1959 in *The International Film Annual*. "The war roused us, as film makers, to a sense of duty; but when peace comes, what happens? The effort gutters out, we go on reflecting the effort, and relapse into decency and evasion, we become again the nonfilm makers that apparently we are."[1]

Whitebait wrote these strong words at a time when he and other observers of the British film scene were speculating whether or not the new movement in British cinema called Social Realism was going to have any real impact on the British film industry or merely "gutter out". As things turned out, Social Realism did not last long as a distinct movement, but it did have a lasting impact on British film making.

British Social Realism has done two things for British cinema. First, in extending the area of interest for British films beyond London and its environs, it brought the film maker out of the insulated atmosphere of the studio and into contact with story material dealing with people of the provinces, who now became subjects for cinema. Second, the language of ordinary people began to replace the inbred theatrical dialogue previously common on the British screen.

Since Bryan Forbes and other directors such as John Schlesinger began their careers just as Social Realism was making its presence felt in the British film industry, it will be helpful to examine this movement briefly. In this way we can better understand the climate in which a director like Forbes began making films.

The roots of British Social Realism go back to the formation of the welfare state in postwar England in the mid-1940s. It was then that the expectations of the working classes were aroused by free education and promises of equality of opportunity. When these expectations were not fully realized, a disillusionment developed that was to be echoed in novels like John Braine's *Room at the Top* (1957) and Alan Sillitoe's *Saturday Night and Sunday Morning* (1958), and in the plays of John Osborne produced at the Royal Court Theater, beginning with *Look Back in Anger* in 1956. Often the setting of these works was a northern industrial community where progress and advancement had remained largely unfulfilled ambitions. In Osborne's *Look Back in Anger*, for example, the working class hero Jimmy Porter spoke in plain language that everyone understood about problems that many in the audience shared.

Bryan Forbes at the camera during the filming of _The Raging Moon_ (1971). (The Bryan Forbes collection)

In 1956, the same year that *Look Back in Anger* premiered at the Royal Court, Lindsay Anderson, who was associated with the Royal Court, joined Tony Richardson and Karel Reisz in launching British Free Cinema, based on ideas that Anderson, Reisz, and others had already been writing about in the Oxford magazine *Sequence*. British Free Cinema would in turn be the genesis of Social Realism in British films.

Looking back on those days, Anderson said that Free Cinema developed into a movement by accident. He and his colleagues wanted "to celebrate the insignificance of every day," as their manifesto put it, to look at factories and youth clubs, people at work and at play. "Yet," Karel Reisz added, "we were not interested in treating social problems, so much as we were in becoming the first generation of British directors who as a group were allowed to work freely on material of their own choosing"; and by so doing they would be implementing a fundamental principle of the *auteur* theory.

A director like Carol Reed, as was noted, achieved this kind of independence only after proving himself by working on low-budget films assigned to him by the stuido. Reisz, Richardson, and Anderson knew that they could only hope to make feature films on their own terms if they could prove themselves by making superior short films. Accordingly they put together a program of shorts and took over the British Film Institute's National Film Theater for a few days in 1956 in order to give their films a showing. Under the banner of British Free Cinema they presented Reisz's and Richardson's *Momma Don't Allow*, Anderson's *O Dreamland*, and other documentaries.

"The films were not intended as social propaganda," Anderson maintained; but the social aspects of these short films made by the group helped to bring the films to public attention sooner than might have otherwise been the case. "Nevertheless, they were not about problems but about people," he emphasized.

Room at the Top (1958), directed by Jack Clayton, extended the trend of Social Realism to feature films. Joe Lampton (Laurence Harvey) is the film's antihero, a bitter young man who, like Jimmy Porter in *Look Back in Anger*, marries across the class barrier. Joe ruthlessly works his way up in the business world until he reaches his goals. The success of *Room at the Top* proved that audiences were ready to accept outspoken motion pictures with unsympathetic heroes, and this encouraged Richardson to film Osborne's *Look Back in Anger* (1958) and *The Entertainer* (1960).

Karel Reisz followed Richardson's lead by making his first feature, *Saturday Night and Sunday Morning* (1960). It was as successful on both sides of the Atlantic as *Room at the Top* had been, despite the fact that both Reisz and his star, Albert Finney, were virtually unknown at the time the picture was made. Reisz's short films had already reflected his concern for young people with assembly-line jobs that made them feel unimportant and rendered their lives sterile and meaningless. Arthur Seaton (Albert Finney) in *Saturday Night* is a young machinist who works off the frustration of his monotonous job by heavy drinking and symbolically expresses his rebellion against society in general and the plant's management in particular by getting the wife of his foreman pregnant.

In contrast to the more polished sytle of *Room at the Top*, Reisz made his film on location in the Nottingham factory district in a documentarylike style that gave the story a vital air of authenticity. The realism that Carol Reed and David Lean had brought to their postwar films was given a strong shot in the arm by films like *Saturday Night and Sunday Morning*. Moreover, audiences heard Finney and the other actors in the film using the ordinary speech with which they were familiar. Reisz was convinced that audiences "no longer wanted to look up to something different. They wanted stars with whom they could identify." The success of his film proved him right.

Although *Saturday Night and Sunday Morning* was looked upon as an excellent example of Social Realism, or "kitchen sink" realism as the movement was nick-named, Reisz did not look upon *Saturday Night* as a social document. "If a director succeeds only in capturing the sociological situation of the moment in a film," he said, "he will find that the film will be dated within a few years. But if he has caught some aspect of the human predicament, something of the spiritual problems that underlie the material ones, then the film will not go out of date, but will have a lasting quality."

By this time critics were beginning to wonder if the rich vein of Social Realism could be exploited indefinitely. Moviegoers were getting a bit tired of the same grimy tenements and the eternal "kitchen sink-drome." The pattern of British Social Realism was changed at this juncture by two of the men responsible for establishing it.

In 1963 Reisz joined Lindsay Anderson as producer of Anderson's first full-length feature, *The Sporting Life*, which pushed Social Realism toward psycho-logical realism. The story is told from the point of view of a good-natured but brutish ballplayer named Frank Machin (Richard Harris) who is at home only on the playing field. He is baffled by other people and usually treats them as members of the opposing team. Anderson intercut the main story with fragmented flashbacks that show the viewer how Frank's past experiences influence his present thought and action. "Telling the story from Frank's point of view was necessary to avoid making the film seem to be about a football player instead of about a man," Ander-son commented. "Football provided important metaphors about the nature of man's struggle in life."

Other British directors followed Anderson's lead in departing from the realms of strict Social Realism in favor of psychological realism, which was more concerned with examining carefully and authentically the inner conflicts that motivate a char-acter's actions than with exploring the external social pressures that influence their behavior. Among these film makers was Bryan Forbes. Reisz also experimented with psychological realism in *Morgan!* (1966). The hero, played by David Warner, is an emotionally unstable young man who tries to win back his estranged wife (Vanessa Redgrave) by acting first like Tarzan and then like King Kong. Reisz treated his hero with humor to avoid making him a case study instead of a human being. "Too often in films dealing with people with neurotic problems the director treats these individuals as specimens to be analyzed, rather than fellow human beings who need to be understood." This is one of the principles that the British

Free Cinema short films were based on; and it is a hallmark of the films of Bryan Forbes, who sometimes deals with emotionally disturbed characters in his films, as in *Seance on a Wet Afternoon* and *The Whisperers*.

Even after Social Realism as a separate movement passed into film history, its original protagonists continued to insist that films should leave their audiences with something to think about. "You may not be able to change anyone's mind with a movie," said Reisz, "but you can change their feelings; you can make them feel differently about a problem, and this will influence their thinking. The way the director distributes the sympathy which he wants to arouse in the audience for various characters and situations in the film will determine this influence."

The 1969 Cannes Film Festival provided what might be called the apotheosis of British Social Realism when Anderson's *If* won the Grand Prize and Vanessa Redgrave won the best actress award in Reisz's *Loves of Isadora*. "We originally fought to secure the director a place in the whole film making process," Reisz pointed out, "and Free Cinema helped to accomplish this." As a result many British directors now have more creative freedom than they would otherwise have had in making a film.

One such film maker is Bryan Forbes, who was born in London in 1926. After playing minor roles in films like Carol Reed's *The Key* (1958), he turned to writing movie scripts. He provided the screenplay for *The Angry Silence* (1960) and for the Peter Sellers vehicle *Only Two Can Play* (1961), as well as for *The League of Gentlemen* (1961), in which he also acted.

The Angry Silence was a crucial film for Forbes since he not only wrote the script but coproduced it with the movie's star, Richard Attenborough, and hence was able to learn a great deal about film production from the inside. The picture was made during the heyday of Social Realism, the same year as Reisz's *Saturday Night and Sunday Morning* and Richardson's *The Entertainer*, and fit neatly into that genre in its uncompromising look at corruption within the unions.

Tom Curtis, a young factory worker (Richard Attenborough), refuses to back a wildcat strike and is "sent to Coventry"—ostracized by his fellow workers. Tom manfully resists the pressures that are brought to bear on him, maintaining that "if people can't be different—there's no point in bringing up kids, no point in anything." Finally, when he is attacked by agitators and loses one of his eyes, the other workers come to their senses and realize how unjustly Tom has been treated.

Forbes's crisp dialogue lent realism to the film, as did the scenes shot on location in a factory with several of the employees appearing as extras. "Credit is due for making this film at all," Roger Manvell comments, "and for the forthrightness of much of its dialogue. There had been almost nothing on the British screen about abuses within the trade unions."[2]

Following the success of *The Angry Silence*, Forbes and Attenborough coproduced three more independent productions together: *Whistle Down the Wind*, *The L-Shaped Room*, and *Seance on a Wet Afternoon*, all of which Forbes directed as well as scripted. Initially *Whistle Down the Wind* (1962) was to have been directed by Guy Green, who had directed *The Angry Silence*; but Green decided to make another film instead. "We were quite near the starting point," Forbes remembers, "and had very little money. We were all scrabbling around because Hayley Mills was the star and the Mills family had director approval; so finally we took our courage in our hands and drove down to the Mills's farm and asked about my doing it. After about two or three hours of discussion, they agreed." Forbes left immediately to look for locations in Northern England. "By the time I got scared about directing my first film," he says, "we were already two weeks into the picture."[3]

In *Whistle Down the Wind* Alan Bates plays a bearded fugitive who is discovered hiding in a barn by three children. When he is asked who he is, the startled criminal bursts out, "Jesus Christ!" The children take him literally and believe him to be Christ come back to earth. The fugitive encourages them in their misconception about him, because they are therefore willing to bring him food secretly. Finally the criminal gives himself up to the police rather than destroy their religious faith. As he stands in the farmyard being frisked by the police, his arms assume a crucifixion pose, indicating that he is sacrificing himself for the children.

Forbes caught perfectly the hauntingly bleak atmosphere of the countryside of Northern England where the film was shot and marked himself as a director of promise. *Whistle Down the Wind* has remained his favorite among the films he has made. "It was a funny film in many ways," he notes, "because it worked on so many levels. Someone writing in a religious magazine said, not unperceptively, that it must have been made by an agnostic. But it wasn't really about religion—it was about innocence." *Whistle Down the Wind* really shows Innocence influencing Evil, quite the reverse of the situation in Losey's *The Servant*. Forbes, like Losey, makes both Innocence and Evil seem tangibly real as they are embodied in his chief characters.

The promise that Forbes showed in his first directorial effort was fulfilled in *The L-Shaped Room* (1963), for which Leslie Caron won a British Academy Award for her performance as Jane Fasset, a French girl living in a London tenement. She has an affair with a handsome young man who deserts her when she becomes pregnant. After considering abortion, she decides to have her child and return to her family. The film was in the mainstream of British Social Realism, with its use of authentic locations in the London slums and its carefully drawn portrayals of the variety of characters that inhabit the boarding house where the girl lives.

There is Mavis, an ancient has-been actress who comments on her lesbian bent to Jane by saying, "Takes all sorts, dear. I hope you have a girl; they're less trouble than boys, really"; Johnny, a homosexual West Indian (Brock Peters); a prostitute who declares, "I love my tea; I don't care much for the other any more, but I do like my tea"; and Toby Coleman (Tom Bell), an unpublished writer who falls in love with Jane, unaware that she is pregnant with another man's child.

Jane's decision not to have an abortion is prompted by the calloused, mercenary attitude of the doctor (Emlyn Williams) whom she consults about it. She tries to hide her pregnancy from Toby, but inevitably he learns of it and disowns his love for her, refusing to accept the responsibility of bringing up a child not his own. He nevertheless visits her in the hospital after the baby is born. He presents her with a short story he has written entitled "The L-Shaped Room," named after the attic

Leslie Caron and Emlyn Williams in *The L-Shaped Room* (1963). (Movie Star News)

garret in which Jane has lived at the boarding house and dealing with their short-lived affair. Jane tells Toby that she has decided to return to her family, but on her terms. "I've had my baby; they can't take it away from me," she says, referring particularly to her father, who had encouraged her to have an abortion.

When Jane returns to her flat to collect her belongings before going back to France, she meets the girl (Nanette Newman) who has rented the L-shaped room. The latter says that she has no intention of making the acquaintance of any of the other tenants in the building. "I won't get mixed up with them," she insists. "First they get friendly, and then your life's not your own any more." Jane can only smile sadly at this remark, for, shortly before, she had said of her relationship with these same people, who had seen her through her ordeal: "It was nice to have love. Without that there's nothing left."

Forbes handled the sexual problems in the film with both frankness and discretion.[4] "I am more concerned about the proper presentation of violence on the screen than sex," Forbes says. "You can't legislate sex out of people's lives in the same way that you can and should violence. Since sex is a part of people's everyday life, I deal with it in a film when it is called for, as in *The L-Shaped Room*; but I always imply that sex must be involved with true love."

Even though the scripts Forbes has written have usually been based on novels or plays, his choice of subject matter consistently reflects his own interests and point of view; hence he clearly qualifies as an *auteur*. The cinema of Bryan Forbes often deals with the world of the loser. Some of his central characters deserve to lose, like the criminal in *Whistle Down the Wind*; others, like the girl in *The L-Shaped Room*, learn the paradox that only in losing skirmishes in life can one ultimately win the battle that is life itself.

Seance on a Wet Afternoon (1964) is about a woman who seems born to lose. Myra Savage (Kim Stanley) is a neurotic medium who persuades her passive and intellectual husband Bill (Richard Attenborough) to help her kidnap a child, ostensibly so that she can win recognition by "divining" where the child has been hidden. But her real, though unacknowledged reason is rooted in the suppressed frustration she feels because she is childless. Indeed, her whole obsession with her supposed visionary powers rests on her belief that she can communicate with her own child, who was stillborn.

Forbes mixed the melodrama of the kidnapping with a touching study of two lonely misfits who are unable to cope with the harshness of reality, a theme that he would continue to develop in other films. He reveals the strange motivation that underlies Myra's behavior very slowly in the film, and yet the picture moves along on the narrative level at a brisk pace. For example, the director skillfully extracts every ounce of suspense from the sequence in which Bill carries out the kidnapping plot. He secures a motorcycle with an enclosed sidecar and hides it behind an abandoned building. Then he proceeds to the school where he is to kidnap the small daughter of a well-to-do family. He arrives just at dismissal time and waits until the chauffeur, who normally takes her home, has put her in the back seat of the family limousine. Then Bill steps forward and sends the chauffeur into the school on a pretext, enabling Bill to get behind the wheel of the limousine and drive off before the chauffeur returns.

As the car speeds down the highway, Forbes quickly cuts back and forth from close-ups of Bill's tense expression to the little girl, whose frightened screams go unheard, shut in by the glass panelling that separates the front seat from the back. Once they arrive at the place where Bill has hidden his cycle, he chloroforms the child and takes her home to Myra in the enclosed sidecar. This is truly a riveting scene, matched only by the sequence in which the ransom money is delivered by the kidnapped child's parents. This latter scene was shot with hidden cameras during the rush hour in and around London subway stations.

Despite all of their meticulous plans, however, Myra and Bill are tracked down by the police. But by this time Myra has withdrawn from reality to the point that she is not even aware the police are arresting her and her husband. As for Bill, he looks almost relieved that the long ordeal is now at an end.

That Forbes was coming into his own as a prominent director was evidenced by Judith Crist's review of *Seance*: "The fascination of the film lies, of course, partly in its ingenious plot, partly in the brilliant photography, and in the subtle and exciting direction of Bryan Forbes, author of the screenplay as well." Crist went on to praise the performance of Kim Stanley and Richard Attenborough as the shabby middle-aged couple. They represent two of "the gray people who surround us unnoticed, but behind whose familiar faces an invisible horror lurks undetected," until it bursts forth in bizarre and terrifying behavior.[5]

Forbes has always been a gifted director of actors, able to elicit powerful performances from his cast. "I think everything should be subordinate to the performance," he says. "I don't believe that you should flash your technique to the detriment of the actors. In the last analysis all that you remember after seeing a film are the performances, whether it's Spencer Tracy or Katharine Hepburn or Garbo. If actors feel that you are only working for them, directing them in the truest sense of the word, then you get first-rate performances."[6] Perhaps that is why actors like Kim Stanley, Richard Attenborough, Leslie Caron, and George Segal have done some of their best work under Forbes's direction.

In *King Rat* (1965) Segal brilliantly underplays the title role of a crafty American in a Japanese prison camp during the Second World War who learns to capitalize on the misery of his fellow prisoners by engineering various crooked deals among them. He is idolized by a naive but good-natured young British inmate (James Fox), for whom he develops a genuine friendship that he promptly disowns, once the camp is liberated: "You did me some favors, and I paid you for them" are King Rat's last words to his comrade.

Forbes was quite successful in creating the degrading atmosphere of prison life. When one sees the merciless sun glaring down on the camp compound and the sweat on the faces of captives and captors alike, it is hard to believe that the film was shot almost entirely in a Hollywood studio. The director builds up the claustrophobic atmosphere of prison life by emphasizing in his visual compositions the cramped conditions in which the prisoners live, in an effort to help the audience understand how narrow a man's view of life can become when his horizon has been so restricted. Discipline and morale are maintained by the senior officers among the inmates, and the situation has become so desperate that someone caught by his fellow prisoners stealing supplies is punished with death—which is officially reported as suicide.

In this atmosphere of fear, suspicion, and loneliness, of course, a scoundrel like King Rat thrives. But it is clear at the end of the film, when he turns away from his one true friend, that a man in whose world there is no place for human feeling and friendship is the real loser in life, regardless of how often he successfully swindles others.

Forbes looks upon *King Rat* as one of his best films. "I think it's my most ambitious film," he says; "and in many ways it was ahead of its time," in that it presented an American soldier as an antihero before it had become fashionable in the film industry to present such a character in an unflattering light.[7]

Back in England, Forbes switched to farce for his next film, *The Wrong Box* (1966). He assembled a remarkable cast, headed by Ralph Richardson and John Mills, to tell a tale about a scramble among some supposedly respectable Victorian gentlemen for a fortune that is to go to the last surviving member of their club.

Two brothers, Sir Joseph Finsbury (Ralph Richardson) and Masterman Finsbury (John Mills), are the last survivors of the club. Sir Joseph's heirs (Peter Cook and Dudley Moore) hatch several plans to see that Sir Joseph outlives Masterman, who

The prison camp in *King Rat* (1965). (Author's collection)

in turn is consistently foiled in his efforts to exterminate his brother in order to win the fortune. The plot becomes hilariously complicated when Sir Joseph is apparently killed in a train wreck. Amid the wreckage, the two nephews find the body of the "Bournemouth Strangler" and mistake the corpse for that of Sir Joseph. They accordingly hide what they take to be Sir Joseph's corpse in a barrel and then seek to give the impression that Sir Joseph is still alive when, in fact, he is! After a series of mad mishaps, none of the principals who are scrambling for the fortune receives it. All of them quite deservedly turn out to be losers.

Although Forbes drew rich comic portrayals from the whole cast, it is Peter Sellers, for whom he had written *Only Two Can Play*, who steals the picture. Sellers enacts the role of a benighted doctor reduced to selling undated death certificates for a living, presumably to potential murderers.

The subject for his next film was suggested to Forbes when he heard about an old woman who died in an apartment building and was not found for several days because no one had missed her. From that time onward he wanted to make a film about lonely old people. When he came upon a novel about such an elderly woman, he adapted it for the screen as *The Whisperers* and secured Dame Edith Evans, Seventy-nine, for the central role of Margaret Ross. Mrs. Ross is an elderly woman who is driven into a world of illusion by loneliness and old age but still goes on coping with life as best she can.

Deserted by her husband Archie (Eric Portman), her only company is the imagined voices she hears whispering to her. She also takes refuge in delusions of grandeur about wealth and a social position she never possessed. These fantasies come to the surface when she signs forms at the welfare office as Margaret Ross, "Dame of the Order of the Garter and Doctor of Laws" and assures a social worker that she will cease to need help from the state once she completes the sale of her pedigreed cattle.

Her daydreams suddenly seem vindicated when she accidentally discovers in her closet a large sum of money hidden there secretly by her thieving son. Inevitably, the money is stolen from her because she brags about having it. Mrs. Ross is drugged by some miscreants and left in an alley overnight. While she recuperates in the hospital, her husband is located and returned to her. But Archie soon disappears again, and Mrs. Ross is left alone once more with her voices.

Yet *The Whisperers* is not a depressing film, for Dame Edith Evans injects humor as well as pathos into her portrayal of Margaret Ross. When a social worker inquires why her closet is stuffed with old newspapers, Mrs. Ross replies grandly, "I keep them—for reference." Dame Edith said at the Berlin Film Festival, where she won the best actress award for her performance, that she took the part because Mrs. Ross seemed to her to be a likeable and compassionate person. When she hears on the radio how many old people there are in Britain who are destitute, Mrs. Ross mutters, with no thought of herself, "The poor old souls."

There is a certain nobility about an old woman who, despite the fact that she is one of life's losers, refuses to feel sorry for herself. Instead she seeks to maintain whatever shreds of respectability are left to her. As Forbes implies in his screenplay, even good social assistance is no substitute for compassion and understanding for the aged. "How do you tell all of the Mrs. Rosses of the world," muses a social worker, "that they are nobody?"

The only fault one can find with the picture is that writer Forbes might have made it easier for director Forbes to pace the film had he written a more tightly knit script. Nevertheless, Forbes has made a movie that never descends into maudlin melodrama and that records on film the best performance of Dame Edith Evans's long career. "I was more than pleased when Dame Edith won recognition for her performance," says Forbes. "But I was very disappointed when the film did not receive a wider distribution, since I believed very much in the picture; and her performance deserved to be seen by more people. I couldn't have conceived of making the film with anyone else but Dame Edith." For Forbes, she brought to the role what he described on another occasion as the kind of "rare, unvarnished honesty" that always distinguished her acting.[8]

The Whisperers was modestly budgeted at $500,000, and Forbes comments, "I've never made a cheaper film in my life. It was even cheaper to make than *Whistle Down the Wind* because all of the artists agreed to come in on a cooperative basis"—that is, to take a percentage of the movie's eventual profits rather than demand a flat salary while the film was in production. This is an indication that others besides Forbes very much believed in the film, and the resulting motion picture is a tribute to that belief.

Deadfall (1968) is a slick suspense movie that, as Forbes told me when I talked with him on the set at London's Pinewood Studios, marked a change of pace for him after the somber drama of *The Whisperers*. *Deadfall* is about a cat burglar (Michael Caine) who in the end goes sour on thievery as a profession when he falls in love with the wife of his partner in crime (Eric Portman). The film reaches a peak of excitement in the scene that depicts one of the cat burglar's typical capers. In this renowned twenty-three-minute burglary sequence, the Caine character must bring off a jewel theft before the man whose mansion is being robbed returns home from a concert at a nearby auditorium. For this complicated sequence Forbes had John Barry, the composer of the movie's musical score, create a complete guitar concerto, which was played throughout the sequence, while the director intercut the scene in the concert hall with the robbery in progress back at the victim's home.

Barry notes that, in general, the film score must be subservient to the movie's action. But in this instance, he says, Forbes elected to have him record the concerto first, and the film was shot and edited to the tempo of the music. Sometimes a musical passage underlined the action; but at other points "the relaxed moments in the concerto were deliberately matched to contrastingly tense shots in the sequence," in order to provide an ironic counterpoint to what was happening on the screen. Needless to say, this setpiece, which was so artfully photographed and cut together, is the highlight of the whole picture.

A strong confirmation of the principle that a director should be involved in the making of a film from the earliest stages of preproduction planning is to be found in Forbes's somewhat unhappy experience in making *The Madwoman of Chaillot* (1969). Forbes took over the picture from John Huston ten days before shooting began because of irreconcilable differences between Huston and the film's producer. He accepted the job, he says, because he could not resist the opportunity to direct Katharine Hepburn. "Huston had not actually begun shooting; but he had hired most of the actors, built a great number of sets, and chosen the locations," Forbes remembers. "Also he had made the decision to use the charming studios at Nice, but they were unfortunately only forty yards from the airport."[9] That decision had been made in the wintertime, when perhaps four planes passed over the studio per day. But by the time Forbes started filming the airport had up to forty takeoffs and landings a day, which meant that about four hours of shooting time were lost daily because of the noise of planes passing overhead.

The Madwoman of Chaillot had an incandescent cast headed by Katharine Hepburn in the title role, with Giulietta Masina and Edith Evans as her equally mad companions, as well as Charles Boyer, Yul Brynner, Danny Kaye, and Paul Henreid. The plot, from Giradoux's play, concerns an insane countess who emerges from her seclusion long enough to foil a plot to destroy Paris for the sake of the oil deposits beneath the city. Like Margaret Ross, the countess lives in a world of illusion; and there is a touch of nobility in the way that she deals with life from her own subjective frame of reference.

But unfortunately Giradoux's wispy play does not hold up well in the realistic atmosphere of the cinema. "Perhaps people today have become too cynical to accept Giradoux's somewhat naive sentiments, and so the film didn't catch on," says Forbes. "Looking back now, I think my major mistake was to put *Madwoman* in period costume; but I didn't have the luxury of time to change things. Today I would say to Kate: 'Don't change. Go straight on the set as you are in your Afrika Corps hat, Spencer Tracy's old pullover, a pair of slacks and tennis shoes. Just bicycle onto the set as you are, Kate, because you are the Madwoman of Chaillot.''[10]

After making *The Madwoman*, Forbes began a two-year term in April, 1969, as production chief at Elstree Studios, which represents one of the few times in the history of cinema that a film director has become a top studio executive. During his tenure in that office he maintained a policy of artistic independence for the directors who made films there. "I suppose one of the most individualist directors is Joseph Losey," Forbes said at the time, "and he completed *The Go-Between* while I was at Elstree; and I don't think we ever had a cross word. I never abused my position with any of my directors. I tried to allow them to work and enjoy the same sort of creative freedom I had fought for myself. . . . What's more, I think we made an atmosphere at Elstree that was far removed from the old factory atmosphere."[11]

When Forbes was presented with the script of *The Raging Moon*, about an athlete who becomes a paraplegic, he decided not only that he would approve it for production at Elstree, but that he would direct it himself. He was obviously happy to be back at work directing once more, after more than a year of purely administrative work. "I suppose that it was rare for the head of a studio to be directing a film at the same time, but Alexander Korda did it at Denham years ago, so it is not that extraordinary," says Forbes. "I didn't find running the studio while directing a film difficult. I had accumulated a very good team of people in whom I had trust and respect. So I was entirely confident that the studio was not going to fall down around our heads."

I visited the set of *The Raging Moon* while Forbes was shooting it at Elstree, and it proved an interesting experience to observe one man running a studio and directing a picture simultaneously. Forbes was directing the scene in which Bruce (Malcolm McDowell) discovers the bruise on his leg that gives him the first indication of the onset of his disease. Forbes began the day's shooting by discussing with McDowell and the other actors the frame of mind he wanted each of them to have during the scene. This was done in a quiet, conversational tone of voice that he never raised, even when calling "action" or "cut." A very considerate man, he even took time to compliment the make-up artist for the realistic bruise on McDowell's leg.

Between takes he had to consult not only with the technicians and actors on the set, as any director does, but also with members of the studio staff who came to the set to discuss problems involved with the overall running of the studio. Yet he still found time to discuss the film with me.

"I wrote one bit of dialogue right on the set the other day," he said. "It was in the scene where Bruce berates the vicar who has come to visit him in the hospital with the fact that God should not have allowed a young athlete like him to contract this disease. It's the 'Why me and not somebody else?' attitude. The vicar, who realizes that he won't be able to reason with Bruce while the lad is upset, says simply,

'These are difficult questions for God too.'" The vicar never loses faith that Bruce will overcome his bitterness; and he is vindicated when Bruce falls in love with Jill, a thirty-year-old woman who is another wheelchair patient.

The role of Jill is played in the film by Nanette Newman, an accomplished actress in her own right who also happens to be Mrs. Bryan Forbes. She has appeared in supporting roles in most of her husband's films, but Jill was her first major role; and her portrayal proved that she deserved it.

The sets designed for *The Raging Moon* were not large, since the film was being made on a small budget, and Forbes compensated for their lack of expanse by using every possible inch of playing space on each set. As the cast and crew moved from the bedroom set where the day's shooting began to the living-room set close by, Forbes surveyed it in silence for a moment, then said, "Let's have that bloody wall out to give us more room to move the camera." With that, carpenters unbolted one wall of the living room set, and Forbes began pacing off the movements of the actors, listening to their suggestions all the while.

The Raging Moon represents a return to the spare realism of Forbes's earlier work. In dealing with the doomed love affair of the invalid Bruce for a polio victim who dies before they can be married, Forbes has drawn what is probably his definitive picture of a loser who refuses to admit defeat. During his first days in the convalescent home Bruce sulks in his dark room, turning his wheelchair in an endless circle of frustration. Later, as he begins to take an interest in the other patients, notably Jill, his life begins to take on meaning once more.

When Jill dies before they can be married, Bruce is again bereft of hope. In the final scene, superbly moving in its understatement, Bruce sits brooding in the game room of the nursing home. Another patient hits a ping pong ball in his direction. At first Bruce refuses to take any notice. Then, realizing that the game of life must go on, Bruce returns the ball when it is served to him again, and the camera pulls away from the scene as Bruce becomes engaged in the game.

When Forbes completed his two-year term as production chief at Elstree, he returned to writing and directing films. "I wanted to go back to being a loner and plowing my own solitary furrow," he explains, "because I think that's how I work best."

Recently he recalled, "After resigning as head of production at Elstree Studios in 1971, I wrote a novel called *The Distant Laughter*," a behind-the-scenes look at the movie business, "and a first volume of autobiography called *Notes for a Life*. Then I went to Connecticut to film *The Stepford Wives* (1975)," a film Leslie Halliwell characterizes as science fiction set in suburbia that treats its intriguing premise with "agreeable sophistication."[12] It tells the story of Joanna, a new wife in a suburban village (Katharine Ross), who finds the behavior of her female friends rather strange. It develops that their husbands have conspired with a suave, sinister evil genius named Dale Coba (Patrick O'Neal) to have them converted into docile automatons. Forbes makes the most of his material, as when he depicts the Stepford wives marching down the aisle of a supermarket like zombies, mechanically filling their carts with groceries. The viewer can only wonder ruefully how long Joanna can avoid a similar fate.

Roger Moore, star of *The Naked Face* (1985). (Museum of Modern Art/Film Stills Archive)

The Stepford Wives was successful enough to spawn no less than two sequels on TV, *Revenge of the Stepford Wives* (1980) and *The Stepford Children* (1987), both of which were made by other directors. To Forbes's credit, neither sequel packs the punch of his original movie.

Following *Stepford Wives* Forbes wrote and directed a sumptuous musical version of the Cinderella fable, *The Slipper and the Rose* (1976), and did some noteworthy work for British television, including a splendid documentary on Dame Edith Evans. He also contributed a farcical segment, featuring Roger Moore, to the anthology film *Sunday Lovers* (1980). Moore later starred in *The Naked Face* (1985), a thriller that Forbes adapted from Sidney Sheldon's novel and shot on location in Chicago.

In *The Naked Face* Moore plays a psychiatrist who is being stalked by a syndicate hit man; in order to discover why the Mafia wants him killed, he desperately turns to an aging private investigator (Art Carney), whose disheveled appearance and squalid lodgings belie his past record as a once-successful detective. With the latter's help, the hero discovers that a powerful Mafia don has ordered his liquidation because the don fears that his wife, who happens to be one of the psychiatrist's patients, has revealed "family secrets" to him in the course of their therapy sessions. This revelation leads to the movie's action-packed finale, when the psychiatrist, with the police close behind, moves in for a showdown with the Mafia boss.

From this melodramatic material Forbes has fashioned a stylish chiller, topped off by Art Carney's marvelous delineation of the down-at-the-heels private eye who can still pull himself together when a challenging case comes his way.

Forbes has continued to write fiction, as well as to work in the motion picture and TV industries. In the summer of 1988 he filmed a four-hour telemovie, which he adapted from his own novel, *The Endless Game*, with Albert Finney and George Segal in the leading roles.

Examining Forbes's varied filmography, one observes that it encompasses a wide range of genres, from social drama to farce. What all of his movies have in common has been succinctly summarized by Roger Manvell: "As a writer, Bryan Forbes has an admirable sense of dialogue; as a director, he has an equally admirable sense of how to get the best out of his actors. His films, which often edge near melodrama and sentimentality, always allow for subtlety and an unhurried exploration of human feeling."[13] Unquestionably this provocative and fascinating director has created a body of work that assures him a place in cinema history.

13
John Schlesinger
Kinds of Loving

John Schlesinger was never an official part of the British Free Cinema movement. Yet, like Bryan Forbes, he began making films when the trend toward Social Realism initiated by Free Cinema was in full swing in Britain.

As a youth Schlesinger, who was born in London in 1926, wanted to become a professional magician, an avocation he feels helped lead him toward a film making career. "The mixture of spoof, technical dexterity, and audience control of the illusionist closely parallels the craft of the film maker," Schlesinger explains. "My interest in magic may well have been the first glimmering of my ambition to translate images and illusions of life onto the screen."

After serving in World War II, Schlesinger turned to acting and directing for the Oxford University Dramatic Society, to amateur photography, and to making experimental films. When these short films failed to arouse interest in any of the film companies, he took up acting again, appearing in minor roles on stage and screen. Finally he began making television documentaries for BBC-TV. Working on these documentaries, Schlesinger believes, helped him to develop his powers of observation and to learn to make decisions quickly: "The speed at which you are obliged to work teaches you a sort of basic film grammar, like weekly repertory in the theater does for an actor."[1]

In the late 1950s Schlesinger made several documentary segments for the BBC television series *Monitor*. The subjects ranged from the circus and the Cannes Film Festival to Brighton Amusement Park and the hi-fi record craze. In each of these cinematic essays Schlesinger sought to probe beneath the surface of the event he was examining in order to get at the human dimension implicit in the situation. In *The Circus*, for example, Schlesinger cuts from the glamour of the performance to the decidedly unglamorous existence that the performers live backstage. His film on the Cannes Film Festival satirizes the publicity stunts that are staged on behalf of would-be superstars to gain the attention of journalists and film executives. "A film festival is a circus," says the commentator, "a self-advertising parade. Those who don't enter films in the festival enter themselves."

One of Schlesinger's best *Monitor* films is *The Innocent Eye: A Study of the Child's Imagination*. As we see a small child wandering through a park in autumn, the narrator muses that, to a youngster, the world is a strange place filled with

John Schlesinger directing *Yanks* **(1978). (The John Schlesinger collection)**

innumerable joys. Then Schlesinger shows us a series of watercolors done in a nursery school by a group of five-year-olds. As the scene shifts to some older boys in an art class, the commentator continues, "At fourteen everything is suddenly difficult. Once the imagination grew wild. Now it has to be coaxed and cultivated. You study things that have grown commonplace, things that were once unique, to recapture that sense of wonder you once had. Does a door within us close as we enter the outside world amid the noise of growing up? We may spend the rest of our lives trying to open it again."

That Schlesinger himself still has his sense of wonder intact is clear from *Terminus* (1961), the best of his documentaries, which he shot in London's Waterloo Station and which won him a prize at the Venice Film Festival. In it he focuses the viewer's attention on the human comedy that everyone passing through a large railway station usually takes for granted.

"I have always been interested in people and their relationships to each other," Schlesinger explains. Therefore he filmed all sorts of situations at Waterloo Station for *Terminus*, from wedding parties to a lost little boy. The forty-five minute film about human beings in a hurry can well serve as the prologue for all of his later work, he says. "We wanted to juxtapose the different kinds of people to be found in a railway station. Under one roof we found all of the misery, happiness, loneliness, bewilderment, and loss to be found anywhere in the world."

Terminus is the type of documentary popularized in England during the late 1950s by the Free Cinema movement, the success of which created the atmosphere in which the Free Cinema directors were able to make feature films that had similar social themes. When, on the release of Reisz's *Saturday Night and Sunday Morning* (1960), both he and his star, Albert Finney, suddenly became internationally known, it was easier for producer Joseph Janni to convince financial backers to allow Schlesinger to make his first feature film. Schlesinger chose for the lead role of Vic the relatively unknown Alan Bates. History repeated itself, and both Schlesinger and Bates gained international attention with *A Kind of Loving* (1962).

Based on Stan Barstow's novel, the film examines the problems of Vic, a young man who is fed up with his dull office job. In addition, Vic hastily marries his girl Ingrid because he has gotten her pregnant; and they are forced for economic reasons to live with her mother, with all of the attendant pressures involved.

Schlesinger's camera accurately captures the stifling environment in which Vic must live by always seeking out significant details. In the coffee bar scence, Vic ignores Ingrid's chatter and looks around the room, where he sees a young couple talking intimately, three lads enjoying each other's friendship, and an old couple sitting contentedly in silence—all sharing a rapport that Vic and Ingrid lack. "There is a serious problem of communication between Vic and Ingrid," Schlesinger comments. "But in the end Vic decides to stay with her, in the hope that 'a kind of loving' will grow up between them."

In Vic's eventual decision to make the best of his marriage we see the principal theme of Schlesinger's work coming to the fore: "My films are about the problem that people have in finding security and happiness in life, and the need for accepting what is second best when that is all that one can hope for." In fact Schlesinger feels that *A Kind of Loving* could serve as the title for just about any of the films that he has made.

Schlesinger told me that, at the time he made *A Kind of Loving*, he preferred location shooting to working on a studio sound stage. He liked to take a unit away from the confines of the studio, he said, to work in genuine locales in which he as director could take advantage of "the unexpected," such as the opportunity to cast real people living in the area in some of the film's bit parts.

But over the years, he continued, his attitude toward extensive location work changed: "I'm getting away from doing lots of location work. It's useful when you're filming out of doors, but I would rather work in a studio for interiors. For one film we used a real house for several scenes; and when we had to reshoot one of the scenes we wound up building part of the original house in the studio after all. At that point I wished that I had shot all of those scenes in the studio; although I miss not being able to see real landscapes through the windows of a studio set, as you can when you shoot on location in a real house."

Looking back on *A Kind of Loving*, its star Alan Bates has said, "I think it's a very pure and honest film. It's not theatrical and overglamorized. It's not full of crosscuts and fancy photography. Of course, it's absolutely true that it came towards the end of the vogue of Social Realism. Even in England people tend to think it was just another of the same school."[2]

Perhaps because Schlesinger felt that Social Realism was becoming too commonplace on the screen, after *A Kind of Loving* he advanced into the realm of psychological realism, as Reisz, Anderson, and Forbes had done. But, like them, Schlesinger continued to give his films a realistic look and to be interested in stories with a social dimension.

Billy Liar (1963) presents a shy clerk (Tom Courtenay) who seeks to make his humdrum life in a small town tolerable by retreating into a world of fantasy. When his girl (Julie Christie) invites him to escape to London with her to try to make something of his life, he purposely misses the train. "Billy has settled for living in a world of fantasy," Schlesinger notes. "He accepts this as a safetyvalve which protects him from facing life's problems, and so he simply gives up trying to communicate with others altogether."

Like *A Kind of Loving*, *Billy Liar* was produced by Joseph Janni, who was associated with Schlesinger on several of his feature films. Schlesinger said after he finished *Billy Liar* that the studio had given Janni and himself "a completely free hand in making our first two films. They never came near us, and we had no disagreement until it came to the posters! Nevertheless, I cannot help feeling that distributors are anxious to cash in, and play safe with a formula which has proved successful. I resisted the suggestion that I should automatically make Stan Barstow's second novel into a film, just because the first one had been successful. I do think it is up to filmmakers to resist every temptation to be stereotyped. It is difficult to be freely creative in something that calls itself an industry."[3]

Julie Christie, whom Schlesinger had met in his television days while making a documentary about the Central Acting School, gained so much attention for her small role in *Billy Liar* that Schlesinger decided to star her as Diana Scott in *Dar-*

ling (1965). She won an Academy Award for her performance, as did Frederic Raphael for his original script for the film. Schlesinger compares the relation of writer and director to a tennis match, in which both strain to return each other's ideas successfully. In developing the story of Diana Scott for *Darling*, Schlesinger recalls that he and Raphael "started with the idea of the ghastliness of the present-day attitude of people who want something for nothing. Diana Scott emerged as an amalgam of various people we had known."

They gave an ironic dimension to the movie by having Diana narrate her life story on the sound track to a reporter from the *Ideal Woman* magazine. Diana attempts to whitewash her sordid past as she describes it to the interviewer on the sound track, but on the screen we see her as she really is, a young woman who uses her attractiveness to men to further her career. By the time the *Ideal Woman* appears on the newstand at film's end, we are very much aware that Diana is something less than anyone's concept of the ideal woman.

Darling was criticized in some quarters for offering a shallow depiction of Diana's character. "But Diana is a shallow person," the director counters. "She will never commit herself to anyone or anything. She always wants something better than what she has, both in her career and in her personal life; and therefore she is always looking forward to her next experience, instead of making the most of the present." Diana discards a TV commentator (Dirk Bogarde) for an advertising executive (Laurence Harvey) and then gives him up for a loveless marriage to an aging Italian nobleman who soon loses interest in her. But she remains married to him simply because she has no other prospects at the moment.

In the closing image of the film, the camera pans away from the *Ideal Woman* on sale at a bookstall on Piccadilly Circus to a tawdry fat woman with a scarf tied under her chin, who begs for coins by singing Italian arias on the sidewalk. To Schlesinger this image embodies "the awful isolation of this poor creature, singing her heart out in a language the passersby do not understand; a familiar, sad figure, someone to stare at, who is unloved and unwanted. She is a symbol, in other words, of Diana, who had failed to communicate with the people in her world." To drive home his point that Diana's selfishness is symptomatic of the materialistic modern age, Schlesinger had Dirk Bogarde in his role as the TV commentator do real interviews on the streets of London, asking questions about the state of contemporary society.

During the filming of *Darling*, a cameraman showed Schlesinger and Raphael a copy of Thomas Hardy's *Far from the Madding Crowd*, and they decided to reach back to the Victorian era for their next collaboration. "I was attracted to Hardy," Schlesinger explains, "because I was tired of presenting negative solutions to current problems. Hardy observed very truly people's relationships. He saw life as an endurance contest, and felt that when Fate or Providence—call it what you will—knocks you down, you must pick yourself up and force yourself to go on. Here is a real affirmation of existence."

Schlesinger shot the color film in 1967 in Dorset, which Hardy called "Wessex," in muted tones that completely capture the landscape. He gave a semidocumentary air to the scenes of English country life in a small farming community, often using real-life townspeople in minor roles. Schlesinger takes his time in building up gra-

Julie Christie and Laurence Harvey in *Darling* **(1965). (Cinema Bookshop, London)**

dually an abundance of seemingly insignificant details of everyday life in the village, while all the time the film is gathering the momentum that will culminate in the dramatic impact of the later scenes.

Like Hardy's other novels, *Far from the Madding Crowd* is basically a gaslight melodrama, in which Hardy often does not provide clear-cut motivations for his characters' actions. We are drawn to probe beneath the surface of the characters for the motives that lurk behind their actions. But Hardy gives us little help, and the film, in being faithful to the novel, follows his lead. One wonders, for example, why the apparently prudent Bathsheba (Julie Christie) spurns the genuine love of the sturdy Gabriel Oak (Alan Bates), a hard-working shepherd, toys with the devoted passion of her rich suitor, William Boldwood (Peter Finch), and then rather unexpectedly succumbs to the silken overtures of the irresponsible Sergeant Troy (Terence Stamp).

"We didn't adapt the novel with sufficient freedom," Schlesinger says. "Hardy's drama when distilled on film doesn't work, though his setting is marvelous." Nevertheless, Schlesinger did try hard to overcome his rather intractable material by spelling out the implications of the plot whenever possible in visual terms. In what must be one of the most extraordinary seduction scenes in all of cinema, Troy wins Bathsheba by a dazzling display of swordsmanship in a sunlit field. This incident helps to illuminate the romantic illusions that lie just beneath the surface of Bathsheba's apparently prudent personality, which render her vulnerable to the flash and dash of a sly charmer like Troy. In interpreting Hardy's novel on film, Schlesinger avoided the pitfalls of the formula superspectacular and came up with a cinematic presentation of a classic novel in terms that are true to the spirit of the original.

Nonetheless, *Far from the Madding Crowd* was a commercial failure, and this made it difficult for Schlesinger to finance another film. In the movie business a director is only as good as the box-office receipts of his last picture. "I was simply out of fashion," he remembers. "It didn't matter that I'd had a previous success." Movie executives "can see the artist coming, cap in hand, with a project that he wants to do," he continues; "and they will say, 'Well, right. He wants to do it very badly, so he's going to have to make a sacrifice because it's a project that hasn't been instigated by us.' If it's something that they are instigating, then there is no problem in obtaining immense amounts of money. It's strange, but it's true."[4]

Schlesinger wanted to make a film of James Leo Herlihy's 1965 novel *Midnight Cowboy*, but when he suggested the project to United Artists, he found that a reader in their story department had already submitted an unfavorable report on the book. The report said that the action of the novel went steadily downhill from the outset and recommended that the company not acquire the book for filming. Schlesinger, on the other hand, saw dramatic possibilities in the story of a Texan named Joe Buck, who comes to New York with illusions that he can make easy money there as a male companion to wealthy women. United Artists decided to let him make *Midnight Cowboy* (1969), and the film eventually won Academy Awards for best director and best film of the year in both America and England and was a huge financial success.

Joe (Jon Voight) is himself taken advantage of repeatedly by the assortment of tough and desperate individuals he encounters in the course of his descent into the netherworld of New York's slums, and at one point it looks as if he will become as ruthless as the rest. But he makes a friend of Ratso Rizzo (Dustin Hoffman), a repulsive-looking bum who needs companionship as much as Joe does; and the two take refuge in each other's friendship. Their relationship is not homosexual, Schlesinger points out; rather the story shows "how two men can have a meaningful relationship without being homosexual."

The film is faithful to the novel on which it is based, but Schlesinger and screenwriter Waldo Salt exercised more freedom in adapting it than had been the case with *Far from the Madding Crowd*. The first third of the novel, dealing with Joe's lonely youth, is compressed into a few fragmented flashbacks as he makes his way cross country by bus. These flashbacks indicate how unsuccessful Joe's search for friendship and love has been up to this point and hence explain why Ratso is fulfilling a real need in Joe's emotional life.

There is an interesting religious dimension that becomes apparent in the film when one examines it in depth. While Joe travels cross country on his way to New York, his Bible-belt religious formation is sketched for us as he listens to a faith healer preaching over his transistor and notices through his bus window the words "Jesus Saves" painted on the roof of an abandoned shed.

Once in New York Joe meets a Mr. O'Daniel (John McGiver), a religious fanatic who tries to force Joe to pray with him before a garish statue of Christ that flashes on and off like a neon sign. As Joe escapes from Mr. O'Daniel's shabby hotel room, Schlesinger intercuts shots of Joe's boyhood baptism in a river. The frightened boy is plunged into the waters while a hymn-singing congregation watches from the bank.

Though Joe's religious experiences have not always been pleasant, there is inbred in him a need for some kind of religious belief to give meaning and purpose to his life. Significantly, the only friend that Joe makes in New York is Ratso, an Italian Catholic from the Bronx, who sleeps in the condemned tenement they share with a picture of Christ hanging over his bed. Small church candles provide illumination at night because the electric power has long since been shut off. Joe, in turn, sings himself to sleep on occasion with one of the old hymns he learned as a boy, about receiving "a telephone call from Jesus."

After a visit to the grave of Ratso's father, Ratso discusses the afterlife with Joe, who tries to dismiss the conversation as "priest talk." Ratso counters that he is not talking "priest talk," but about what people believe in. Joe, somewhat embarrassed, admits that he thinks about such things too. At another point Joe accepts a medal of Saint Christopher, patron of travelers, from a pathetic middle-aged homosexual, who gives him the assurance that "you don't have to be a Catholic to wear it."

These and other religious references in the film have a cumulative effect on the viewer. "Is God dead?" a bishop asks rhetorically in a TV sermon we see at one point. One might be tempted to answer "yes"—at least in the corrupt world in which Joe finds himself among the low life of New York's slums. And yet these

Dustin Hoffman and Jon Voight in *Midnight Cowboy* **(1969). (Movie Star News)**

isolated bits and pieces of religious ritual that appear throughout the film are like so many souvenirs of a faith that has somehow been mislaid, but that the owners have never completely abandoned hope of finding again. It is true that Joe does not have his faith in God strengthened in any explicit way in the picture. But, through his friendship for Ratso, he does have his faith in mankind restored, and that in itself is significant.

As their various money-making schemes ludicrously fail, Joe and Ratso begin to care about each other's welfare—something that has never happened to either of them before. Joe literally gives his blood for Ratso as a donor in order to buy medicine for his tubercular friend. Joe and Ratso are like two orphans in a storm, huddling together for safety. More than once they are photographed through a fence, implying that they are imprisoned together in a cruel and indifferent world and must stick together for survival.

It is all the more poignant, therefore, when Joe and Ratso both begin to realize that Ratso's illness is fatal and that he is never going to recover. Joe frantically steals money to take Ratso to Florida before he dies, since they have both looked forward to going there as to a kind of benign earthly paradise. But Ratso dies aboard a bus just before they reach their destination. Joe, tears in his eyes, puts his arm around Ratso in the only overt gesture of affection in the film. The ending, nonetheless, is not pessimistic. Having experienced the friendship denied him in youth, Joe is ready to embark on a more mature way of life. His adolescent illusions about the easy life are now shattered.

Schlesinger says that he tried to breathe into the film "the mixture of desperation and humor" he found all along Forty-second Street in New York while filming there, and in fact he did. It is noteworthy that a British director could bring such a sense of Social Realism to a film made in what for him is a foreign country. He has captured the atmosphere of New York, Miami Beach, and the Texas Panhandle in *Midnight Cowboy* as surely as he captured the atmosphere of the Hardy country in *Far from the Madding Crowd* or of an English factory town in *A Kind of Loving*.

Schlesinger returned to England for his next film, *Sunday, Bloody Sunday* (1971). In this movie Schlesinger once again explores the problem of human relations, and how people must settle for second best in their search for security and happiness in life. But he has never treated this theme more straightforwardly than in this film. Daniel Hirsh, a Jewish doctor (Peter Finch), and Alex Greville, a divorcee (Glenda Jackson), find themselves in love with the same young man, Bob Elkin (Murray Head). Schlesinger originally conceived the story and then asked screenwriter Penelope Gilliatt to work it out and set the tone for the script. "She prefers to underplay conflicts and it was good discipline for me to follow this approach in making the film," he says. "I had no dramatic climaxes in which to take refuge. Every nuance and every detail had to be there in the film, in order to make the underplayed emotions of the characters come across the audience. I wanted the whole film to give the audience a chance to feel something deeply, since we live in an unfeeling, mechanized age. That is why *Sunday* is perhaps the most intimate film I have made."

Alex's basic conflict in her relationship with Bob is her fear that he is incapable of making a commitment to her or to anyone else. "Bob represents those young people today whose lives consist in having an experience and then taking the nearest exit to some other experience," Schlesinger comments. "Their whole lives are filled with exits. Bob is not so much bisexual as uncommitted and unformed. He can switch experience on and off, just as he switches on and off between Alex and Daniel. Whenever a conflict arises with one of them, he takes refuge in the other."

Schlesinger treats the fact that Daniel is a homosexual in a very matter-of-fact way in the film. "*Sunday* is not about the sexuality of these people," he says. "The film asks the audience to try to understand them. I am tired of homosexuals being portrayed in films as either hysterical or funny. *Sunday* is the first film that I know of that asks the audience to try to understand the homosexual character along with the others in the film. I didn't want to preach in the picture that we must be tolerant of others, but rather to imply the kind of understanding that I mean."

In one scene Daniel goes to his nephew's bar mitzvah, which serves to remind him how out of touch he has become with his family and its traditions. "I am Jewish myself," the director notes, "and I wanted to show in the synagogue scene the traditional tug of Daniel's religion on him; what it means to belong to the family of Judaism." At the bar mitzvah reception one of Daniel's aunts warns him that, if he does not marry, he will be very lonely as he gets older. Daniel already knows what she means, for his house has begun to fill up with the expensive bric-a-brac that affluent bachelors tend to collect to make their homes seem less empty.

The device Schlesinger uses in the film to tie together the stories of Alex and Daniel and Bob is the telephone, the means by which Alex and Daniel try to keep in contact with the elusive Bob. "I used the telephone imagery because we are all at the mercy of telephones," remarks Schlesinger. "I wanted to visualize the vast network of wires and connections which people depend on today to keep in touch with one another." The telephone system thus becomes symbolic of the efforts of the characters to communicate with each other, and the metaphor of wrong connections is everywhere in the film.

Alex resents having to give so much more in her relationship with Bob than she receives, just as she resents the way her father ignores her mother most of the time because he is preoccupied with business. Referring to Alex's divorce and her subsequent affairs, her mother says to her, "You keep throwing in your hand because you haven't got the whole thing. There *is* no whole thing—you have to make it work." This is the most important line in the whole picture, the director feels: "*Sunday* is a film about love and compromise. Lots of people hang on to someone in the hope that things may get better. And if not, then at least they feel that perhaps what they have is better than nothing. Therefore I see the film as positive rather than pessimistic, because it deals with people coping with life."

This point is made strongly at the end of the film. Bob has gone off to America and left a gap in the lives of both Daniel and Alex. We see Daniel spending a bloody Sunday afternoon trying to learn Italian from a record, in preparation for a vacation on the Continent that he was to have taken with Bob. This circumstance once more recalls how the film centers on the lack of communication in the characters' lives. Daniel is sitting in the patient's chair in his office; suddenly he looks across the desk into the camera, as if he were himself asking a doctor for advice. He confesses his loneliness, now that Bob is gone, and wonders what to do about it. Others tell him that he is better off without Bob, he muses aloud. "People say, 'What's half a loaf?' And I say, 'I know that. I miss him, that's all.'" He continues, "All my life I've been looking for someone courageous and resourceful, not like myself; and he wasn't it. But . . . we were something."

This little monologue, which closes *Sunday, Bloody Sunday*, is as near as Schlesinger has ever come in one of his motion pictures to stating explicitly his recurring theme that the security and happiness that people achieve in life always falls short of their expectations and that they must make the best of it.

As a change of pace, Schlesinger hearkened back to his documentary days by agreeing to direct one segment of *Visions of Eight* (1973), an anthology film that producer David Wolper made of the 1972 Munich Olympic Games, to which several other internationally known directors also contributed. Schlesinger centered his episode, entitled "The Longest," around the British entry in the marathon race, Ron Hill, intercutting shots of his long-term preparation and training for the event with the actual race. The director found it interesting to return temporarily to documentary film making, but he prefers fiction films in which he can tell a strong story and manipulate characters according to their individual motivations.

Schlesinger's thriller, *Marathon Man* (1975), recalls his segment on the marathon in *Visions of Eight*, in that the hero of *Marathon Man*, Babe Levy (Dustin Hoffman), is a part-time marathon runner. He is also a full-time graduate student at Columbia University, who all of a sudden finds himself being pursued by a fugitive Nazi and his henchmen. Schlesinger said, when I was on the set of *Marathon Man* in Hollywood, that one of the things which attracted him to filming the marathon race for *Visions of Eight* and likewise to adapting *Marathon Man* to the screen was his abiding fascination with the virtue of endurance that must characterize the long-distance runner perhaps more than any other kind of athlete.

Indeed, the motto that helps Babe to endure all of the grueling experiences which confront him throughout the film is the creed of all marathon runners: "If you're a marathon runner, you don't give in to pain." By that standard Babe has become at film's end a genuine marathon man, for he has truly gone the distance and outlasted his adversaries. Babe's chief foe is Christian Szell (Laurence Olivier), a Nazi war criminal still at large, whom Babe's older brother Doc, an intelligence agent (Roy Scheider), knows to be temporarily hiding out in New York City.

When Doc forces a confrontation with Szell, the latter summarily knifes him and flees; but the mortally wounded Doc lives just long enough to make it to Babe's apartment building, where he dies at his brother's door. The paranoid Szell assumes that, before Doc died, he shared with Babe some secret information that would imperil Szell; and he accordingly has Babe kidnapped and carried off to his hideout for interrogation.

One of the most frightening sequences in the movies is the celebrated torture scene. Since Szell was once a dentist by trade, he methodically utilizes his professional skill to force Babe to reveal information about Doc. Capitalizing on the viewer's native terror of dentists, Schlesinger stimulates maximum audience iden-

Timothy Hutton as a young American who betrays his country in *The Falcon and the Snow-man* **(1985). (Author's collection)**

tification with Babe by photographing Szell from his victim's subjective point of view, as he implacably trains his drill on a fresh, live nerve in Babe's mouth. The menacing drill thus moves closer and closer to the camera, as if Szell were aiming the gruesome instrument at the viewer.

Later Babe gets a chance to make a run for it and manages to get away from Szell's torture chamber. Once free, he sees to it that Szell meets the kind of fate he deserves. When last we see Babe, he is walking down the path along which he used to jog, ignoring the other joggers who now pass him by. Babe has apparently lost interest in training for the marathon, for he knows that he has already won the most important race of his life—one which will never be chalked up in the official records—when he literally outran his captors and escaped from Szell's lair, which marked the beginning of the end for Szell.

Since *Marathon Man* was a box-office bonanza, Schlesinger was able to find the financing to make a more personal film, *Yanks* (1979). For this venture he decided to go back to his roots and make a movie set in England during World War II. This film would mark not only a return to his native land, but a return to his cinematic roots as well; for *Yanks* is principally a work of Social Realism very much akin to his first British films. As a matter of fact, part of the movie was shot in Stockton, the town in the north of England where *A Kind of Loving* was filmed.

"The Yanks are overpaid, oversexed, and over here." That was the wry slogan of the British families who lived near the American army camps that were established in Britain during World War II, just prior to the launching of the D-Day armada on 6 June 1944. Schlesinger's film deals with this period, in which the English attitude toward the Americans on their doorstep gradually melted from suspicion to acceptance, and with the romantic entanglements that were an inevitable part of the involvement of American servicemen in British family life.

When I watched the filming of *Yanks*, Schlesinger was shooting on location in a quiet residential section of London. In conversation between takes, the director pointed out that the movie primarily focuses on the manner in which the clash of cultures colors the relationship of an American soldier named Matt (Richard Gere) and his British girlfriend Jean (Lisa Eichhorn). Jean's family assumes that their daughter will marry her childhood sweetheart when he returns from the front, but she meets Matt and falls in love with him. "When the prospect of their eventually going to America together finally seems to become a real possibility, however, Matt is no longer certain that he is committed to taking Jean home with him," Schlesinger continued; "while Jean, on the other hand, is still completely committed to going with him."

In the movie's last sequence, the troop train crowded with American soldiers on their way to the beaches of Normandy pulls out of the station, amid the tears and cheers of Jean and the rest of the girls who are being left behind. As the train begins to move, Matt and his buddies, who are waving furiously from the windows, seem to evaporate in a cloud of steam and smoke, as quickly and as miraculously as they had materialized at the beginning of the movie when they arrived in the little British town. This final tableau symbolizes the painfully fleeting quality of wartime relationships and once more demonstrates Schlesinger's strong visual sense, which never deserts him when he is filming.

Perhaps the most moving visual image in the entire film occurs when Jean hitches a ride to the train depot in a troop truck to see Matt off. The strong arms of several obliging GIs reach down to lift her up into the truck. This is a beautiful symbol of the way that the American soldiers as a group have in the course of their stay extended a helping hand to their British compatriots with both affection and good will. Jean's final acceptance of Matt and of his American ways is reflected in her look of calm contentment as she sits in the truck, completely surrounded by friendly American soldiers on their way to the station.

Although some critics characterized *Yanks* as a routine World War II movie, the picture is really a supreme example of Social Realism; for it has the genuine look and feel of a documentary about the war. Indeed, it is a film in which Schlesinger succeeds in evoking the past as a vividly living present. This is likewise true of *The Day of the Locust* (1975), in which the director created a film about the legendary past of Hollywood that recalls Cukor's *What Price Hollywood?* and *A Star is Born.*

Locust was derived from the book by novelist-screenwriter Nathanael West. As Schlesinger noted while I was observing the filming on the studio back lot in Hollywood, it is a dark fable about a group of Hollywood types who have come to the film colony to fulfill their dreams of success; but they wind up being cheated "by their own false hopes and fantasies of what Hollywood could do for them." There is, for example, Tod Hackett (William Atherton), a studio artist who aspires to be a great painter. Tod Hackett is aptly named, since his first name (the German word for death) implies that, if he becomes the Hollywood hack which his last name suggests, such artistic prostitution will mean the demise of his creative talent.

Among Todd's acquaintances is Faye Greener (Karen Black), a full-time movie extra and part-time call girl who dreams of being a superstar. Faye is an elusive creature whom many men pursue in the course of the story, including Tod Hackett and Homer Simpson, a stolid, withdrawn studio bookkeeper from the Midwest (Donald Sutherland). But none of the males who trail after Faye ever catches her for long, because Faye, whose last name implies that "the grass is always greener on the other side of the fence," is an inaccessible love goddess who consistently promises more than she delivers.

The most elaborate sequence in *Locust* is the gala Hollywood premiere at Graumann's Chinese Theater, near the end of the picture, at which the mass of movie fans erupts into a riot. Trouble starts during the premiere festivities when Homer, deeply disturbed by being rejected by Faye once and for all, is moping past Graumann's, intent on taking the next bus back to Iowa. Adore Loomis, a monstrous, mother-ridden child actor who has been tormenting Homer throughout the picture, begins baiting him sarcastically about Faye, causing Homer's simmering anger and frustration to explode into violence.

Homer goes berserk and madly stomps Adore to death in the gutter. The frantic fans milling around the theater get wind of the murder and, smelling the scent of blood, turn into a raging mob. At first they are bent only on avenging Adore's death by killing Homer; but, having done so, they move on to wreak general havoc and senseless destruction everywhere, as the situation explodes into a riot.

From the beginning of his sojurn in Hollywood, Tod had suspected Tinsel Town's glittering facade might one day crack open and reveal the latent forces of violence lurking beneath. In fact, he has been working throughout the film on a gigantic painting entitled *The Burning of Los Angeles*, which has gradually taken shape on the wall of his apartment, and which is designed to portray just such a cataclysmic event.

Furthermore, Tod has sensed all along that these dark forces would undoubtedly be unleashed by the "locusts" who have swarmed into Hollywood from all over the country, hoping that the phony fantasies of easy success and happiness that they have watched flickering before them on the silver screen will somehow be actualized in their own lives, if they can but get close to the source of supply. Tod has also suspected that they would eventually come to realize that the shaky illusions of fame and fortune on which Hollywood was founded are not even realized in the lives of those who make the movies, much less in the lives of those who see them. At this point, he concluded, the locusts would have their collective day of revenge on Hollywood, in retaliation for not making their counterfeit dreams come true in the way that similar dreams come true in the movies.

In Tod's overwrought imagination it seems that the riot he is witnessing at Graumann's has equivalently brought his prophetic painting of *The Burning of Los Angeles* to life; and he fantasizes that the grotesque figures in his mural have stepped down from his wall to destroy the movies capital. In Tod's apocalyptic vision, then, when Graumann's theater goes up in flames, the destruction of this lavish cinema shrine, which epitomizes the magnificent movie temples of the past, is emblematic of the passing of the old Hollywood.

Inevitably, the disillusioned Tod Hackett leaves Hollywood for good at film's end, finally convinced that Tinsel Town will never fulfill his own dreams—both of winning Faye and of using the movie industry as a stepping stone to becoming a major artist.

Day of the Locust was underrated at the time of its release; but it has since deservedly gained a reputation as a film that presents a richly detailed tapesty of the Hollywood of yesteryear. With films like *Honky Tonk Freeway* (1981), a rather off-center social satire on life in present-day America, and *The Falcon and the Snowman* (1985),the true story of two young Americans convicted of selling government secrets to the Russians, Schlesinger has returned to the contemporary scene.

The Falcon and the Snowman revolves around Christopher Boyce (Timothy Hutton) and Daulton Lee (Sean Penn), two young men who have known each other since their days as altar boys in a parochial school in an affluent Los Angeles suburb. By the time they have both reached their early twenties, Boyce, who has become an expert falconer in his spare time, is employed by a message-routing center attached to the CIA, and Lee has become a drug dealer. In the course of his duties at the center, Boyce is shocked to discover evidence that the CIA is meddling in the internal affairs of other nations by, for example, attempting to discredit the Labor government in Australia.

Boyce decides to punish the CIA for its transgressions by selling some of its information to the Russians, by way of the Russian embassy in Mexico City. He enlists the aid of his old buddy Lee, who has some contacts in Mexico, where he goes to obtain drugs. In due course the two amateur spies make an arrangement with the KGB in Mexico City, whereby Boyce (code name: Falcon) will supply information to Lee (code name: Snowman), who in turn will peddle it to the Russians on his visits to Mexico. Eventually the Falcon and the Snowman learn to their great cost that the world of international espionage is no place for amateurs, and they are inevitably apprehended by American agents and given stiff prison terms. As Schlesinger has since said in correspondence, "It was amazing they got away with what they did for so long."

Like Schlesinger's other film about international intrigue, *Marathon Man*, this movie won a wide audience, although some critics complained that the director did not lay out the motives that prompted the two young Americans to betray their country with sufficient clarity in the course of the film. Noting this criticism in a letter at the time, Schlesinger responded to it thus: "So many of the press seem to need explanations for an inexplicable and ill-thought-out act."[5]

Discussing this controversial point about the movie, critic Roger Ebert said in his review that Boyce and Lee hardly seemed to be clear in their own minds about precisely how they got around to committing treason, as is evident in Robert Lindsey's carefully researched book, on which the film is based. One of the strengths of the film, Ebert continued, is that it succeeds in showing us how Boyce and Lee simply drifted into becoming spies through a murky mixture of motives that included "naivete, inexperience, misplaced idealism, and greed." What started out as an adventurous lark, Ebert concluded, gradually turned into a challenge, "and finally into a very, very bad dream," once they realized that they had gotten in way over their heads.

For his part, jounalist Robert Lindsey, who consulted with scriptwriter Steven Zallian about the screenplay, was pleased that the film was so faithful to the story of Boyce and Lee as he had related it in his book. "I was very impressed with the integrity of Zallian and Schlesinger for trying to stick as much as they could to the facts," he said. "They seemed to feel a sense of responsibility for not only making a good picture, but adhering to the truth."[6] In the end Schlesinger proved that it was possible to do both.

After making another film with an American setting, a horror picture called *The Believers* (1987), Schlesinger shot *Madame Sousatzka* (1988) in London. The movie features Shirley MacLaine in the title role of a dedicated, demanding piano teacher. The venerable lady reaches a personal crisis in her life when her exacting standards threaten to drive her most promising pupil away. Schlesinger's talent for bringing out the best in his actors in exemplified in the performance of Shirley MacLaine, who has never been better—as evidenced by the best actress award for her performance, which she won at the Venice Film Festival.[7]

In addition, Schlesinger's acutely observed depiction of the ramshackle old rooming house where Madame lives, with its colorful assortment of diverse tenants, lends to the film an authentic atmosphere that once more recalls the heyday of Social Realism. While shooting *Madame Sousatzka* in and around London, Schlesinger supervised every phase of the production, as is his custom, since he believes that the director must be the controlling factor in the making of a film, as the *auteur* theory maintains.

Nevertheless, he still looks upon film making as a collaboration. "There are few total creators in the cinema," he points out, "since film making is really a corporate effort. But collaboration can mean a healthy conflict which produces creative results. The various people that the director works with, whether they be the script writer, technicians, or actors, have confrontations throughout the film making process; and we make discoveries together. Still it is up to the director to make the final selection of material and to see that it all works together into a finished film. That's the most challenging thing about film making: creating a unified work of art out of the contributions of so many different people."

Because of his contribution to British film art, Schlesinger has been named a Commander of the British Empire. He is pleased with the honors he has received, but he feels Oscars and other awards are important primarily because they enable him to get financial backing for future projects. Schlesinger wants to continue to make films that provide something more than mere escapism. In fact, in his corpus of films he has proved as well as any director can that, in his own words, "it is possible to give people entertainment in a film that will also provoke thought, stimulate the imagination, and disturb the mind."

14
Ken Russell
The Past as Present

If Stanley Kubrick has enabled us to understand the present better by looking into the future, Ken Russell has given us some insights into the present by taking us into the past. "Historical films are often made as if the people living in the past thought of themselves as part of history already, living in museums," Russell explains. "But people in every century have thought of themselves as contemporary, just as we think of ourselves as contemporary."

Russell gravitates toward the past in choosing subjects for filming because, as he says, "topics of the moment pass and change; besides, one's feelings towards contemporary topics tend to distort one's presentation of them. We can be much more dispassionate and objective, and therefore more truthful, in dealing with the past. To see things of the past from the vantage point of the present is to be able to judge what effect they have had on the present."

He became interested in portraying historical material for contemporary audiences while making documentaries about great artists of the past for BBC-TV, where John Schlesinger also received his principal training as a director. Russell was born in Southampton, England, in 1927; and, like Schlesinger, he also tried photography and acting before turning to directing.

In all Russell made thirty-five documentaries for television. "My first TV documentaries coincided with the accepted textbook idea of what a documentary should be. You were supposed to extol the great artists and their work; and I did this in my film about the composer Edward Elgar, for example," Russell recalls. "Finally I decided to dispel the preconceived idea of what a documentary should be by presenting the life of a great artist in a way that showed how he transcended his own personal problems and weaknesses in creating great art. Showing the personal struggles out of which an artist's work grew is more of a tribute to him than making believe that he had led an easy life, and worked without any obstacles in his path. I took this more controversial approach in my later TV films about such artists as Isadora Duncan and Richard Strauss. In all of these biographies I tried to condense the essence of an artist's life into the brief span of a telefilm."

The films that Russell made for television were done on tiny budgets, and Russell therefore had to tax his artistic ingenuity to find ways of creating the atmosphere of a historical setting when, as he says, "I couldn't afford period costumes for more than six extras. I had no way to create nineteenth-century Paris in my film on

Ken Russell, the director of *The Rainbow* (1989), on the set. (The Russell collection)

Debussy, for example." Russell solved the latter problem by building his film *Debussy* (1965) around a group of actors who are making a movie about the composer. In this way he was able to set the film virtually in the present.

In making all of these TV films, Russell sought to find imaginative ways to present the lives of these artists as he saw them. In his documentary on Elgar (1962), Russell projected Elgar's consternation about his "Pomp and Circumstance March" being used as a patriotic marching song to send soldiers off to die at the front in World War I through accompanying the march with newsreel shots of wounded soldiers dying ignominiously amid the mud and barbed wire of the battlefield.

Russell directed a one-hour television version of the life of Isadora Duncan called *The Biggest Dancer in the World* (1966), two years before Karel Reisz made his film *The Loves of Isadora*. "Reisz's film version used most of the incidents in Isadora's life that I used," says Russell; "but I managed to tell her story with a little more economy in about half the time that his film runs." This is partially due to the fact that Russell begins his TV biography by running through the whole of Isadora Duncan's life in a kind of kaleidoscopic newsreel. Russell is able thereby to give the audience a capsule view of her life that provides a frame of reference for the series of flashbacks that make up the balance of his film.

"Since Isadora's life was so pathetic and tragic, I tried to lighten the material at times," Russell explains. "For example, I used the old Betty Hutton recording of "The Sewing Machine" from the 1947 Hollywood film *The Perils of Pauline* on the sound track when Isadora was falling in love with Paris Singer, the sewing machine manufacturer." Nonetheless Russell's *Isadora* has some darker moments that are not in Reisz's film. For instance, Russell indicates that Isadora's Russian husband, the only one of her several lovers that she ever married, was an epileptic and a kleptomaniac, further complicating their already tragic relationship.

Russell's television biography of Richard Strauss, *The Dance of the Seven Veils* (1970), caused a considerable amount of controversy in England when it was aired, and it foreshadowed the controversies that would erupt over his later motion pictures, *The Music Lovers* and *The Devils*. Russell is convinced that he had to make *The Dance of the Seven Veils* in the way that he did: "I saw that television biographies were becoming filled with terrible clichés that had grown out of imitation of my earlier TV films. Deification of the artist is wrong; he should be presented as a human being who, despite his faults, managed to create lasting works of art. *The Dance of the Seven Veils* begins with an announcement that what is to follow is a harsh and violent personal interpretation of Strauss's life and work, but one which is nevertheless based on real events. I built up the portrait of Strauss from the man himself, and ninety-five percent of the things he said in the film were his actual words.

"In every film which I make the style is always dictated by the subject. *The Song of Summer* (1968), my biography of Frederick Delius, was an austere and restrained film because it was about an aging composer who was cared for by his faithful wife and his amanuensis. Since it dealt mainly with three people in a bare, white room, that was the way to do that particular story. Strauss, on the other hand, was a self-advertising, vulgar, commercial man. I took the keynote of the film from his music, a lot of which is bombastic."

Russell feels that those who were offended by *The Dance of the Seven Veils* took the film much too literally and therefore failed to realize that it was working on a deeper symbolic level. This is illustrated in the way that Russell presents Strauss's relationship to the Nazi regime. Strauss (Christopher Gable) thought of himself as an ageless superman, Russell points out; the composer based his *Zarathustra* (which has since become identified with Kubrick's use of it as a theme in *2001*) on Nietzsche's concept of the superman. Then in later years, when he was out of favor with Hitler, Strauss wrote an obsequious letter to him. "At this point," as Russell describes it, "I have his wife put on Strauss the mask of an old man, for Strauss has finally admitted his weakness and dependence on Hitler's favor. Later, after the war, when he is conducting the *Zarathustra* in London after he has been completely exonerated by the allies of having endorsed the Nazi regime, the music swells to a crescendo and I have Strauss rip off the mask of the old man. He is still the crypto-Nazi with the superman fantasy, underneath the facade of the distinguished elderly composer."

Russell maintains that "if Strauss, who was one of the most prestigious Germans of his day, had taken a stand against the Nazis, it would have had a tremendous effect. I was trying to shock people into a realization of their responsibilities." As for the complaints that the BBC received about *The Dance of the Seven Veils*, Russell remarks, "The members of the television audience are all asleep in their armchairs; it's a good thing to shake them up occasionally, even if it only moves them as far as the telephone."

Most of Russell's television films were shot on location because, as he says, "the indoor sets in a TV studio always seemed to me to look like sets: four blinking flats with pictures hung on them. In general, I always disregarded the fact that documentary films which I made were being done for television; I simply thought of myself as a film maker."

Russell's first venture into the world of cinema was *French Dressing* (1964). He remembers it as "a kind of seaside comedy which was an ill-conceived project from the start. The chemistry of the characters was wrong and the story never quite jelled." It was a flop; so it was back to television for Russell. Then, in 1967, Russell signed a contract with producer Harry Saltzman to film the life of the Russian dancer Vaslav Nijinsky, but the project was shelved when Rudolf Nureyev lost interest in playing the lead. So Russell directed the spy film *The Billion Dollar Brain* for Saltzman instead, with Michael Caine playing secret agent Harry Palmer, who Saltzman hoped would inspire a cult the way James Bond had done. But by this time moviegoers had had their fill of spy films for the time being, and so *The Billion Dollar Brain* did not catch on.

Because of the consistent interest that Russell's telefilms occasioned, however, United Artists decided to ask him to direct another motion picture. He chose to do a screen version of D. H. Lawrence's *Women in Love* (1969), and this brought him to the attention of serious filmgoers at last. Like John Schlesinger, Russell found that his experience in the television medium proved invaluable to him when he began making feature films.

Oliver Reed and Glenda Jackson, in her Oscar-winning role, in *Women in Love* (1969). (The John Baxter collection)

"Working in television, you learn how to cut costs and prune down the project to essentials," Russell says. "When you work fast you get a certain spontaneity from your cast and crew, and they make suggestions about how to improve a scene during shooting. I only work with people who understand what I am trying to do because of the short time we have to work. In order to make a period picture on the same budget as a film in a contemporary setting you have to sacrifice something, and I sacrifice time. I assemble around me a cast and crew that can intuit what I want, and to whom, therefore, I have to say very little." Actors like Oliver Reed and Glenda Jackson have worked for Russell several times and therefore are clearly Russell's kind of performers.

Although the actual time he had to shoot *Women in Love* was limited, Russell spent a great deal of time in preparing to direct the film beforehand, immersing himself totally in Lawrence's novel. The two women of the title are the Brangwen sisters, Ursula (Jennie Linden) and Gudrun (Glenda Jackson). Gudrun is in love with the wealthy Gerald (Oliver Reed) and Ursula with his friend Birkin (Alan Bates). Gerald becomes the pivotal character inasmuch as he cannot give himself totally to Gudrun in a love relationship, any more than he can give himself in a different way in friendship to Birkin. He consequently causes frustration and unhappiness all around and finally takes his own life.

At the end of the film, just as at the conclusion of the novel, Birkin tells Ursula, now his wife, that he has found fulfillment with her, but that he nonetheless regrets that Gerald was incapable of fulfilling him on the level of friendship. "You can't have two kinds of love," she responds, "because it's false, impossible." "I don't believe that," he answers. Nor, one infers, does Lawrence.

Russell decided to include the nude wrestling scene from the novel in his film because of its symbolic importance in the narrative. "I originally thought of a swimming context for the scene, since how else could you explain the two men stripping off for the match? Then Oliver Reed said that that setting would be too poetic. He suggested that it should be more of a real physical confrontation between the two men locked in a room sweating and straining; and that is how we finally did it."

At its conclusion Birkin says to Gerald, "We are mentally and spiritually close. Therefore we should be physically close too." "This is not a plea for a homosexual relationship," Russell explains. "Birkin is rather expressing to Gerald the same point of view about love relationships that he expresses to his wife at the end of the film. He believes that two men can each get married and yet maintain an intimate relationship with each other that is different from, but which nevertheless complements the heterosexual relationship that each has in marriage. Gerald could not commit himself to Birkin on this level, not only because he thought such a relationship unconventional, but because he really could not reveal himself or commit himself to anyone."

Several critics commented on how carefully Russell preserved the spirit of Lawrence's novel in making his film. In recalling the various stages through which the script passed, Russell says that the first version was done by a competent screen writer who unfortunately believed "that unless a script writer changes his source beyond recognition, he is not being creative. As a result this first script had little to do with D. H. Lawrence. At the final fade out Alan Bates and Jennie Linden were to gallop off into the sunset. At this point I took a hand in writing the script. I used as much of Lawrence's dialogue as I could. Nearly all of the conversation is verbatim from the novel. For the story line, I pulled out of the novel's action the bits that would hang together as a narrative. So I suppose that I am as responsible as anyone for the film's fidelity to Lawrence."

Lawrence's novel *Women in Love* was actually the sequel to his earlier book *The Rainbow*, which depicts the past history of Ursula's and Gudrun's family, the Brangwens. When Russell came to film his admirable version of *The Rainbow* two decades later, he again wanted to be faithful to his literary source. He noted in a letter at that time that his film of *The Rainbow* (1989) accordingly concentrates on "the last section of the book, when Ursula and Gudrun are teenagers," and by-passes much of the Brangwen family's previous history as the most effective way of compressing the long novel for the screen.[1]

At all events, the success of *Women in Love* during its initial release in 1969 vindicated United Artists' confidence in Russell; and hence the studio offered to finance his next project. But this time Russell demanded and got the same artistic control of his upcoming movie as he had enjoyed at the BBC. "While I was at the BBC I was my own boss," he remarks. "And immediately after *Women in Love* I was ready to go back to television for good, since I wasn't allowed to act as my own producer on that film, or on any of my previous feature films. I found that when someone else is producing, I have a battle royal with him most of the time. After one has poured his lifeblood into a project, it is difficult to accept the fact that someone else is really controlling it. But when I was finally granted the same artistic freedom in making theatrical features that I had had in television, I decided to stick with motion pictures."

Oddly enough, there is a hint in *Women in Love* of what Russell's next film would be. In one scene in *Women in Love* Gudrun and Loerke, a homosexual artist, parody the relationship of Tchaikovsky and his wife Nina, referring to it as the marriage of a "homosexual composer and a scheming nymphomaniac." "That is a flip way of putting it," says Russell, "but basically that's what the story of Tchaikovsky's marriage boiled down to." And that is what became the subject of Russell's next film, *The Music Lovers* (1970).

Glenda Jackson, who won an Academy Award for her performance as Gudrun in *Women in Love*, plays Nina, and Richard Chamberlain is Tchaikovsky. A Russian film on the life of Tchaikovsky was being made at the same time as Russell was directing *The Music Lovers*, but he assured United Artists that his approach to the composer's life would be different from the Russian version. "For one thing, the Russians have never admitted that Tchaikovsky was homosexual," Russell notes. "Tchaikovsky himself said that his inner conflicts are there in his music and so they are. His Sixth Symphony is tortured and tragic. In making *The Music Lovers* I followed the practice that I had established in my television biographies of great artists by making a definite connection between the man's life and his work. There is not one piece of Tchaikovsky's music that is used in the film that is there for its own sake. It's all there to reflect some aspect of Tchaikovsky's life and personality."

The Music Lovers covers only two years in the composer's life—the period of his marriage, which was the turning point of his life. When the film begins Tchaikovsky is involved with the rich Vladimir Chilovsky (Christopher Gable), whose possessiveness helps to turn Tchaikovsky's thoughts toward marriage, as does Tchaikovsky's long cherished desire to have a family.

Tchaikovsky believes that man is governed by fate, and he is in the midst of composing an opera on this theme entitled *Eugene Onegin*, in which a girl writes love letters to a man who turns her down, thereby ruining both his life and hers. Hence, when Tchaikovsky receives love letters from Nina Milyukova, he decides that the situation is too much of a coincidence to be ignored. He meets and marries Nina, and the marriage, of course, is a disaster.

In his essay "The World of Ken Russell," Michael Dempsey writes that Russell's central characters "seek to change, deny, or flee their identities. Those who fascinate him most are romantic idealists struggling against their own personalities in order to achieve a level of existence that they regard as higher, more noble." This is true of Gerald in *Women in Love*, and it is true of Tchaikovsky in *The Music Lovers*. Gerald mistakenly flees from his own human instincts to reach out to others with love because he is afraid of self-giving. Instead of trying to come to terms with his homosexuality, Tchaikovsky seeks to deny it by becoming entangled in a hopeless marriage. Nina, too, deceives herself, thinking that marrying a famous composer will automatically bring her happiness and prestige, with the result that her marriage to Tchaikovsky renders him an embittered neurotic and drives his wife into the asylum where she ends her days. Richard Chamberlain accordingly comments on the movie: "The film's central theme, that the avoidance of truth leads to insanity, was deeply felt."[2]

Russell's direction is masterly in the way that he cuts back and forth between the lives of his characters, using Tchaikovsky's music as a bridge. Early in the picture, at the premiere of Tchaikovsky's First Piano Concerto, Russell shows the daydreams the piece inspires in its composer as he plays it and in Nina, whom Tchaikovsky has not yet met, as she listens.

Tchaikovsky recalls in sumptuously beautiful images the past summer he spent with his married sister and her family, an idyllic interlude into which the figure of Chilovsky suddenly intrudes. In this way Russell brilliantly visualizes the conflict in Tchaikovsky between his wish to have a family and his homosexual tendencies. For her part, Nina imagines herself marrying the handsome Russian officer who happens to be sitting near her at the concert. The pair are pictured galloping along in a carriage gleefully drinking champagne, accompanied by an appropriate passage of the concerto. The romantic illusions of both Tchaikovsky and Nina, which have been inspired by the composer's romantic music, are soon to be shattered; for life seldom lives up to the aspirations of art, Russell suggests.

Perhaps the most perfect visual symbol in the film occurs in the scene in which Tchaikovsky's wealthy patron, Madame Von Meck, who is secretly infatuated with him, gives a birthday party in his honor. As he and her children dance amid a dazzling display of fireworks, Chilovsky cruelly tells her of Tchaikovsky's homosexuality, just as a likeness of the composer, made of fireworks, lights up the sky. As Chilovsky finishes his revelation and Mme. Von Meck turns away from him with a cynical smile on her face, the image in the sky dwindles into darkness. It is not surprising that, soon after, she withdraws her financial support from Tchaikovsky, for Russell has already symbolically pictured her disillusionment with the man to whom she had been attracted.

Filmgoers not familiar with Russell's highly imaginative television biographies were unsettled when *The Music Lovers* did not turn out to be a conventional cinematic biography of a composer, as they had anticipated. They were even more unprepared for Russell's baroque rendering of the story of religious conflicts in seventeenth-century France, *The Devils* (1971), which Russell based on John Whiting's play of the same name and on Aldous Huxley's book *The Devils of Loudun*.

The central character of *The Devils* is Father Urbain Grandier (Oliver Reed), who leads the people of the city of Loudun in opposition to Cardinal Richelieu's plan to destroy the walls that make their city independent of the crown and therefore able to resist Richelieu's efforts to centralize the French government. Richelieu's minions take advantage of the fact that Grandier is known to have been guilty of several sexual indiscretions to accuse him of having corrupted, as Satan's agent, an entire convent of Ursuline nuns, starting with the Prioress, Mother Jeanne (Vanessa Redgrave). In the ensuing hysteria, Grandier is tried, convicted, and burned at the stake, and the city walls are reduced to rubble.

"What particularly drew me to the subject matter of *The Devils*," Russell says, "was the fact that it reflected an instance of the collision of the individual with the State. We know from history that the State usually survives while the individual loses out in these cases; but I wanted to examine what lasting impact the individual still has, even when he loses."

Russell, who was converted to Roman Catholicism in 1957 and still regards himself fundamentally as a Catholic, insists that *The Devils* is a Christian film about a sinner who becomes a saint. "The film has some things to say about the Church," he says, "but the Church will survive it." Like Gerald in *Women in Love* and Tchaikovsky, Grandier wants to achieve a more noble level of existence. "Grandier is a mixture of good and bad qualities," Russell says; "he knows what he should do, but he often doesn't do it, as Saint Paul once said. Then he gets the opportunity to stand up against Richelieu in order to preserve the rights of the city and he does so. In this crisis his good qualities come to the surface and he dies a Christian martyr for his people."

Asked about the vividness with which he portrayed the bizarre events in *The Devils*, Russell replied, "Once I had decided to do *The Devils*, I had to go along with the truth as it was reported. I had to show the violent atmosphere that the plague had created at the time, for instance, in order to explain how ordinary people could stand by and allow a man they knew to be innocent to die a hideous death. They had become calloused as the result of the plague. When there is death on every doorstep, the death of a man like Grandier becomes inconsequential, an everyday occurrence. That is why the crowd behaved at his burning as if they were attending a football match."

The film, he continued, "is a jolly sight less ugly than Aldous Huxley's book.

When one reads these events in Huxley's account, one can sift the words through one's imagination and filter out as much of the unpleasantness as one cares to. You can't do this when you are looking at a film. I was reading another book of Huxley's, *Ape and Essence*, and I said to myself, this is ugly stuff and were I to film it people would probably say that I had exaggerated the presentation of the material of that book. But it really couldn't be exaggerated."

Because Russell believes that people living in the past thought of themselves as contemporary in the same way that we think of ourselves as contemporary, the sets in *The Devils* look curiously modern. The church, the convent, the government buildings are not edifices of grey medieval stone, but sleek, all-white buildings towering above the city. Moreover, the anachronistically modern settings help to give more immediacy to the religious and political issues dealt with in the picture.

Russell as always uses visual symbols as a method of telegraphing messages to his audience. The physical deformity of Mother Jeanne, who is hump-backed, symbolizes her spiritual deformity, of which she is unaware. "Look at me and learn the meaning of love," Grandier, disfigured by torture, shouts at her before he dies. He wants her to confront her sins as he has finally come to terms with his. But she cannot or will not; for her twisted love for him, which she has never admitted even to herself, has long since turned to an irrational hatred, a hatred that has led her to accuse him falsely of the crimes for which he is being executed.

Russell feels that not only *The Devils* but all of his serious films have been influenced by his Catholicism. "When I was young, I really didn't know where I was going," he comments; "but when I came into the Faith, my work gained direction. Almost all my films are Catholic in outlook, dealing with sin, forgiveness, and redemption—movies that could only have been made by a Catholic."

Russell's next film, *The Boy Friend* (1971), is a complete change of pace for him, since it is a screen version of Sandy Wilson's musical toast to the 1920s. Even this film, however, is something of a departure from established ways of movie making. Russell was out to prove that a lush-looking musical can be made for two million dollars—twenty million less than was spent on *Hello, Dolly!*. "After the strain of making a violent film like *The Devils*," says Russell, "I thought I would try making a musical just for fun. But *The Boy Friend* turned out to be the most complicated project that I have attempted, given the time and money I had to work with."

While I was on the set of *The Boy Friend*, Russell was directing a musical number that was designed to be a homage to the Busby Berkeley musical extravaganzas of the 1930s. A group of girls were arranged in geometric patterns on a gigantic phonograph record, as technicians scurried around out of camera range. At the end of the day's shooting, Russell recounted how his script for *The Boy Friend* had evolved.

He had gotten hold of a 16mm film of the original 1954 British production of the show, which had been made to assist the New York company during rehearsal. "It was funny and touching at first, with everyone striking poses," he recalls; "but as the film went on, one got bored with the cardboard characters in a way that one didn't when watching them on stage. That's when I realized that I would have to do the original musical as a show within a show, if I were going to sustain the audience's interest throughout the film. I decided to frame the original show within the context of a backstage musical of the sort that Hollywood turned out in the 1930s." The opening credits of the film set this tone by announcing "Ken Russell's Talking Picture of *The Boy Friend.*"

Polly, the heroine of the film (Twiggy), is the understudy of the leading lady in a tacky stock company that is putting on *The Boy Friend.* When the star of the company (Glenda Jackson, in a cameo appearance) breaks her leg, the director of the troupe pushes Polly on stage as her replacement with Warner Baxter's line from the Berkeley musical *Forty-Second Street* (1932), "You're going out there as a chorus girl, but you're coming back a star!" The rest of the cast is jealous of Polly and tries to sabotage her performance. Furthermore, Cecil B. De Thrill, a Hollywood director interested in making a film of the show, is present at the performance; and all of the performers try to upstage each other, as well as Polly, in an effort to gain his attention. The production numbers in the film are projections of how De Thrill imagines that he would stage some of the songs in a lavish Hollywood film.

"I tried to get the extravagant, imaginative flair of the Busby Berkeley musicals into these production numbers," says Russell; "but it was difficult to accomplish in a British studio, where they've forgotten how to do an old-fashioned musical. Of course they've done things like *Oliver!*, where you build naturalistic sets and the chorus dances around them. But I am referring to the kind of musical number which involves a lot of special effects and camera tricks. Take the song in *The Boy Friend*, 'There's Safety in Numbers.' By means of optical effects the chorines seem to spin into pinwheels, and then turn into dancing dominoes. That took some doing."

As luck would have it, Polly is the only girl in the troupe to whom De Thrill offers a career in pictures, but she turns down the opportunity to go to the Hollywood dream factory, in favor of staying on in the company and falling in love with the company's male lead (Christopher Gable). Unlike Tchaikovsky and the central characters of other Russell biopics, Polly is not a romantic idealist who wants to be more than she is. Hence one finds in *The Boy Friend* resonances of the theme that Russell has treated more seriously in other films. It is clear, then, that Russell's great variety of films, although superficially quite different, has, after all, sprung from the same creative consciousness.

In addition to *The Boy Friend*, Russell has done a couple of other movie musicals, including his essay in rock opera, *Tommy* (1975). But *The Boy Friend* remains his best effort in this genre.

Russell again returned to the past with *Savage Messiah* (1972). Like *The Music Lovers*, it is a biographical film (or biopic, as the genre has come to be called) of the kind that he pioneered on BBC-TV, this time built around sculptor Henri Gaudier, who died in World War I. Gaudier (Scott Antony) lived in a one-room flat with an older woman, Sophie Brzeska (Dorothy Tutin), and was forced to steal tombstones to provide raw material for his work.

Henri and Sophie are very different in many ways. Henri is exuberant and impetuous; Sophie is more genteel and mature. The one thing that draws them together is their mutual loneliness. Their complicated relationship is partially that of a mother and son, of a sister and brother, and of two lovers, although Sophie refuses to allow Henri to make love to her or to marry her, because of some unpleasant amorous experiences in her past.

Henri loses himself in his work when he gets the chance to have a one-man exhibition. One day he reaches through the grating that separates him from the rest of the world while he is sculpting in his basement flat and buys a newspaper. It tells him that Rheims Cathedral and other monuments of art and architecture are being destroyed in the war. He therefore leaves his work and goes off to join the army, fortified with Sophie's promise to marry him on his return. After his death in battle, the exhibition of his sculpture is held posthumously. We see Sophie standing in tears before the unfinished statue on which Henri was working on the day that he decided to enlist, and the film ends with the camera examining various pieces of sculpture we had seen Henri creating at different times in the course of the film.

In some ways *Savage Messiah* is one of Russell's best biopics; for it completely captures the spirit of the euphoric young artist Gaudier, without trying to offer any facile explanations either for his life or for his work. As for the latter, Henri comments while working on a statue, "The stone must lead you. Every blow of the hammer is a risk. It's as much a mystery to the one who's doing the sculpture as to the one who will look at it."

There are some fine cinematic touches in the film: the hand of the young man clasped in that of the older woman the first time that they express affection for each other; Henri leaping about barefoot on the seashore as he shouts of his love for Sophie and asks her to marry him, and then limping away across the beach like a wounded bird, as if feeling the pebbles for the first time, when she turns him down yet again.

Russell believed in the project of making a film on Gaudier's life to the extent of investing in the production himself. "Otherwise it would have taken me much longer to finance the film," he explains. "I then set out to make the film as good as possible for as little as possible." Because Russell has found that the smaller the budget a film has, the less likely the front office is to interfere with its production, he trimmed the budget for *Savage Messiah* as much as he could and shot it in a small studio he refers to jokingly as a "derelict biscuit factory, on the banks of a stagnant canal."

Continuing in the biopic genre, Russell did *Mahler* (1974), about the nineteenth-century Austrian composer Gustav Mahler, and *Valentino* (1977), inspired by the life of the matinee idol of the silver screen, Rudolph Valentino. The latter film, of course, parallels the Cukor and Schlesinger movies about the film colony, already treated.

In making *Valentino*, Russell, who cowrote as well as directed the movie, contrasts the public image of Valentino, the superstar of the silent cinema, with the private image of the man that he was in his personal life. Thus Valentino the private individual is portrayed as valuing very much the personal code of honor that he brought with him to America from his native Italy. It seemed shopworn and old-fashioned to the progressive modern Americans with whom he came into contact during the balance of his short life, which ended with his untimely death at thirty-

(Top) Rudolph Valentino, the silent film star; (bottom) Rudolf Nureyev playing Valentino in *Valentino* **(1977). (The Ken Russell collection)**

one in 1926. But, as Russell has drawn him in the movie, Valentino was willing to live and, if necessary, to die for that code.

As Valentino's life unfolds, Russell emphasizes the enormous hostility that Valentino (Rudolf Nureyev) unwittingly evoked in the American male population, who had become increasingly jealous of the sexual prowess he exhibited on the screen. It is a matter of record that such male antipathy toward Valentino's virile screen image did exist and that it culminated in a snide editorial in the *Chicago Tribune* which charged him with being both impotent and homosexual and as such unworthy to represent genuine manhood on the screen.

Valentino retaliated with an open letter denouncing the editorial for slurring his family name and Italian ancestry by casting doubts upon his manhood. Moreover, he challenged the anonymous author of the editorial to a boxing match as a test of honor. His challenge went unacknowledged by anyone at the *Tribune*; but Frank O'Neil, the boxing writer for the *New York Evening Journal*, offered to take Valentino on in a private sparring match—which Valentino uncontestably won.

In the movie Valentino's challenge is picked up by Rory O'Neil, a sports writer who also happens to be a retired Navy boxing champion. Russell stages O'Neil's bout with Valentino, not in private, but in a packed arena, in order to underline its importance to Valentino, who sees the fight as the equivalent of a traditional duel, whereby he can vindicate both his personal honor and his public image. At first the ex-champ gets the best of his novice opponent; but O'Neil is out of shape and finally caves in under Valentino's fervent onslaught.

Valentino staggers home, weary but triumphant. Nevertheless, the strenuous exertions of the night have taken their toll on the already critically ailing man, and he slumps to the floor of his living room as he reaches for an orange from the bowl on the table. As he dies, his unsteady hand grasps for the orange, which remains tantalizingly out of reach, just as Valentino's dreams of retiring some day to the seclusion of a farm to raise oranges has likewise eluded his grasp to the end.

Valentino was not a hit, but Russell then made a highly commercial science-fiction film, *Altered States* (1980). The plot revolves around the experiment that Eddie Jessup, a Harvard psychologist (William Hurt), conducts on himself by submerging himself in a sensory deprivation tank while under the influence of hallucinogenic drugs. His purpose is to propel himself backward to the birth of his own consciousness and beyond that to the dawn of human consciousness itself in order to comprehend more deeply the meaning of human existence as it has evolved down through the centuries.

When I spoke with Russell on the set in Hollywood, he said that *Altered States* reflects the religious preoccupations that often surface in his movies. Jessup goes to great lengths to obtain an experimental knowledge of the mysteries of the universe such as God has not vouchsafed to grant to any other human being, Russell explained; and the film implies that "Jessup is wrong in arrogantly trying to wrest from God by force a grasp of divine truth that can only be God-given."

In effect Jessup is succumbing to the temptation of Adam and Eve in the Garden of Eden. They ate the forbidden fruit of the Tree of Knowledge because of the blandishments of the satanic tempter who appeared to them in the guise of a serpent and advised them that, if they did so, they would become as wise as God Himself. Russell visualizes this concept in one of the fantasy sequences that punctuate *Altered States*. This particular hallucination is the result of Jessup's having eaten some mysterious mushrooms as part of an ancient tribal rite, in which we see him participate in the film's Mexican sequence.

In this dream vision Jessup and his wife Emily (Blair Brown) appear as a twentieth-century Adam and Eve, sitting under a beach umbrella but dressed in nineteenth-century outfits that give the vision a timeless quality. The serpent about to tempt the latter-day Adam and Eve in this fantasy is coiled around the spokes of the mushroom-shaped umbrella, which in turn erupts into the mushroom cloud of an atomic explosion. This image symbolizes the sin of pride Adam and Eve committed in the Garden of Eden as the source of war and other kinds of large-scale disasters throughout human history, as well as causing personal calamities in the lives of individuals like Jessup, who nearly destroys himself and everything he loves because of his prideful obsession with piercing the mysteries of the universe. Happily in Jessup's case he finally comes to his senses, both literally and figuratively, with the aid of his devoted wife, whose love for him finally helps him to triumph over his inner compulsions.

Russell then directed *Crimes of Passion* (1984), an unflinching look at the underside of modern American life, in which he trained his camera on a sordid world of drugs and debauchery. In 1986 he released *Gothic*, a film centering on the English

Blair Brown and William Hurt in *Altered States* (1980). (The Ken Russell collection)

Romantic poets Byron (Gabriel Byrne) and Shelley (Julian Sands). The movie takes place one stormy night in 1816 when the pair, along with Mary Godwin, Shelley's wife-to-be (Natasha Richardson) and some others, get together to conduct a weird seance. The upshot of this harrowing evening, during which the participants experience several drug-induced hallucinations, is the seance's ultimately inspiring Mary to write the classic monster tale *Frankenstein*.

Russell conjures up some overwhelming dream visions in the movie, filled with a wide assortment of grotesque, ghostly creatures, in order to visualize the macabre hallucinatory experiences that are visited upon Byron and his entourage. "But," writes Lloyd Sachs, "in order for Russell's cylinders to be pumping at maximum efficiency, he needs a strong narrative to go along with his nightmare images; and neither he nor scriptwriter Stephen Volk has found it in *Gothic*."[3] Nonetheless, any movie made by a venturesome director like Russell, whose reach sometimes exceeds his grasp, is still of interest; and *Gothic* is no exception.

Although the film's fantasy sequences tend to overshadow its story line, as Sachs indicated, *Gothic* is still a biopic in that it portrays an incident that happened to a group of historical personages, and that thought brings one back to Russell's cinematic biographies. When one recalls the director's uncompromising biopics about Tchaikovsky, Gaudier, and others, it is abundantly clear that Russell has almost singlehandedly revolutionized the conventional movie biography to the point where that genre will never be quite the same again.

In addition to experimenting with the nature of biographical films, Russell has at the same time sought by trial and error to discover in all of his films, biopics or not, to what extent a motion picture can be cut loose from the moorings of conventional storytelling, as in his mind-bending science fiction film *Altered States*. If these experiments in narrative technique account for occasional lapses in the narrative logic of a Russell movie, they also account for the intricate and arresting blend of past and present, fact and fantasy, in his best work.

A case in point is *The Lair of the White Worm* (1988), Russell's lively, streamlined adaptation of a horror tale by Bram Stoker, author of *Dracula*. The story gets going when Lord James D'Ampton (Hugh Grant) gives a party in his castle in commemoration of a knightly ancestor of his celebrated for having slain a gigantic serpent, which is represented in ancient lore as an enormous, savage white worm. One of his guests, an archeology student named Angus Flint, and James both agree that there is an eerie connection between the legend of the white worm, some mysterious cases of "snakebite" that have turned up in the area, and the strange disappearances of some of the locals near the forbidding mansion of the sultry Lady Silvia Marsh (Amanda Donohoe).

Among the baleful revelations that come to light as the film unreels, Lady Silvia is discovered to be the monstrous vampire that has been prowling the countryside. Indeed, her spooky domain serves as the "lair" from which she ventures forth in search of her victims; moreover, she fosters a secret pagan cult dedicated to the legendary monster, with whom she harbors a grim kinship. By the time this vile villainess gets her just deserts, Russell has treated his audience to a number of genuinely scary, blood-splattered episodes. In sum, he has skillfully managed to fashion a fresh retelling of the old vampire legends, that has all the earmarks of a topnotch horror movie, as *Variety* sagely observed.[4]

Russell then shot *The Rainbow* (1989), from the D. H. Lawrence novel. As noted above, Lawrence wrote *Women in Love*, which Russell filmed two decades earlier, as a sequel to *The Rainbow*. Accordingly, Ursula and Gudrun, the two heroines of *Women in Love*, are still in their teens in Russell's film of the earlier book. In the present movie Ursula (Sammi Davis, in a winning performance), asserts her independent spirit by leaving home to teach in a slum school. "It's about a girl who won't stay within the comforting womb of her family," Russell explains, "but goes off alone to find her own way of life." As the story develops, Ursula has an affair with Anton, a Polish officer (Paul McGann), which ends tragically. While she is trying to come to terms with this unhappy experience, a rainbow appears in the sky, which offers the promise of the reintegration of human values in her life once more. The rainbow, then, symbolizes the promise of the future. "It's a timeless parable," Russell concludes, "terribly simple but very effective, about growing up."

Russell mentioned in correspondence that the film reunited him with some of the actors and creative team who had been involved in *Women in Love*—notably Glenda Jackson, who played Ursula's sister in that film and appears as Anna, the girl's mother, in *The Rainbow*. It was "just like old times," said Russell, working with the same people again; he added that their participation augured that the film just might turn out as well as its earlier companion piece.[5] And so it did. Indeed, Russell's two Lawrence films, taken together, will in time be recognized as an outstanding achievement of the cinematic art.

In considering his career as a whole, one realizes that Russell has never lost the conviction which he said he learned from the short life of Henri Gaudier. Russell expresses it this way: "Everyone is a potential artist who has a little spark of something special in him, which he can transmit to his fellows, which might well be of use to them. I am still striving to accomplish this in my work, and will go on doing so—despite the fact that after every film I always say I'll never make another one. Somehow I always do."[6]

Epilogue:
Artists in an International Industry

All of the film makers in this book learned during their careers that a director not only has to work hard to achieve the kind of artistic independence that qualifies him to be an *auteur*, but that he has to work just as hard to keep it. For example, although a director like Ken Russell has often been looked upon as a maverick who makes films perhaps more subjective and personal than those of many of the other directors treated here, it is important to realize that his motion pictures have often been financed by some of the oldest and largest of Hollywood studios: MGM, Columbia, and Warner's. That these companies have been willing to allow him such a great degree of artistic freedom is yet another indication that the big Hollywood studios are well aware they must make an effort to present contemporary audiences with fresh material and not just a rehash of the old commercial formulas long since overfamiliar to moviegoers.

On the other hand, a canny director like Russell realizes that a film maker must cooperate with the studio that has invested in his film if he expects to get backing in the future. In other words, the cooperation must be on both sides; and Russell does not mind meeting company demands, as long as he can meet them in his own way. Thus he has it stipulated in his contracts that any cuts the studio wants to make in a film of his are to be made under his supervision.

The relationship of artist and industry will always be a difficult one, since the director is primarily concerned with preserving his artistic integrity while the industry is primarily interested in safeguarding its investment. This conflict of interest will inevitably lead to compromise; but as has been seen in the film makers covered in this book, the compromise can often be one enabling the director to produce a film that is recognizably his own, and yet one from which the studio can expect a return on its investment.

As television becomes to an ever increasing degree the medium that claims the largest segment of the mass audience in the way the cinema once did, motion pictures are being thought of more and more in the same category as the legitimate theater: a medium that can afford to appeal to a more discriminating audience which wants fare a bit more challenging than what they can usually find on the tube. As this happens, film directors are more frequently being given a freer hand in making films that are more inventive and personal than has usually been the case in the past.

After all, the major studios began to extend artistic freedom to independent film makers in the first place because studio executives realized that they were losing touch with the moviegoing public's taste. The great virtue the directors in this book as a group have in common is that they have for the most part been able to make films their own way, while at the same time remaining aware of what would appeal to their audience. They have, in short, shown their respect for the creative freedom they have achieved by working so hard to win it and by using it so well.

In surveying the international film scene, one notices a trend among British film makers like Forbes, Schlesinger, and Russell to work in the United States as well as in their native England. "I like the cross-fertilization that comes from making films in both England and America," John Schlesinger responded when this question was raised with him. But a more critical reason for English directors returning to American shores to make movies, he added, has been the steady decline of the British film industry as a significant force in world cinema since the 1960s. "British audiences tend to stay home and watch television even more than Americans do," he continued, simply because British TV is, on the whole, of a higher caliber than American TV. "As a result, the television industry in Britain is flourishing in a way that the film industry is not; and therefore the younger British film makers can only get financing for the little screen mostly, not often for the big screen."

Because American capital has continued to be the principal source of financing for production in England as well as in America, British film makers come often to the United States, where projects are generated and decisions about the financing of film productions are primarily made. After all, only a relatively small part of the British film industry has remained independent of American capital; and, according to film historian Leslie Halliwell, the part that has retained its independence is committed to turning out movies that, with few exceptions, are made on low budgets for a quick three-week showing on the art house circuit, followed soon after by a screening on TV.

For his part, Schlesinger says, "Although I am English and I do like to work in England, I have gotten used to regarding myself more and more as mid-Atlantic." As a matter of fact, foreign directors, precisely because they are not native Americans, are sometimes able to view American life with a vigilant, perceptive eye for the kind of telling details that home-grown directors might easily overlook or simply take for granted.

Still, regardless of where a film maker works, he must reconcile himself to the fact that he is usually going to have difficulties in securing studio backing for a project he has developed. In the present setup, a director must negotiate with movie executives who operate a given studio as part of some larger conglomerate and who are therefore wary of rocking the corporate boat by providing financing for a property that departs in varying degrees from the kind of safe, commercial subject matter they tend to favor. Yet, as more than one director has suggested, it is precisely the risky, offbeat projects that often capture a large audience; and movies like *2001*, *Midnight Cowboy*, and *Altered States* bear out this contention.

More than ever, movies made by serious directors are mirroring the attitudes and problems of society at large and hence possess the potential to appeal to an international audience. In fact, directors like Kubrick, Schlesinger, Russell, and their colleagues have learned to survive in the increasingly complicated world of movie making by forging themselves reputations that transcend national boundaries. In reality, therefore, they are in a true sense members of an international community of film makers who are trying to speak to an equally international audience. That is the way world cinema has been headed for some time, and the major directors of the American and British cinema have helped to lead it in that direction.

Notes

Any direct quotations in this book that are undocumented are derived from the author's personal interviews with the subjects; direct references to their personal correspondence are documented.

Prologue: Artists in an Industry

1. Ben Hecht, "Enter the Movies," in *Film: An Anthology*, ed. Daniel Talbot (Berkeley: University of California Press, 1966), p. 258.
2. Andrew Sarris, *Confessions of a Cultist: On the Cinema* (New York: Simon and Schuster, 1971), p. 363.
3. Peter Wollen, *Signs and Meaning in the Cinema* (Bloomington: Indiana University Press, 1969), p. 74.
4. Pauline Kael, "Circles and Squares," in *I Lost It at the Movies* (New York: Bantam, 1966), pp. 273–75; Sarris, *Confessions*, p. 361.
5. Pauline Kael, *Deeper into Movies* (New York: Bantam, 1974), p. 98.
6. Gordon Anders Kindem, *Toward a Semiotic Theory of Visual Communicantion: The Color Films of Alfred Hitchcock* (New York: Arno, 1980), p. 75; Maurice Yacowar, *Hitchcock's British Films* (Hamden, Conn.: Archon Books, 1977), p. 14; see also Jeffrey Chown, *Hollywood Auteur: Francis Coppola* (New York: Praeger, 1988), pp. 9–10 and 214, on the interaction of the *auteur* and his collaborators, and also John Schlesinger's extended remarks at the end of chapter 13.
7. Gerald Mast, *A Short History of the Movies*, rev. ed. (New York: Macmillan, 1986), p. 262.
8. Arthur Knight, *The Liveliest Art* (New York: New American Library, 1957), p. 269.
9. Mast, *Short History*, p. 67; cf. Alanna Nash, "Remembering D. W. Griffith," *Take One* (Special Griffith Issue) 4, no. 7 (1975): 15.
10. David Robinson, "The Twenties," in *Hollywood: 1920–70*, ed. Peter Cowie, rev. ed. (New York: Barnes, 1977), p. 26.
11. Knight, *Liveliest Art*, p. 270.
12. Louis Giannetti, *Masters of the American Cinema* (Englewood Cliffs, N.J.: Prentice-Hall, 1981), p. 76.

Chapter 1. Charles Chaplin: The Little Fellow in a Big World

1. Richard Meryman, "Ageless Master's Anatomy of Comedy," *Life*, 3 April 1967, p. 25; the centennial of Chaplin's birth received international attention—see Walter Kerr, "A Master's Centenary," *New York Times*, 9 April 1989, sec. 2, pp. 1, 20, 21.
2. Charles Chaplin, *My Autobiography* (New York: Pocket Books, 1966), p. 148. Chaplin's autobiography is not to be confused with *Charlie Chaplin's Own Story* (1916), a spurious autobiography written by one Rose Wilder Lane, a San Francisco journalist, without the subject's collaboration; see David Robinson, *Chaplin: His Life and Art* (New York: McGraw-Hill, 1989), pp. 180–85.
3. Theodore Huff, *Charlie Chaplin* (New York: Pyramid, 1972), p. 9.

4. Chaplin, *My Autobiography*, p. 184.

5. Ibid., p. 225.

6. Huff, *Charlie Chaplin*, p. 103.

7. Ibid., p. 154.

8. Chaplin, *My Autobiography*, p. 327.

9. Meryman, "Ageless Master," p. 29.

10. Bosley Crowther, *The Great Films* (New York: Putnam's, 1967), p. 52.

11. Huff, *Charlie Chaplin*, p. 173.

12. Chaplin, *My Autobiography*, p. 351. For the record, the sound era was officially inaugurated on October 6, 1927, with the premiere of Alan Crosland's *The Jazz Singer*, which had a musical score and four musical numbers, but no dialogue sequences; it was followed in July, 1928, by Bryan Foy's *The Lights of New York*, the first all-talking picture; and by 1929 the sound era was in full swing.

13. Ibid., p. 353.

14. Meryman, "Ageless Master," p. 27; cf. Charles Silver, *Charles Chaplin: An Appreciation* (New York: Museum of Modern Art, 1989), p. 37.

15. Huff, *Charlie Chaplin*, p. 208.

16. Peter Cotes and Thelma Niklaus, *The Little Fellow* (New York: Citadel, 1965), p. 124.

17. Chaplin, *My Autobiography*, p. 397

18. Huff, *Charlie Chaplin*, p. 214.

19. Meryman, "Ageless Master," p. 26.

20. Cotes and Niklaus, *The Little Fellow*, p. 131.

21. George Wallach, "Charlie Chaplin's *Monsieur Verdoux* Press Conference," *Film Comment* 5, no. 4 (Winter 1969): 36.

22. Meryman, "Ageless Master," p. 26.

23. Sarris, *Confessions*, p. 295.

24. Huff, *Charlie Chaplin*, p. 231.

Chapter 2. Howard Hawks: Lonely Are the Brave

1. Manny Farber, "Underground Films," in *Film: An Anthology*, ed. Daniel Talbot pp. 165, 168; Penelope Houston, *Contemporary Cinema* (Baltimore: Penguin, 1969), p. 66; Andrew Sarris, *The American Cinema*, rev. ed. (Chicago: University of Chicago Press, 1985), p. 53.

2. For more on Rudolph Valentino, see the treatment of Ken Russell's film *Valentino* in chapter 14.

3. Robin Wood, *Howard Hawks* (New York: Doubleday, 1968), p. 21; p. 57.

4. Ibid., p. 93.

5. Jacques Becker, Jacques Rivette, and François Truffaut, "Howard Hawks," in *Interviews with Film Directors*, ed. Andrew Sarris (New York: Avon, 1969), p. 232.

6. Becker et al., "Howard Hawks," p. 237; p. 234.

7. James Agee, *Agee on Film*, vol. 1 (New York: Grosset and Dunlap, 1969), 354.

8. Joseph Blotner, "Faulkner in Hollywood," in *Man and the Movies*, ed. W. R. Robinson (Baltimore: Penguin, 1969), p. 289; Pico Iyer, "Private Eye, Public Conscience," *Time*, Dec. 12, 1988, p. 98.

9. Blotner, p. 302; for Hawks's extended reflections on working with Faulkner, see Joseph McBride, "William Faulkner," in *Hawks on Hawks* (Berkeley: University of California Press, 1982), pp. 56–60; see also Gerald Mast, *Howard Hawks, Storyteller* (New York: Oxford University Press, 1984), pp. 5–10.

10. Peter Wollen, *Signs and Meaning in the Cinema*, p. 91.

11. Pauline Kael, *Kiss Kiss Bang Bang* (New York: Bantam, 1969), p. 350; there are two subsequent, somewhat less effective remakes of this venerable property, as noted in Leonard

Maltin, ed., *TV Movies*, rev. ed. (New York: New American Library, 1988), pp. vii, 374, and 1042: Billy Wilder's *The Front Page* (1974) and Ted Kotcheff's *Switching Channels* (1988), which was updated to the era of TV reporting.

12. Blotner, "Faulkner in Hollywood," p. 299.

13. Wood, *Howard Hawks*, p. 115; for the response of the director of *High Noon* to Hawks's remark, see chapter 6.

14. Review of *El Dorado*, 28 July 1967, p. 80.

Chapter 3. Alfred Hitchcock: Through a Glass Darkly

1. Pete Martin, "Alfred Hitchcock," in *Film Makers on Film Making*, ed. Harry M. Geduld (Bloomington: Indiana University Press), pp. 127–28.

2. See François Truffaut, *Hitchcock*, rev. ed. (New York: Simon and Schuster, 1985), pp. 26–27, for his training in film making.

3. Martin, "Hitchcock," p. 128.

4. Charles Higham and Joel Greenberg, "Alfred Hitchcock," in *The Celluloid Muse* (New York: New American Library, 1972), p. 103.

5. Peter Cowie, *Seventy Years of Cinema* (New York: A. S. Barnes, 1969), p. 235; cf. Charles Derry, *The Suspense Thriller: Films in the Shadow of Hitchcock* (Jefferson, N.C.: McFarland, 1988), pp. 49–50.

6. "*Frenzy*," *Variety*, May 31, 1972, in *Variety: Film Reviews, 1907–80*, vol. 13 (New York: Garland, 1983).

7. Charles Chaplin, "Paying Homage to 'King Alfred'" *Los Angeles Times*, 7 March 1979, sec. 4, p. 18.

Chapter 4. George Cukor: A Touch of Class

1. Sarris, *American Cinema*, pp. 89–90.

2. Letter to the author, Aug. 13, 1980.

3. Crowther, *Great Films*, p. 120.

4. Adela Rogers St. Johns, "The Private Life of Katharine Hepburn," *Liberty*, 6 January 1934. Reprinted in *Liberty: The Nostalgia Magazine*, Spring 1972, p. 54.

5. Gary Carey, *Cukor and Company* (New York: Museum of Modern Art, 1971), p. 69.

6. Virtually all of the missing footage was recovered in the vaults at Warners Brothers, and a restored version of the film was given a limited rerelease in 1983; see Ronald Haver, *A Star is Born: The Making of the 1954 Film and Its 1983 Restoration* (New York: Knopf, 1988), pp. 227–84.

7. For the record, there was another non-musical film of *A Star is Born*, made between the two Cukor versions by another director in 1937. But, as mentioned, Cukor's musical remake remains the best of the lot.

8. Richard Schickel, *The Men Who Made the Movies* (New York: Athenaeum, 1975), p. 164.

Chapter 5. George Stevens: In Search of a Hero

1. Donald Richie, *George Stevens: An American Romantic* (New York: Museum of Modern Art, 1970), p. 34.

2. Elliott Sirkin, "*Alice Adams*," *Film Comment* 7, no. 4 (Winter 1971): 66.

3. Ibid., p. 68.

4. Ritchie, *George Stevens*, p. 11; see Katharine Hepburn, "Get a Tough Director," *Panorama* (March 1981), p. 60, where Hepburn singles out Stevens for his assured direction of *Alice Adams*, a point endorsed by her costar, Fred MacMurray, in conversation with this writer.

5. Kael, *I Lost It at the Movies* (New York: Bantam, 1966), p. 217.

6. *Agee on Film*, vol. 1, 385.

7. Kael, *I Lost It at the Movies*, p. 216.

8. See Max Hastings, "Dachau," in *Victory in Europe*, photographed by George Stevens (Boston: Little, Brown, 1985), pp. 164–71. The book is illustrated with shots from Stevens's filmed record of the war.

Chapter 6. Fred Zinnemann: Darkness at Noon

1. *Agee on Film*, vol. 1, 302.

2. Roger Manvell, *New Cinema in the USA* (New York: Dutton, 1968), p. 12.

3. Carl Foreman, "What Film Shall We Make Next?" in *International Film Annual*, ed. William Whitebait (New York: Doubleday, 1958), p. 118.

4. Alan Stanbrook, "A Man for All Movies, Part II," *Films and Filming* 13, no. 6 (June 1967): 13; cf. Stuart Y. McDougal, *Made Into Movies* (New York: Holt, Rinehart, and Winston, 1985), pp. 47–50.

5. Ed Fischer, *Film as Insight* (Notre Dame: Fdes Press, 1971), p. 78.

6. John Howard Reid, "A Man for All Movies, Part I," *Films and Filming*, 13, no. 5 (May 1967): 10.

7. Judith Crist, *The Private Eye, the Cowboy, and the Very Naked Girl* (New York: Paperback Library, 1970), p. 229.

8. Benedict Nightengale, "Fred Zinnemann Distills a New Film from an Old Dream," *New York Times*, 7 November 1982, sec. 2, p. 1; letter to the author, 23 May 1988.

Chapter 7. Stanley Kubrick: Stop the World

1. Peter Cowie, *Seventy Years of Cinema* (New York: A. S. Barnes, 1969), p. 222.

2. Kael, *I Lost It at the Movies*, p. 184.

3. William Kloman, "In 2001 Will Love be a Seven-Letter Word?" *New York Times*, 14 April 1968, sec. 2, p. 15.

4. Gene Siskel, "Stanley Kubrick," *Chicago Tribune*, 14 February 1972, sec. 2, p. 9.

5. "Anthony Burgess," *Evening News* (London), 31 January 1972.

6. Tom Burke, "Malcolm McDowell," *New York Times*, 31 January 1972, sec. 2, p. 13.

7. Thomas Allen Nelson, *Kubrick* (Bloomington: Indiana University Press, 1982), p. 211.

8. Letter to the author, 5 December 1981.

9. Gene Siskel, "Candidly Kubrick," *Chicago Tribune*, 21 June 1987, sec. 13, p. 5; see *Literature/Film Quarterly* 16, no. 4 (Fall, 1988) which has a special section of four articles on *Full Metal Jacket*.

Chapter 8. Francis Coppola: The Lower Depths

1. Robert K. Johnson, *Francis Ford Coppola* (Boston: Twayne, 1977), p. 74; p. 73.

2. Ibid., p. 98; p. 125.

3. Pauline Kael, *Reeling* (New York: Bantam, 1977), p. 528.

4. Ibid., p. 532.

5. Johnson, *Coppola*, p. 148; p. 155.

6. Rob Edelman, "Francis Ford Coppola," in *The International Dictionary of Films and Filmmakers*, rev. ed., ed. Christopher Lyon, James Vinson, and Nick Thomas (London: St. James Press, 1989), vol. 2, 93.

7. Jean-Paul Chaillet and Elizabeth Vincent, *Francis Ford Coppola*, trans. Denise Raab Jacobs (New York: St. Martin's, 1985), p. 93.

8. Gene Siskel, "Flick Picks," *Chicago Tribune*, 24 October 1986, sec. 7, p. C.

9. Gene Siskel, "Celluloid Godfather," *Chicago Tribune*, 5 October 1986, sec. 13, p. 4.

10. Richard A. Blake, "Apocalypse Within," *America*, 8 September 1979, p. 96.

11. Joy Gould Boyum, *Double Exposure: Fiction into Film* (New York: Universe, 1985), p. 111.

12. Bob Strauss, "*Tucker*," *Chicago Sun-Times*, Aug. 8, 1988, 2:5; Robert Lindsey, "Francis Ford Coppola: Promises to Keep," *New York Times Magazine*, July 24, 1988, pp. 26–27.

13. See Jeffrey Chown, *Hollywood Auteur: Francis Coppola* (New York: Praeger, 1988), pp. 1–5 and 213–15, on Coppola as an *auteur* director.

Chapter 9. Carol Reed: The Disenchanted

1. On the quota system, see Roy Armes, *A Critical History of British Cinema* (London: Secker and Warburg, 1978), pp. 73, ff.

2. Knight, *Liveliest Art*, p. 209.

3. Kael, *Kiss Kiss Bang Bang*, p. 440; for a further treatment of Reed's early British films, see Robert F. Moss, *The Films of Carol Reed* (New York: Columbia University Press, 1987), pp. 88–114.

4. *Graham Greene on Film: Collected Film Criticism, 1935–40*, ed. John Russell Taylor (New York: Simon and Schuster, 1972), p. 265.

5. For a more extensive critique of *Night Train to Munich* by the same author, cf. William K. Everson, "Rediscovery: *Night Train to Munich*," *Films in Review* 38, no. 12 (December 1987): 619–21; James DeFelice, *Filmguide to Odd Man Out* (Bloomington: Indiana University Press, 1975), p. 14.

6. *Agee on Film*, vol. 1, 269; Graham Greene, "Introduction to *The Fallen Idol*," in *The Third Man* and *The Fallen Idol* (New York: Viking, 1950), p. 146.

7. Quoted in Robert Emmett Ginna, "*Our Man in Havana*," *Horizon* 2, no. 2 (November 1959): 38.

8. Houston, *Contemporary Cinema*, p. 38; in conversation Reed mentioned that it was his hand that was photographed reaching through the sewer grating, since Welles had not as yet arrived on location.

9. Kael, *Kiss Kiss Bang Bang*, p. 13.

10. Ginna, "Reed's *Our Man in Havana*," 122.

11. Carl Foreman, "What Film Shall We Make Next?", p. 118.

12. Pauline Kael, *Going Steady* (New York: Bantam, 1971), p. 251.

13. Ginna, "*Our Man in Havana*," p. 31.

14. Marion Fawcett, "Sir Carol Reed," *Films in Review* 10, no. 3 (March 1959): 141.

Chapter 10. David Lean: The Undefeated

1. Gerald Pratley, "Interview with David Lean," *Interviews with Film Directors*, p. 319.

2. David Lean, "The Film Maker and the Audience," in *Film Makers on Film Making*, ed. Harry M. Geduld (Bloomington: Indiana University Press, 1969), p. 282.

3. Houston, *Contemporary Cinema*, pp. 39–40; Michael Anderegg, *David Lean* (Boston: Twayne, 1984), p. 21.

4. *Great Expectations: A Study Guide* (New York: National Center for Film Study, 1972), p. 2.

5. Lean, "Film Maker and Audience," p. 285.

6. John Huntley and Roger Manvell, *The Technique of Film Music* (London: Focal Press, 1957), pp. 74–75.

7. Lean, "Film Maker and Audience," p. 285; cf. Michael Anderegg, *David Lean* (Boston: Twayne, 1984), pp. 58–60, concerning the "Fagin controversy."

8. Gordon Gow, "The Fifties," in *Hollywood: 1920–70*, p. 190.

9. For the record, after the premiere of *Lawrence*, the studio cut the film from 222 minutes to 202 minutes. The missing footage has been recovered from the vaults at Columbia, and a restored version of the film was rereleased in 1989; see Janet Maslin, "*Lawrence* Seen Whole," *New York Times*, 29 January 1989, sec. 2, pp. 1, 13.

10. "Oscar Bound," *Time*, 24 December 1965, p. 44.

11. Richard Schickel, "Lean's *Dr. Zhivago*," *Life*, 21 January 1966, p. 62A.

12. Harlan Kennedy, "'I'm a Picture Chap,'" *Film Comment*, 21, no. 2 (January–February 1985), 28.

13. Pratley, "Interview with David Lean," p. 321; Kennedy, "'I'm a Picture Chap,'" p. 32.

Chapter 11. Joseph Losey: Decline and Fall

1. Tom Milne, *Losey and Losey* (New York: Doubleday, 1968), p. 128.

2. Ibid., p. 61.

3. James Leahy, *The Cinema of Joseph Losey* (New York: A. S. Barnes, 1967), p. 60; for further background on the House Unamerican Activities Committee, see Bernard Dick, *Radical Innocence* (Lexington: University Press of Kentucky, 1989), pp. 1–9.

4. Milne, *Losey on Losey*, p. 44.

5. Leahy, *Cinema of Losey*, p. 76.

6. Ibid., p. 79.

7. Milne, *Losey on Losey*, p. 158.

8. Leahy, *Cinema of Losey*, p. 109.

9. Ibid., p. 11

10. Reed, *Conversations in the Raw* (New York: World, 1969), p. 144.

11. Tom Milne, "*Accident*," *Sight and Sound* 36, no. 2 (Spring 1967): 57.

12. Richard Roud, "Going Between," *Sight and Sound* 40, no. 3 (Summer 1971): 158.

13. Gow, "Reflections: Alan Bates," *Films and Filming* 17, no. 6 (June 1971): 28.

14. When *Secret Ceremony* was released to TV, the studio added a prologue and epilogue, in which a psychiatrist "explains" the emotional problems of the principles to a colleague, and cut the original film to make room for the added material. Losey disowned the TV version of the film, and the original version is now the only one shown on TV.

15. Michel Ciment, *Conversations with Losey* (New York: Methuen, 1985), p. 339; letter to the author, Sept. 30, 1980.

16. Ibid., p. 387, p. 390; Reed, *Conversations in the Raw*, p. 141.

Chapter 12. Bryan Forbes: The Kitchen Sink-Drome

1. William Whitebait, "A Dawn in British Films?" in *International Film Annual*, ed. William Whitebait (New York: Taplinger, 1959), p. 11.

2. Roger Manvell, *New Cinema in Britain* (New York: Dutton, 1969), p. 62.

3. "Bryan Forbes; "An Interview," *Films Illustrated*, July 1971, p. 10; cf. Bryan Forbes, *Notes for a Life* (London: Collins, 1974), pp. 295–305, for Forbes's account of his transition from screenwriter to film director.

4. "Forbes: An Interview," p. 10; see Vito Russo, *"The L-Shaped Room,"* in *The Celluloid Closet: Homosexuality in the Movies* (New York: Harper, Row, 1987), pp. 146–47, where Russo notes the nuanced handling of the homosexual characters in the film.

5. Judith Crist, *The Private Eye, the Cowboy, and the Very Naked Girl*, p. 100.

6. John Gruen, "He Says, 'Yes, yes, Nanette,'" *New York Times*, 24 October 1971, sec. 2, p. 11.

7. Forbes, "An Interview," p. 10.

8. Bryan Forbes, *That Despicable Race: A History of the British Acting Tradition* (London: Elm Tree, 1980), p. 299.

9. Ivan Butler, *The Making of Feature Films* (Baltimore: Penguin, 1971), p. 159; Gruen, "He Says, 'Yes, yes, Nanette,'" p. 11.

10. Bryan Forbes, "An Interview," p. 10.

11. Bryan Forbes, "Report on Elstree," *Films Illustrated*, July 1971, pp. 6–8; cf. Alexander Walker, "The Last Tycoon," in *Hollywood, England: The British Film Industry in the Sixties* (London: Michael Joseph, 1974), pp. 426–40.

12. Letter to the author, 15 February 1985; Leslie Halliwell, *Film Guide*, rev. ed. (New York: Scribner's, 1989), p. 981.

13. Manvell, *New Cinema in Britain*, p. 90.

Chapter 13. John Schlesinger: Kinds of Loving

1. See Schlesinger's remarks, in the epilogue of this book, on TV as a training ground for younger directors; also cf. Martin Auty, "But is It Cinema?" in *British Cinema Now*, ed. Martin Auty and Nick Roddick (London: British Film Institute, 1985), pp. 57–70.

2. Gow, "Reflections: Alan Bates," *Films and Filming* 17, no. 6 (June 1971): 23.

3. John Schlesinger, "Blessed Isle or Fool's Paradise?" *Films and Filming* 9, no. 5 (May 1963): 8.

4. Gow, "A Buck for Joe," *Films and Filming* 15, no. 11 (Nov. 1969): 6.

5. Letters to the author, 19 July 1988; 15 February 1985.

6. Roger Ebert, "Schlesinger's *Falcon and the Snowman* Turns Life into Art," *Chicago Sun-Times*, 25 January 1985, sec. 2, p. 37; Stephen Rebello, "Spies Like Us," *Saturday Review* 67, no. 1 (Jan.–Feb. 1985): 38.

7. Harold C. Schonberg, in *"Madame Sousatzka* Strikes a Chord," *New York Times*, 9 October 1988, sec. 2, pp. 23, 30, places the film among the screen's significant works about musicians, such as *Intermezzo* (1939) and *The Seventh Veil* (1945).

Chapter 14. Ken Russell: The Past as Present

1. Letter to the author, 23 May 1988; *The Rainbow* is treated at the end of this chapter.

2. Michael Dempsey, "The World of Ken Russell," *Film Quarterly* 26, no. 4 (Spring 1972): 14; Ken Hanke, *Ken Russell's Films* (Metuchen, N.J.: Scarecrow, 1984), p. x.

3. Lloyd Sachs, *"Gothic,"* *Chicago Sun-Times*, 22 May 1987, sec. 2, p. 24.

4. *"The Lair of the White Worm,"* *Variety*, 31 August 1988, p. 15.

5. Michael Billington, "Just Right for D. H. Lawrence," *New York Times*, 30 April 1989, sec. 2, p. 17; letters to the author, 23 May 1988; 25 April 1989.

6. For further reflections by the director on his career, see Ken Russell, *The British Picture: An Autobiography* (London: Heinemann, 1989).

Bibliography

Only the more significant and substantial research materials are included here. Thus books and articles alluded to in the text that are only tangential to the films of the directors dealt with in this study are not included below.

Charles Chaplin

Chaplin, Charles. *My Autobiography*. New York: Pocket Books, 1966.

Cotes, Peter, and Thelma Niklaus. *The Little Fellow: The Life and Work of Charlie Chaplin*. New York: Citadel, 1965.

Huff, Theodore. *Charlie Chaplin*. New York: Pyramid, 1972.

Kerr, Walter. "A Master's Centenary: The Centennial of Chaplin's Birth." *New York Times*, 9 April 1989, sec. 2, pp. 1 and 20–21.

Meryman, Richard. "Ageless Master's Anatomy of Comedy." *Life*, 3 April 1967, pp. 22–29.

Robinson, David. *Chaplin: His Life and Art*. New York: McGraw-Hill, 1989.

Silver, Charles. *Charles Chaplin: An Appreciation*. New York: Museum of Modern Art, 1989.

Wallach, George. "Charlie Chaplin's *Monsieur Verdoux* Press Conference." *Film Comment* 5, no. 4 (Winter 1969): 34–42.

Howard Hawks

"*El Dorado*." *Time*, 28 July 1967, p. 80.

Iyer, Pico. "Private Eye, Public Conscience." *Time*, December 12, 1988, p. 98.

McBride, Joseph, ed. *Focus on Hawks*. Englewood Cliffs, N.J.: Prentice Hall, 1972.

———. *Hawks on Hawks*. Los Angeles: University of California Press, 1982.

Mast, Gerald. *Howard Hawks, Storyteller*. New York: Oxford University Press, 1984.

Phillips, Gene D. "Faulkner as Screenwriter: The Five with Howard Hawks." In *Fiction, Film, and Faulkner: The Art of Adaptation*, pp. 7–56. Knoxville: University of Tennessee Press, 1988.

Poague, Leland A. *Howard Hawks*. Boston: Twayne, 1982.

Wood, Robin. *Howard Hawks*. New York: Doubleday, 1968.

Alfred Hitchcock

Derry, Charles. *The Suspense Thriller: Films in the Shadow of Alfred Hitchcock*. Jefferson, N.C.: McFarland, 1988.

Phillips, Gene D. *Alfred Hitchcock*. Boston: Twayne, 1984.

Rothman, William. *Hitchcock: The Murderous Gaze*. Cambridge: Harvard University Press, 1982.

Schickel, Richard. "Alfred Hitchcock: Afternoon of an *Auteur*." In *Schickel on Film*, pp. 70–81. New York: Morrow, 1989.

Spoto, Donald. *The Dark Side of Genius: The Life of Alfred Hitchcock*. Boston: Little, Brown, 1983.

Taylor, John Russell. *Hitch: The Life and Times of Alfred Hitchcock*. New York: Pantheon, 1978.

Truffaut, Francois. *Hitchcock*. Rev. ed. New York: Simon and Schuster, 1985.

George Cukor

Carey, Gary. *Cukor and Company: The Films of George Cukor*. New York: Museum of Modern Art, 1971.

Clarens, Carlos. *George Cukor*. London: Secker and Warburg, 1976.

Estrin, Allen. "George Cukor." In *The Hollywood Professionals,* vol. 6, pp. 88–136. New York: A. S. Barnes, 1980.

Haver, Ronald. *A Star is Born: The Making of the 1954 Film and Its 1983 Restoration*. New York: Knopf, 1988.

Lambert, Gavin. *On Cukor*. New York: Putnam's, 1972.

"The 1939 Classic Films." *Life* (Special Hollywood Issue) 12, no. 5 (Spring 1989): 25–49. (Cukor's direction of *The Women* and his uncredited work on *Gone with the Wind* are noted.)

Philips, Gene D. *George Cukor*. Boston: Twayne, 1982.

George Stevens

Hastings, Max. *Victory in Europe: D-Day to V-E Day*. Photographed by George Stevens. Boston: Little, Brown, 1985.

Hepburn, Katharine. "Get a Tough Director." *Panorama*, March 1981, pp. 58–61, 77. (Includes some top directors, notably Stevens.)

Petri, Bruce. "George Stevens: The Wartime Comedies." *Film Comment* 11, no. 4 (July–August 1976): 52–56.

Reed, Rochelle, ed. *Dialogue on Film: George Stevens*. Beverly Hills : American Film Institute, 1975.

Richie, Donald. *George Stevens: An American Romantic*. New York: Museum of Modern Art, 1970.

Sirkin, Elliott. "*Alice Adams*." *Film Comment* 7, no. 4 (Winter 1971): 66–69.

Fred Zinnemann

Buckley, Michael. "Fred Zinnemann." *Films in Review* 34, no. 1 (January 1983): 25–40.

McDougal, Stuart Y. "*Member of the Wedding*." In *Made Into Movies: From Literature to Film*, pp. 44–50. New York: Holt, Rinehart, and Winston, 1985.

Nightengale, Benedict. "Fred Zinnemann Distills a New Film from an Old Dream." *New York Times*, 7 November 1982, sec. 2, p. 1.

Reid, John Howard. "A Man for All Movies: Fred Zinnemann, Part I." *Films and Filming* 13, no. 5 (May 1967): 11–15.

Stanhope, Alan. "A Man for All Movies: Fred Zinnemann, Part II." *Films and Filming* 13, no. 6 (June 1967): 11–15.

Zeitlin, David I. *Fred Zinnemann.* Los Angeles: Directors Guild of America, 1966.

Stanley Kubrick

Coyle, Wallace. *Stanley Kubrick: A Guide to References and Resources.* Boston: G. K. Hall, 1980.

"*Full Metal Jacket*" (special section). *Literature/Film Quarterly* 16, no. 4 (Fall 1988). (Four articles on the film.)

Kloman, William. "In 2001 Will Love be a Seven-Letter Word?" *New York Times,* 14 April 1968, sec. 2, p. 15.

Nelson, Thomas Allen. *Kubrick: Inside a Film Artist's Maze.* Bloomington: Indiana University Press, 1982.

Phillips, Gene D. *Stanley Kubrick: A Film Odyssey.* New York: Popular Library, 1975.

Siskel, Gene. "Candidly Kubrick." *Chicago Tribune*, 21 June 1987, sec. 13, pp. 4–5, 22–23.

———. "Stanley Kubrick." *Chicago Tribune*, 14 February 1972, sec. 2, p. 9.

Walker, Alexander. *Stanley Kubrick Directs.* Rev. ed. New York: Harcourt, Brace, Jovanovich, 1972.

Francis Coppola

Blake, Richard A. "Apocalypse Within." *America*, 8 September 1979, p. 96.

Chaillet, Jean-Paul, and Elizabeth Vincent. *Francis Ford Coppola.* Translated by Denise Raab Jacobs. New York: St. Martin's, 1985.

Chown, Jeffrey. *Hollywood Auteur: Francis Coppola.* New York: Praeger, 1988.

Coppola, Eleanor. *Notes.* New York: Simon and Schuster, 1979. (A diary about the making of *Apocalypse Now*.)

Johnson, Robert K. *Francis Ford Coppola.* Boston: Twayne, 1977.

Kael, Pauline. "*The Gardens of Stone*." In *Hooked*, pp. 303–6. New York: Dutton, 1989.

Lindsey, Robert. "Francis Ford Coppola: Promises to Keep." *New York Times Magazine*, 24 July 1988, pp. 23–27.

Pye, Michael and Lynda Myles. "Francis Ford Coppola." In *The Movie Brats: How the Film Generation Took Over Hollywood*, pp. 66–111. New York: Holt, Rinehart, and Winston, 1979.

Siskel, Gene. "Celluloid Godfather." *Chicago Tribune*, 5 October 1986, sec. 13, pp. 4–5.

Wise, Naomi, and Michael Goodwin. *On the Edge: Francis Coppola.* New York: Morrow, 1989.

Carol Reed

Coultass, Clive. *Images for Battle: British Film and the Second World War.* Newark: University of Delaware Press, 1989.

Davies, Brenda. *Carol Reed*. London: British Film Institute, 1978.

DeFelice, James. *Filmguide to Odd Man Out*. Bloomington: Indiana University Press, 1975.

Everson, William K. "Rediscovery: *Night Train to Munich*." *Films in Review* 38, no. 12 (December 1987): 619–21.

Fawcett, Marion. "Sir Carol Reed." *Films in Review* 10, no. 3 (March 1959), 134–41.

Ginna, Robert Emmett. "*Our Man in Havana*." *Horizon* 2, no. 2 (November 1959): 26–31, 122–26.

Moss, Robert F. *The Films of Carol Reed*. New York: Columbia University Press, 1987.

Phillips, Gene D. "Our Man in Vienna: The Three with Carol Reed." in *Graham Greene: The Films of His Fiction*, pp. 44–89. New York: Columbia University Teachers College Press, 1974.

David Lean

Anderegg, Michael A. *David Lean*. Boston: Twayne, 1984.

Day, Ernest, "*A Passage to India*." *American Cinematographer* 66, no. 2 (February 1985), pp. 56–62.

Kennedy, Harlan. "'I'm a Picture Chap.'" *Film Comment* 21, no. 1 (January–February 1985), 28–32.

McInerney, John M. "*Zhivago*: A Reappraisal." *Literature/Film Quarterly* 15, no. 1 (Winter 1987), 43–48.

Maslin, Janet. "*Lawrence* Seen Whole." *New York Times*, 29 January 1989, sec. 2, pp. 1, 13.

"Oscar Bound." *Time*, 24 December 1965, pp. 44–45.

Schickel, Richard. "A Work of Serious, Genuine Art." *Life*, 21 January 1966, p. 62A.

Joseph Losey

Ciment, Michel. *Conversations with Losey*. New York: Methuen, 1985.

Dick, Bernard. "Introduction." In *Radical Innocence*, pp. 1–11. Lexington: University Press of Kentucky, 1989. (On the blacklisting era in Hollywood.)

Hirsch, Foster. *Joseph Losey*. Boston: Twayne, 1980.

Leahy, James. *The Cinema of Joseph Losey*. New York: A. S. Barnes, 1967.

Milne, Tom. "*Accident*." *Sight and Sound* 36, no. 2 (Spring 1967): 56–69.

———. *Losey on Losey*. New York: Doubleday, 1968.

Roud, Richard. "Going Between." *Sight and Sound* 40, no. 3 (Spring 1971): 158–59.

Bryan Forbes

"Bryan Forbes: An Interview." *Films Illustrated*, July 1971, p. 10.

Forbes, Bryan. *Notes for a Life*. London: Collins, 1974.

———. "Report on Elstree." *Films Illustrated*, July 1971, pp. 6–9.

———. *That Despicable Race: A History of the British Acting Tradition*. London: Elm Tree, 1980.

Gruen, John. "He Says, 'Yes, yes, Nanette.'" *New York Times*, 24 October 1971, sec. 2, p. 11.

Russo, Vito. "*The L-Shaped Room*." In *The Celluloid Closet: Homosexuality in the Movies*, pp. 146–47. New York: Harper, Row, 1987.

Walker, Alexander. "The Last Tycoon." In *Hollywood, England: The British Film Industry in the Sixties*, pp. 426–40. London: Michael Joseph, 1974.

John Schlesinger

Brooker, Nancy J. *John Schlesinger: A Guide to References and Resources*. Boston: G. K. Hall, 1978.

Gow, Gordon. "A Buck for Joe." *Films and Filming* 15, no. 11 (November 1969), 4–8.

Phillips, Gene D. *John Schlesinger*. Boston: Twayne, 1981.

Rebello, Stephen. "Spies Like Us." *Saturday Review* 67, no. 1 (January–February 1985), 34–38.

Schlesinger, John. "Blessed Isle or Fool's Paradise?" *Films and Filming* 9, no. 5 (May 1963): 8–10.

Schonberg, Harold C. "*Madame Sousatzka* Strikes a Chord." *New York Times*, 9 October 1988, sec. 2, pp. 23, 30.

Ken Russell

Baxter, John. *An Appalling Talent: Ken Russell*. London: Michael Joseph, 1973.

Billington, Michael. "Just Right for D. H. Lawrence—Russell's *Rainbow*." *New York Times*, 30 April 1989, sec. 2, p. 17, 20.

Dempsey, Michael. "The World of Ken Russell." *Film Quarterly* 26, no. 4 (Spring 1972): 13–25.

Hanke, Ken. *Ken Russell's Films*. Metuchen, N.J.: Scarecrow, 1984.

"*The Lair of the White Worm*." *Variety*, 31 August 1988, p. 15.

Phillips, Gene D. *Ken Russell*. Boston: Twayne, 1979.

Rosenfeldt, Diane. *Ken Russell: A Guide to References and Resources*. Boston: G. K. Hall, 1978.

Russell, Ken. *The British Picture: An Autobiography*. London: Heinemann, 1989.

General Studies

Armes, Roy. *A Critical History of British Cinema*. London: Secker and Warburg, 1978.

Auty, Martyn, and Nick Roddick, eds. *British Cinema Now*. London: British Film Institute, 1985.

Cowie, Peter, ed. *Hollywood: 1920–70*. Rev. ed. New York: A. S. Barnes, 1977.

Keyser, Les. *Hollywood in the Seventies*. New York: A. S. Barnes, 1981. (An extension of the volume in the previous entry up to 1980.)

Lyon, Christopher, James Vinson, and Nick Thomas, eds. *The International Dictionary of Films and Filmmakers*. Rev. ed. 4 vols. London: St. James Press, 1989–90.

Mast, Gerald. *A Short History of the Movies*. Rev. ed. New York: Macmillan, 1986.

Sarris, Andrews. *The American Cinema: Directors and Directions, 1929–68*. Rev. ed. Chicago: University of Chicago Press, 1985.

Variety: Film Reviews, 1907–80. 13 vols. New York: Garland, 1983.

Unpublished Materials

Letters, typed and handwritten, signed to Gene Phillips, dated from Los Angeles and London, from various directors represented in this book. The correspondence contains information about the films they were making at the time of writing, as well as about their previous pictures. The correspondence received is as follows:

George Cukor (1971–80); Fred Zinnemann (1972–80, 1987–89); Stanley Kubrick (1970–76, 1980–83, 1988); Carol Reed (1975); Joseph Losey (1967–84); Bryan Forbes (1973, 1985–88); John Schlesinger (1967–89); Ken Russell (1970–89).

Filmography

Charles Chaplin

1921	The Kid	1940	The Great Dictator
1923	A Woman of Paris	1947	Monsieur Verdoux
1925	The Gold Rush	1952	Limelight
1928	The Circus	1957	A King in New York
1931	City Lights	1967	A Countess from Hong Kong
1936	Modern Times		

Howard Hawks

1926	The Road to Glory, Fig Leaves	1940	His Girl Friday
1927	The Cradle Snatchers, Paid to Love	1941	Sergeant York, Ball of Fire
1928	A Girl in Every Port, Fazil, The Air Circus	1943	Air Force
		1944	To Have and Have Not
1929	Trent's Last Case	1946	The Big Sleep
1930	The Dawn Patrol	1948	Red River, A Song Is Born
1931	The Criminal Code	1949	I Was a Male War Bride
1932	The Crowd Roars, Scarface, Tiger Shark	1952	The Big Sky, Monkey Business, O'Henry's Full House (one segment)
1933	Today We Live		
1934	Twentieth Century, Viva Villa! (with Jack Conway)	1953	Gentlemen Prefer Blondes
		1955	The Land of the Pharaohs
1935	Barbary Coast	1959	Rio Bravo
1936	Ceiling Zero, The Road to Glory, Come and Get It (with William Wyler)	1962	Hatari!
		1964	Man's Favorite Sport
		1965	Red Line 7000
1938	Bringing up Baby	1967	El Dorado
1939	Only Angels Have Wings	1971	Rio Lobo

Alfred Hitchcock

1926	The Pleasure Garden, The Mountain Eagle (American title: Fear O'God), The Lodger	1942	Saboteur
		1943	Shadow of a Doubt
		1944	Lifeboat
1927	Downhill (American title: When Boys Leave Home), Easy Virtue, The Ring	1945	Spellbound
		1946	Notorious
		1947	The Paradine Case
1928	The Farmer's Wife, Champagne	1948	Rope
1929	The Manxman, Blackmail	1949	Under Capricorn

1930	*Juno and the Paycock, Murder!*
1931	*The Skin Game*
1932	*Number Seventeen, Rich and Strange* (American title: *East of Shanghai*)
1933	*Waltzes from Vienna* (American title: *Strauss's Great Waltz*)
1934	*The Man Who Knew Too Much* (first version)
1935	*The Thirty-nine Steps*
1936	*Secret Agent, Sabotage* (American title: *A Woman Alone*)
1937	*Young and Innocent* (American title: *The Girl Was Young*)
1938	*The Lady Vanishes*
1939	*Jamaica Inn*
1940	*Rebecca, Foreign Correspondent*
1941	*Mr. and Mrs. Smith, Suspicion*
1950	*Stage Fright*
1951	*Strangers on a Train*
1952	*I Confess*
1954	*Dial M for Murder, Rear Window*
1955	*To Catch a Thief, The Trouble with Harry*
1956	*The Man Who Knew Too Much* (second version), *The Wrong Man*
1958	*Vertigo*
1959	*North by Northwest*
1960	*Psycho*
1963	*The Birds*
1964	*Marnie*
1966	*Torn Curtain*
1969	*Topaz*
1972	*Frenzy*
1976	*Family Plot*

George Cukor

1930	*Grumpy* (with Cyril Gardner), *The Virtuous Sin* (with Louis Gasnier), *The Royal Family of Broadway* (with Cyril Gardner)
1931	*Tarnished Lady, Girls about Town*
1932	*One Hour with You* (with Ernst Lubitsch), *A Bill of Divorcement, What Price Hollywood?, Rockabye*
1933	*Dinner at Eight, Little Women, Our Betters*
1935	*David Copperfield, Sylvia Scarlett*
1936	*Romeo and Juliet*
1937	*Camille*
1938	*Holiday* (British title: *Free to Live* or *Unconventional Linda*), *Zaza*
1939	*The Women*
1940	*The Philadelphia Story, Susan and God* (British title: *The Gay Mrs. Trexel*)
1941	*A Woman's Face, Two-Faced Woman*
1942	*Her Cardboard Lover*
1943	*Keeper of the Flame*
1944	*Gaslight* (British title: *Thornton Square*), *Winged Victory*
1947	*A Double Life*
1949	*Adam's Rib; Edward, My Son*
1950	*A Life of Her Own, Born Yesterday*
1952	*The Model and the Marriage Broker, The Marrying Kind, Pat and Mike*
1953	*The Actress*
1954	*A Star Is Born, It Should Happen to You*
1956	*Bhowani Junction*
1957	*Les Girls, Wild Is the Wind*
1960	*Heller in Pink Tights, Let's Make Love, Song without End* (with Charles Vidor)
1962	*The Chapman Report*
1964	*My Fair Lady*
1969	*Justine*
1973	*Travels with My Aunt*
1976	*The Blue Bird*
1981	*Rich and Famous*

George Stevens

1933	*The Cohens and Kellys in Trouble*
1934	*Bachelor Bait, Kentucky Kernels*
1942	*Woman of the Year, The Talk of the Town*

1935	Alice Adams, Laddie, Nitwits,	1943	The More the Merrier
	Annie Oakley	1948	I Remember Mama
1936	Swing Time	1951	A Place in the Sun
1937	Quality Street, A Damsel in	1952	Something to Live for
	Distress	1953	Shane
1938	Vivacious Lady	1956	Giant
1939	Gunga Din	1959	The Diary of Anne Frank
1940	Vigil in the Night	1965	The Greatest Story Ever Told
1941	Penny Serenade	1970	The Only Game in Town

Fred Zinnemann

1942	Kid Glove Killer, Eyes in the Night	1955	Oklahoma
1944	The Seventh Cross	1957	A Hatful of Rain
1946	Little Mr. Jim, My Brother Talks to	1959	The Nun's Story
	Horses	1960	The Sundowners
1948	The Search, Act of Violence	1963	Behold a Pale Horse
1950	The Men	1966	A Man for All Seasons
1951	Teresa	1973	The Day of the Jackal
1952	High Noon, The Member of the	1977	Julia
	Wedding	1982	Five Days One Summer
1953	From Here to Eternity		

Stanley Kubrick

1953	Fear and Desire	1968	2001: A Space Odyssey
1955	Killer's Kiss	1972	A Clockwork Orange
1956	The Killing	1975	Barry Lyndon
1957	The Paths of Glory	1980	The Shining
1960	Spartacus	1987	Full Metal Jacket
1962	Lolita		
1964	Dr. Strangelove, or: How I learned to Stop Worrying and Love the Bomb		

Francis Coppola

1963	Dementia 13	1982	One from the Heart
1967	You're a Big Boy Now	1983	The Outsiders, Rumble Fish
1968	Finian's Rainbow	1984	The Cotton Club
1969	The Rain People	1986	Peggy Sue Got Married
1972	The Godfather	1987	Gardens of Stone
1974	The Conversation, The Godfather-Part II.	1988	Tucker: The Man and His Dream
1979	Apocalypse Now	1989	New York Stories (one segment)

Carol Reed

1935	*Midshipman Easy* (American title: *Men of the Sea*)	1947	*Odd Man Out*
1936	*Laburnum Grove*	1948	*The Fallen Idol*
1937	*Talk of the Devil, Who's Your Lady Friend?*	1949	*The Third Man*
		1952	*Outcast of the Islands*
1938	*Bank Holiday* (American title: *Three on a Weekend*), *Penny Paradise, Climbing High*	1953	*The Man Between*
		1955	*A Kid for Two Farthings*
		1956	*Trapeze*
1939	*A Girl Must Live*	1958	*The Key*
1940	*The Stars Look Down, Night Train to Munich* (American title: *Night Train*)	1959	*Our Man in Havana*
		1963	*The Running Man*
		1965	*The Agony and the Ecstasy*
1941	*The Girl in the News, Kipps* (American title: *The Remarkable Mr. Kipps*)	1968	*Oliver!*
		1970	*Flap* (British title: *The Last Warrior*)
1942	*Young Mr. Pitt*	1971	*The Public Eye* (British title: *Follow Me*)
1944	*The Way Ahead*		
1945	*The True Glory* (with Garson Kanin)		

David Lean

1942	*In Which We Serve* (with Noel Coward)	1954	*Hobson's Choice*
		1955	*Summertime* (British title: *Summer Madness*)
1944	*This Happy Breed*		
1945	*Blithe Spirit, Brief Encounter*	1957	*The Bridge on the River Kwai*
1946	*Great Expectations*	1962	*Lawrence of Arabia*
1948	*Oliver Twist*	1966	*Dr. Zhivago*
1949	*Passionate Friends* (American title: *One Woman's Story*)	1970	*Ryan's Daughter*
		1984	*A Passage to India*
1950	*Madeleine*		
1952	*The Sound Barrier* (American title: *Breaking the Sound Barrier*)		

Joseph Losey

1948	*The Boy with Green Hair*	1963	*The Servant*
1949	*The Lawless* (British title: *the Dividing Line*)	1964	*King and Country*
		1966	*Modesty Blaise*
1951	*The Prowler, M, The Big Night*	1967	*Accident*
1952	*Stranger on the Prowl* (British title: *Encounter*)	1968	*Boom*
		1969	*Secret Ceremony*
1954	*The Sleeping Tiger*	1970	*Figures in a Landscape*
1955	*The Intimate Stranger* (American title: *Finger of Guilt*)	1971	*The Go-Between*
		1972	*The Assassination of Trotsky*
1956	*Time without Pity*	1973	*A Doll's House*

1957	*The Gypsy and the Gentleman*
1959	*Blind Date* (American title: Chance Meeting)
1960	*The Criminal* (American title: *The Concrete Jungle*)
1961	*These Are the Damned*
1962	*Eve*
1975	*Galileo, The Romantic Englishwoman*
1976	*Mr. Klein*
1978	*Southern Routes*
1979	*Don Giovanni*
1982	*The Trout*
1985	*Steaming*

Bryan Forbes

1962	*Whistle Down the Wind*
1963	*The L-Shaped Room*
1964	*Seance on a Wet Afternoon*
1965	*King Rat*
1966	*The Wrong Box*
1967	*The Whisperers*
1968	*Deadfall*
1969	*The Madwoman of Chaillot*
1971	*The Raging Moon* (American title: *Long Ago, Tomorrow*)
1975	*The Stepford Wives*
1976	*The Slipper and the Rose*
1978	*International Velvet*
1980	*Sunday Lovers* (one segment)
1982	*Better Late Than Never*
1985	*The Naked Face*

John Schlesinger

1962	*A Kind of Loving*
1963	*Billy Liar*
1965	*Darling*
1967	*Far from the Madding Crowd*
1969	*Midnight Cowboy*
1971	*Sunday, Bloody Sunday*
1973	*Visions of Eight* (one segment)
1975	*Day of the Locust*
1976	*Marathon Man*
1979	*Yanks*
1981	*Honky Tonk Freeway*
1985	*The Falcon and the Snowman*
1987	*The Believers*
1988	*Madame Sousatzka*

Ken Russell

1964	*French Dressing*
1967	*Billion Dollar Brain*
1969	*Women in Love*
1970	*The Music Lovers*
1971	*The Devils, The Boy Friend*
1972	*Savage Messiah*
1974	*Mahler*
1975	*Tommy*
1977	*Valentino*
1980	*Altered States*
1984	*Crimes of Passion*
1987	*Gothic, Aria* (one segment)
1988	*Salome's Last Dance, The Lair of the White Worm*
1989	*The Rainbow*

Index